P9-CJZ-147
ex libris

FIRST EDITION

The Collectors Encyclopedia of

HULL POTTERY

by
BRENDA ROBERTS

EDITED BY SHARON AND BOB HUXFORD

Collector Books
P.O. Box 3009
Paducah, Kentucky 42001

In Memory of
Annie "Kate" Garrett,
the special lady who launched my pottery collection.

The information in this publication has been brought together specifically for the collector, and is so dedicated . . .

To the future of Hull collecting,
and Hull collectors everwhere . . .
especially,
13-year-old Amy Ward
of Zanesville, Ohio

Additional copies of this book may be ordered from:

COLLECTOR BOOKS
P.O. Box 3009
Paducah, Kentucky 42001

or

The author: Brenda Roberts
Route 2
Marshall, Missouri 65340

$19.95 Plus $2.00 for postage and handling

TABLE OF CONTENTS

ACKNOWLEDGMENTS

In production since 1905, Hull Company wares continually gain the favor of both collectors and dealers alike. Hull's collecting possibilities are nearly limitless and the growing field of collectors seem to be enthusiastically accepting its challenge. Interest has grown by leaps and bounds, thus making a volume such as this indispensable.

In acknowledging the assistance given and the courtesies shown me, I express my appreciation to all who have contributed in any way toward the gathering of the collection and the compiling of this publication.

My sincere appreciation to Collector Books' Pottery Editors, Sharon and Bob Huxford, who have aided me with their experience during the making of this volume. Bob did the artistic arrangements for the pottery photographs you are about to see, and Sharon, with her keen eye, kept him busy shuffling pieces, turning handles, and straightening lids, for just the "right" set ups. To two very special people, a very special thanks for your help, but most of all, for your friendship.

To a person we couldn't have done without... a hearty "thanks" to the man behind the camera, Ted Wright of Zanesville, Ohio, whose services can hardly be measured. Ted, the photos are just great; many thanks for your long hours of work to make everything look so beautiful.

There are many others to whom I am indebted; but to the following, I am under special obligation:

With deepest gratitude, my appreciation is given to Byron and Robert Hull, and the Hull Pottery Company of Crooksville, Ohio, where I have been welcomed many times. My sincere thanks to the company for consenting to this work.

I wish to acknowledge the aid of the Ohio Historical Society who allowed the reproduction of original company brochure pages housed in the Archives Library in Columbus.

Of valuable assistance with printed company materials were: Mrs. Nelson McCoy of Zanesville, Ohio; Antiques Research Publications, Mentone, Alabama; Shulton, Inc., Clifton, New Jersey; and Duke Coleman, Editor of American Art Pottery, Silver Springs, Maryland.

Most items pictured in this volume are from my private collection. However, several pieces were loaned by Jim and Osna Fenner of Fenner's Antiques, Brooklyn, New York; a handful were photographed from the collection of Joan Hull, Huron, South Dakota; and a lovely piece was loaned by Robert Campbell, Columbus, Ohio. A warm thank you to all who made these things available.

To Linda and Amy Ward of Zanesville goes a special note of gratitude for the use of several interesting items from their collection.

FOREWORD

By the early 20th century, Ohio was the largest producer of clay products in the United States.

Many factors contributed to Ohio's supremacy in the field of ceramics: an abundant supply of raw materials necessary to the marketing of pottery, a growing transportation network reaching markets far beyond the state's borders, a sound local market, and a pool of skilled workers.

Credit for a large portion of the history of the clay industry rightfully belongs to Addis Emmet Hull, founder of the A.E. Hull Pottery Company, and his descendents. The pottery he founded in 1905, continues yet today to manufacture useful and beautiful pottery wares.

Years of vigorous competition with hundreds of area potteries, the lean years of the Stock Market Crash of 1929 and resulting depression, and even total destruction by flood and fire have not persuaded the Hull Pottery firm to close its doors.

The Hull Company name is synonomous with the term "diversification," and the design and development of items having popular appeal is one key element to the company's 75-year-old success story. Market trends have been anticipated, and even guided by Hull's skillful abilities and dynamic leadership.

Stoneware and semi-porcelain art and utilitarian wares, garden ware, tile, florist ware, art pottery and dinnerware are a sampling of the items produced during the history of the Hull Pottery Company. My aim is to guide you through these Hull years...

ABOUT THE AUTHOR

I've been antiquing nearly ten years, and in 1974, focused my attention on The Hull Pottery Company of Crooksville, Ohio. Here I began the pursuit which continues to maintain my interest and challenge my collecting abilities. To date, my collection numbers over 1600 items and is one of the largest Hull collections in the country.

Brenda Roberts

My attraction to Hull wares was accompanied by an avid interest in the company's background and its operations. In 1977, my search for information began in the volumes at The Ohio Historical Society Archives Library and soon after, I made visits to the Ohio pottery region's "clay cities," in which I eagerly sought out potteries in operation in order to gain knowledge of the processes involved in pottery manufacture. Of course, my main stop has always been The Hull Pottery, where I have been granted several V.I.P. tours. Here I have met company officials: J.B. Hull, company president until his death in 1978, and today's Hull president, Henry Sulens, along with others who have aided me with their experience of the pottery trade.

Contact with Hull Company personnel proved to be a fascinating segment in this research and the extensive correspondence conducted nation-wide regarding the company's operations, wares, and price trends has been a valuable aid in the preparation of this study.

THE HULL POTTERY COMPANY

ADDIS EMMET HULL

Addis Emmet Hull was born at Todd's Post Office, Morgan County, Ohio, in 1862. He was the scion of old pioneer stock; his father, Henry M. Hull, who was born in Ireland in 1809, came to the Ohio Valley in the very early days to spend the remaining years of his life as a farmer, before his death in 1884.

After finishing country schools, Addis Hull attended Parsons Business College in Zanesville, Ohio, and upon graduation became a traveling salesman for his brother, J.J. Hull, who at that time operated the Star Stonery Company, which had been organized in 1892. A well established firm, the Star's trade extended from the Atlantic Ocean to the Mississippi River at the turn of the century, and increased steadily.

A.E. Hull's business training and persuasive personality made him a successful salesman, and during his travels he recognized the continually increasing demand for stoneware items. His first venture into the field of manufacturing stoneware was in 1901, as founder and manager of The Globe Stoneware Company. E.O. Watts served as President of the firm, William A. Watts as Secretary, and Jeptha Darby Young as Superintendent.

Success was not far away, for in their first year of production, The Globe Stoneware Company was reported to have developed a grade of ware that was second to none in the valley.

Workers at The Globe Stoneware Company

Among those on the front row are Addis Hull and William Watts. J.D. Young is on the third row. Others identified in this photograph are Ruben Dailey, Albert Aichele, John Wilson, Fred Young, George Aichele, Fat Spring, Frank Watts, Howard Spring, Walter Brown, George Watts, and Frank Wilson.

ORGANIZATION OF THE ACME POTTERY COMPANY

During the time Addis Hull managed the Globe, his brother, J.J., along with a number of business men, met together and enthusiastically decided that Crooksville could support another dinnerware pottery.

In 1903, a group headed by Lewis Springer, Granville Springer, J.J. Hull, W.H. Dunn, W.A. Showers, and A.E. Smith pledged their financial support along with several others and petitioned the Secretary of State for permission to organize, in accordance with the general laws of the State of Ohio, a corporate body under the name of the Acme Pottery Company for the purpose of manufacturing a line of semi-porcelain plain and decorated dinnerware. The authority was granted and the charter received. A meeting of the stockholders was held, a Board of Directors elected, and the organization was affected by electing J.J. Hull as President, and Lewis Springer as Secretary-Treasurer and General Manager.

An incorporator of the Acme Pottery Company, J.J. Hull also served as President of the Board of Directors.

The location for the plant was selected; plans and specifications for kilns were drawn up. The contract was let, and the completion of the plant was speedily effected. Thomas McNichol of East Liverpool, Ohio, a practical pottery man, was secured as General Superintendent. Crooksville had an abundance of stoneware potters, but skilled dinnerware mechanics had to be imported from the West Liverpool pottery district.

The Acme was soon turning out a very fine grade of semi-porcelain dinnerware, and within a few months its products were on the market. Business was humming in Crooksville.

The Acme Pottery Company

THE A.E. HULL POTTERY COMPANY IS FORMED

A.E. Hull continued management and operation of The Globe Pottery until 1904, when he sold his interest in the company and became instrumental in organizing the A.E. Hull Pottery Company. William Watts and J.D. Young also left Globe and served the Hull Pottery Company as Secretary-Treasurer and Superintendent respectively. G.E. McKeever, General Salesman of The Star Stoneware Company, accepted a sales position with Hull.

Organized in July, 1905, The A.E. Hull Pottery Company, located at the north end of China Street, had four kilns, each twenty-two feet in diameter, which were heated with natural gas produced near the plant. (This primary location will be referred to as Plant No. 1 throughout this text.) The company's production centered on stoneware and stoneware specialties. Hull quickly established a firm market and an excellent reputation in the field of ceramics.

HULL EXPANDS: PURCHASE OF THE ACME POTTERY COMPANY

In 1907, The A.E. Hull Company purchased The Acme Pottery which then became Hull's Plant No. 2. Over two hundred skilled men were required to serve the two plants, and nearly the same number of unskilled men and women.

With The Acme Pottery also came Crooksville's first electric light plant, The Acme Electric Light Company. One 75 K.W. two-phase generator had been installed in the pottery in 1905. The engine that was used for the pottery through the day was also used for the lighting generator at night. The light company purchased a new location, constructed a building, and installed a boiler and other equipment necessary to the production of electricity. The generator was moved from the pottery in 1908.

During Hull's early years, a local newspaper boasted of their success.

"We are now without question the largest manufacturers of Stoneware Specialties in the United States. We have grown from four kilns, to a capacity of ten kilns, and two decorating kilns. All the officers are native of Perry County except Mr. Griswold, Vice President, whose home is in Boston, Mass., and all are men of practical worth in the business."

One account states that during the late 1920's, A.E. Hull, Sr., in addition to managing the Hull Plants No. 1 and No. 2, served as President and Director of the Crooksville Pottery, and also was a stockholder in The Muskingum Pottery. L.A. Springer, a Hull Company Director, was also a stockholder in, and General Manager of, The Muskingum Pottery Company. A.E. Hull, Jr., graduated from Ohio State University and was assistant manager to his father at the Crooksville Pottery. J.B. Hull, another son, was connected with the Crooksville Pottery as accountant and bookkeeper, having charge of the order department.

HULL'S EARLY YEARS

In the 1920's, with general offices and factories in Crooksville, an eastern warehouse in Jersey City, New Jersey, a New York office and showroom in 200 Fifth Avenue Building, a Chicago office located at the Morrison Hotel, and a Branch House in Detroit, A.E. Hull's Pottery was "big business."

James Felz managed the New Jersey warehouse, which was eighty-six by two hundred and twenty-five feet in dimension. Guy Cooke served as Hull's New York representative, and D.W. Worthington worked out of the Chicago office. G.E. McKeever, a director of the company, managed the branch house in Detroit, Michigan. Western and northern areas were represented by G.W. Springer, and western and southern areas by N.W. Leland. Serving as a traveling salesman was V.D. Kinnon, a member of the board of directors.

A full line of quality stoneware, semi-porcelain in plain and embossed shapes, decorated with bands and stamps underglaze and overglaze, art pottery with both air-brushed and blended glazes, plain and decorated florists' pots and saucers, garden ware and their special lusterware in a rainbow of iridescent colors are a sampling of the many items produced by Hull at that time.

Lusterware items were marketed in colors of orange, shammy, lavender, slate, emerald, light blue, iridescent blue, and golden glow. Persian and Chinese Red Cracquell were lustre lines designed outside the company to be sold to distributors in the Chicago area.

Hull was a large manufacturer of toilet and kitchenware in the early years. Practically styled, made of absolute white bodied semi-porcelain fired at high temperatures to assure strength and durability, the toilet and kitchenware was made in such a large volume that it was priced very reasonably at all times, and was used by both residences and hotels alike.

Kitchenware items such as salt boxes, jugs, cereal sets, nested bowls, custard cups, and 1 to 6 gallon food containers were staple products in stoneware. Clay bodies varied from that of absolute white, to ivory white, to dark ivory buff, and yellow ware. Much of the material used in Hull's manufacture consisted of what was then known as yellow home clay mined at Crooksville.

Hull supplied many utilitarian wares to both outside markets, and farms and households within the Ohio area. Green glazed stew and bake pans with metal bails were used by nearly every area farm wife. Douglas Young, grandson of Jeptha Darby Young, began his work with the company around 1925. He recalled that at that time he put the bails on those pans for 25¢ a hundred.

That may sound like a meager wage but at Plant No. 2, total employment was 160 people with a payroll of $175,000.00 annually. When operating normally, Plant No. 2's capacity was 650,000 dozen, or 7,800,000 pieces of utility and art ware per year.

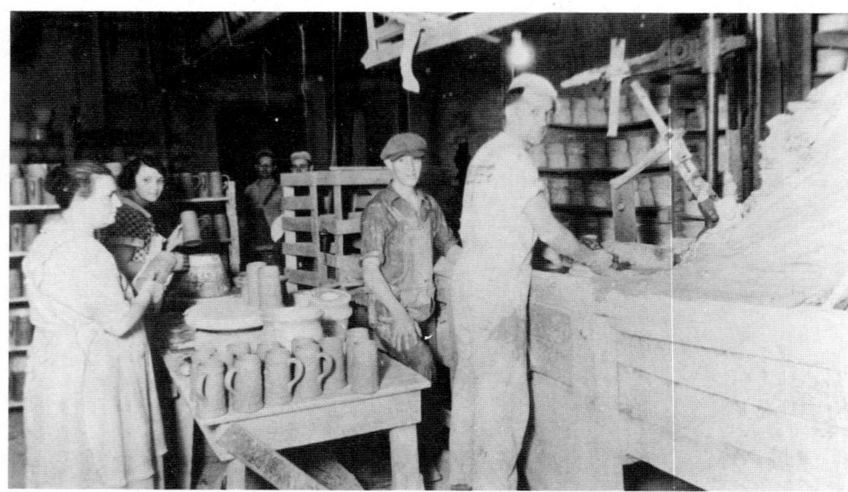

This early photo pictures H in circle steins and pitchers. Workers are identified as follows: Finishers, Iona Lauderbach and Zetta Wilson; Castor, Ray Conaway; and Richard Rosser, Ralph Sherlock and Ken Haymen.

Carloads of ware were shipped daily, on the Pennsylvania and the New York Central Railroads. Being located on both, the company was afforded unexcelled shipping facilities.

All Hull Company orders were accepted subject to and contingent upon strikes, legislation, fire, accidents, or other causes beyond the company's control.

All goods were carefully packed, inspected and delivered to the transportation company in good condition. Accidents, delays in delivery, and loss by transportation companies were beyond the pottery's control, and all claims were made on the transportation companies. However, Hull offered assistance to the purchaser in claim adjustments against the transportation companies.

A.E. Hull Pottery advertised that due to variation in materials used to manufacture it was impossible to produce earthenware (either porous, or semi-vitreous,) that would not craze eventually; therefore, their products were not guaranteed against crazing after a long period of time. The guarantee to withstand crazing was for a reasonable period of time only, and the pottery firm reserved the right to refuse to adjust claims when in their judgment the merchandise had remained in stock too long.

Hull advertised their products to be fired with "stilts" and with the distinct understanding that stilt marks might be visible on any piece. For buyers who required pieces without these marks, special prices applied.

Shrinkage in the manufacture of pottery could not be exactly controlled due to varying materials and conditions, including the human element. Therefore, A.E. Hull could not guarantee sizes, capacities, and weights to be exact. They were approximate, but the margin of error was very small. Hull advertised sizes in inches, capacities in U.S. Pints, and all weights in pounds avoirdupois.

Early bowl sizes were advertised as follows:

42's — 4 inch	9's — 10 inch
36's — 5 inch	6's — 11 inch
30's — 6 inch	4's — 12 inch
24's — 7 inch	3's — 13 inch
18's — 8 inch	2's — 14 inch
12's — 9 inch	1's — 15 inch

Hull's interest had turned toward art pottery by the early 1920's. Addis Hull investigated the possibility of importing European pottery items and learned that some items could be delivered to New York at half the cost of their production in the U.S.A.

The demand for pottery products was on the rise, and in order to supply the increasing market, Addis Hull purchased earthenware china and pottery items from Czechoslovakia, England, Germany, Italy, and France, to stock the eastern warehouse. Each year from 1921 to 1929, a Hull Vice President was sent to Europe to purchase pottery.

The Jersey City warehouse provided storage for imports, while the New York City office became headquarters and distribution center for both domestic and imported wares. This eastern office is said to have imported more than the entire output of domestic wares.

The Stock Market Crash of 1929 ended the demand for imports, and closed the doors of the Jersey City warehouse. Hull was concentrating efforts on domestic pottery of their own manufacture during those "lean years." Although interest in stoneware items had decreased slightly, it continued to be manufactured in great volumes.

TILING OPERATIONS

Emphasis was now on the manufacture of tile in Plant No. 1, which had been converted to tiling operations in 1927.

J.D. Young, an able and experienced man thoroughly schooled in his profession, who had been associated with the company since 1905, was Superintendent of Plant No. 1. Earl Watts Young was assistant to his father. Plant No. 1 began tile production with 125 employees and an annual payroll of $125,000.00. Hull's largest tile customer was The William H. Jackson Company of New York, but they also supplied buyers in the Chicago and Detroit areas. Hull tile at that time was considered rather expensive. In 1927, a dust-pressed 4¼×4¼ flat tile was bringing 65 cents per square foot. Much of the company's tile business was on "special order" basis. Tony Dunlavy was tile designer, and Bill McClellan was Ceramic Engineer during this period. Two types of tile were manufactured; plain and faience; either was available with "cushion" or rounded surface. Decorative tiling for floors, walls, fireplace mantles, etc., was made in a wide array of colors — both solid and stippled, including pastels and black, with high gloss or matte finishes. Accessory items such as towel bars and soap dishes were made in coordinating colors.

THE AMERICAN CLAY PRODUCTS COMPANY

During the early depression years, many Hull items were distributed by The American Clay Products Company, organized in 1929. The short-lived American Clay Products Company was formed by several area pottery firms in an effort to share orders. The president of The American Clay Products Company was Frank Ransbottom of the Ransbottom pottery firm, Roseville, Ohio, with A.E. Hull, Sr., serving as vice president. Companies combined so that any one salesman was able to represent the products of any pottery firm involved. As listed in *"The Collectors Encyclopedia of McCoy,"* by Sharon and Bob Huxford, other companies involved in this merchandising campaign besides Hull were: Burley Pottery Company, Burley Winter Pottery, Crooksville Pottery, Logan Pottery, Muskingum Pottery, Nelson McCoy Sanitary Stoneware Company, Ransbottom Bros. Pottery and Star Stoneware.

The American Clay Products Company marketed many stoneware and semi-porcelain items that had served as staples of The A.E. Hull Pottery Company for several preceeding years. Reproduced in this volume is a catalogue of The A.E. Hull Pottery Company lines as distributed by The American Clay Products Company. These pages will serve as a valuable identification tool for early stoneware and semi-porcelain Hull wares, but identification should be made very cautiously, as some items closely resemble utility wares made by other Ohio area potteries of the day.

NEW MANAGEMENT AND A NEW LOOK AT ART POTTERY

After the death of Addis E. Hull, Sr. in 1930, Addis E. Hull, Jr., succeeded his father in the management of the business and successfully carried it through the great depression.

During the 30's in a definite move to produce a larger volume of art pottery, the A.E. Hull Pottery Company began importing about 20% of their clay for special items and glazes. Please keep in mind, however, that much of the company's production still consisted of stoneware, kitchenware, garden ware, and florist ware. It was to be several years before art pottery lines were fully established and would maintain their largest output.

Hull wares during this time were divided into Earthenware and Stoneware classifications. In 1935, Hull presented this plan of identification:

Earthenware classification — that part of Hull production manufactured of white semi-porcelain body, in every instance, represented by a prefix number of three digits — i.e., 300/13 Casserole, or 610/33 Vase;

Stoneware Classification — that part of Hull production manufactured of buff body, in every instance, represented by a prefix number of two digits — i.e., 34/30 Jardinier, or 34/35 Flower Pot. Earlier wares, in some cases, also follow this plan.

Earlier art pottery shows a consistency in the following marking pattern: second digit numbers — 30, jardiniers; 31, hanging pots; 32, flower bowls; 33, vases; 34, information unavailable; and 35, flower pots and saucers. The later matte finished pastel art pottery line, Calla Lily, most nearly corresponds to this pattern of identification; Tulip somewhat corresponds.

HULL'S CONTRACT WITH SHULTON

In 1937, The A.E. Hull Pottery Company reports, their firm accepted a contract with Shulton of New York for production of pottery cosmetic containers. Pottery containers produced for Shulton by the Hull firm included Old Spice shaving mugs, and Old Spice after shave lotion, cologne, and after shave talc bottles. The Hull Company began production of these containers in 1937, and Old Spice men's products were introduced to the market in 1938. Shulton was relatively small at this time, and it can be said with certainty that the Hull Company was the only producer of pottery containers for their firm during this period.

The following is an excerpt from an article which appeared in the September, 1953 issue of MODERN PACKAGING MAGAZINE, and describes the evolution of Shulton's Hull Pottery.

> Introduced in 1938, at a time when the mere mention of "men's cologne" was a signal for loud guffaws, Old Spice demonstrated how simplicity, good taste, and strong masculine appeal in packaging could build a world market for quality men's products in the dollar-and-up price bracket."
>
> The appeal of the packages as gift items was so great that by 1939, the men's line was outdistancing the women's items and accounting for 22% of the company's gross. Sales were reported at more than $3,000,000. Its success was perhaps even a little surprising to William Lightfoot Schultz.

HULL ACCEPTS MANAGEMENT OF THE SHAWNEE POTTERY

In 1937, A.E. Hull, Jr., resigned to accept the management of The Shawnee Pottery Company located at Zanesville, Ohio.

The following is an excerpt from The Shawnee Pottery Company Prospectus:

> Addis E. Hull, Jr. of Zanesville, Ohio, the President and General Manager, is a graduate of Ohio State University and holds the degree of Ceramic Engineer. He has been actively engaged in the pottery manufacturing business for more than twenty years, the last six as President and General Manager of A.E. Hull Pottery Company of Crooksville, Ohio, which was founded by his father and five associates in 1903.* Mr. Hull has been devoting part of his time and attention to the affairs of the company since its organization. His resignation from Hull Pottery Company will be effective not later than March 14, 1937, or at such prior time as may be convenient to Hull Pottery Company.
>
> *Even though the A.E. Hull Pottery was not founded until 1905, it was not unusual for newspaper accounts, etc., to refer to this plant as The Acme (which dated from 1903) even as late as the 1950 fire, due to the fact that Hull occupied the old Acme Pottery building from 1907.
>
> Mr. Hull has been employed by the Company as General Manager under an agreement terminating December 31, 1941, at a salary of $6,000 annually, plus 5% of the net profits for each fiscal year, resulting after deduction of all operating charges, including interest, depreciation and taxes, but excluding state and Federal income, excess profits and undistributed profits taxes. It is expected that life insurance in the amount of $100,000 payable to the company will be placed on his life.
>
> Mr. Hull will devote his entire time to the affairs of the Company. His principle activities will be market research by contact in the field with buyers and the design and development of new products. The success of pottery manufacture is greatly dependent upon the design and development of products having popular appeal, so that current sales trends may be anticipated and guided. Mr. Hull has outstanding ability as a designer and is thoroughly acquainted with the buyers of the large chain and department stores and wholesalers of pottery products.

HULL'S FABULOUS FORTIES

Gerald F. Watts, son of William Watts, was to succeed A.E. Hull, Jr., in the management of the Hull firm. The company had been clearly established as a giant in the field of ceramics by A.E. Hull, Sr., and A.E. Hull, Jr., and continued to project that same image.

From the late 1930's and into the mid 1940's, Hull vases in many lines appeared relatively simplistic in style. These shapes were repeated usually three, and sometimes four times in a single pattern, each vase gradually enlarging, i.e., Orchid, Tulip, Iris, and Poppy to name a few. This treatment was also shown on several baskets, bowls, and ewers. Although the pottery firm was determined that each design keep its individual identity, shapes and ideas were none-the-less traded from one line to another.

Although the trend at this time was towards art ware, Hull continued to produce down-to-earth utilitarian kitchenware items which were now surfacing with updated shapes and glazes. In keeping utility wares on the market along with its art designs, Hull remained in a position that nearly always pleased the customer.

The Red Riding Hood cookie, patented June 29, 1943, was made in great volumes, and stole the hearts of many. Design Patent Number 135,889 was issued to Louise E. Bauer of Zanesville, Ohio, assignor to the A.E. Hull Pottery Company, Inc., of Crooksville, Ohio, for "Cookie Jar." The Red Riding Hood character proved to be a tremendous seller and before long, a multitude of shapes appeared which continued to be made into the 1950's. The initial patent expired June 29, 1957. Blanks manufactured by Hull were sent to the Royal China and Novelty Company in Chicago for floral decal and decoration.

The early years of 1940 brought about novelty items in the form of foot-long decorated piggy banks. Hull also manufactured an elephant and pig figural liquor bottle with a patented Leeds marking.

Lamps were made within the Hull plant. These lamps are not so rare as has been reported, but do remain a premium to the collector, and usually gather a premium price for the dealer. Hull Company employee Burley Channels jiggered lamps and another, Russell Lee, cut them out and finished them. Fittings were added to lamp bases if the buyer so desired. In addition to lamps made during working hours on company time, "Sunday" or "lunch-hour" lamps were decorated at the whim of some of the workers, and these too are being located. Buck Brothers of Chicago, Illinois, purchased and marketed many Hull lamps.

At that particular time there was a growing resentment toward both Japan and Germany. American produced items were outdistancing the sales of any foreign imports. "Buy American" campaigns were being pushed by every media — radio, newspapers, and magazines. Retail stores throughout the country stocked Hull Pottery, some of which were Federated Stores, F.W. Woolworth Company, McCrory Stores Corporation, G.C. Murphy, Kresges, and Mattinglys.

Hull's pastel tinted art wares embossed with realistic floral sprays began flooding the market; it is these for which the Hull Company is best remembered. Hull's massive arrayment of art pottery shapes included vases, baskets, ewers, wall pockets, rose bowls — and the list goes on... The company reports a "run" in console bowls, which were offered in nearly every design.

Numbering systems were nearly always kept separated; but the pastels that tinted the 1940's art lines were very similar in color, tending toward the prominent blue and rose hues, along with others which included Peach, Almond, Apricot, and Sweet Pink, to name but a few. The duo-tones even infiltrated the stark white mattes of Open Rose.

Even though matte finished lines dominated this period of art pottery production, there were exceptions. The Rosella pattern offered a high gloss ivory or coral finish. The pink-based clay of coral Rosella was made up at the factory. Because of the higher costs incurred in its manufacture, Rosella's term of production was relatively short.

Another pre-1950 high gloss artware line was Magnolia. Although marketed in matte shaded pastels, Magnolia also offered an updated allover transparent pink glaze.

All items produced by Hull have been cast in plaster molds. After removal from a sectional mold, pottery items show lines or seams where the mold fits together. This necessitates a trimming process for all items produced. Many of Hull's intricately shaped art wares required special care in this process. Several molds — for example, the Magnolia and Wild Flower baskets — were quite difficult to trim. These items having cut-outs in the handle sections, were "laced" after the ware was cast.

Many items of this period, due to fancy shapes, and double or triple handles, were trimmed in a special fashion to keep the piece from cracking during the remaining manufacturing processes. Trimming was done while the ware was still green, or unfired, and was a very delicate operation. Too little pressure did not give a thorough finish, while too much resulted in breakage.

PLANT DESTRUCTION: FLOOD AND RESULTANT FIRE

Hull's pastel art pottery lines flourished for over a decade, with production suddenly ending on June 16, 1950, when a four-hour downpour sent Jonathan and Moxahala Creeks out of their banks over a 25-square-mile area in Muskingum, Perry, and Morgan Counties. The water ran seven feet deep through the Crooksville village of about 3000. The red hot pottery kilns of the Hull Company exploded when covered by water and set the plant afire. While the water filled the tunnel kiln firing at 2,000 degrees, the steam pressure forced expansion joints apart causing the roof to ignite.

The flood was devastating and the only pottery in the village not affected by the high water retained the use of its kiln. An estimated 1,500 pottery workers were affected by the flood; approximately 350 of these were Hull Company employees.

More serious than the total destruction of factory equipment was the damage to office records, accounts, and even payroll. Employees lined up at a vacant room on Main Street in Crooksville and declared what was due them. Each and every one of Hull's workers received his pay.

Nearly one week later, the pottery village was back in action, and the first shipment of pottery ware out of Crooksville since the disastrous flood was sent out on the Pennsylvania Railroad by the Worthington Pottery.

RECONSTRUCTION: THE HULL POTTERY COMPANY

Hull's foundation of good will was sound, their reputation among buyers was strong, and other towns were quick to offer inducements to secure the plant. But Hull stockholders felt an obligation to stay in Crooksville where the firm had been founded. Ninety-five per cent of the stockholders wanted to rebuild a new and modern plant. Vice President of the firm at that time, James Brannon Hull, strongly voiced his opinion that it was necessary to rebuild the plant... Hull Company President, Gerald F. Watts was not in favor of reconstruction.

Hull creditors felt an obligation to the company, and satisfied customers hurried to pay their bills before they were due. Over $100,000 came in immediately after the fire.

Insurance provisions enabled the firm to retain the key officials and engineers on the payroll during reconstruction of the new plant. A pilot plant was operated during the months of waiting where new bodies and glazes were formulated.

While the engineers were busy planning future processes and designing a modern plant, the sales department was not idle. The Hull Company maintained their usual display spaces at all shows for a year and a half. They had nothing to display, but they met their customers and promised resumption of production; $150,000 worth of new orders awaited the company's reopening.

NEW PLANT, NEW LEADERSHIP, AND NEW LINES

On January 1, 1952, under the direction of James Brannon Hull, the pottery was restored and the name changed from the A.E. Hull Pottery Company to The Hull Pottery Company. J.B. Hull was elected President, Robert W. Hull, Vice President, and E.D. Young, Secretary-Treasurer and credit manager.

Air floated clay could now be used to prevent imperfections in finished ware. Two 50-ton ram presses were forming ware many times faster than the old jigger and mold methods. Conveyor belts carried ware to workers who finished and glazed it. Other belts lifted ware to overhead drying ovens. The circular Allied kiln, firing at 2,000 degrees, operated 24 hours a day, seven days a week. One car entered and exited every 25 minutes to turn out approximately 100,000 pieces of ware per week.

Production was soon in "full swing" as these photos taken inside the newly constructed plant in the early 1950's indicate.

Casting is the technique used in making a series of identical pottery items. All Hull ware involves this process. As shown, a plaster mold is made from the piece to be reproduced.

These photos were taken inside the mold room.

In casting, a liquid form of clay, called either slip or soup is poured into the plaster molds which have a large number of very small pores that absorb the water from the slip wherever the mold is in contact with it. In this way, a wall of solid material gradually builds up along the face of the mold. When this wall has reached the desired thickness, the excess slip is poured out of the mold leaving the layer of the slip solids in contact with the mold surface. This layer still contains a considerable amount of water, although sufficient water has been removed from it by the mold to render it essentially solid. As this water dries out, both by evaporation and by further absorption, the layer starts to shrink and breaks away from the mold. The cast piece can then be removed and after further drying is ready for the finishing processes.

During Hull's years, other methods besides casting were used to produce the desired shapes. Many of Hull's kitchenware items were formed by jiggering. This method is very similar to hand turning, but is faster and easier and produces ware that is more uniform in shape and thickness. A wheel is used which has on it a plaster mold. The clay is pressed against the sides of the mold by a "bat," sometimes called a pull-down or paddle.

Another method, ram pressing, involves the compressing of moist clay into molds under great pressure to form hollow-ware items. Many shapes such as casseroles and plates are produced this way in today's plant.

These photos illustrate finishing techniques.

The delicate operation of trimming is done by hand as the ware is still green, or unfired.

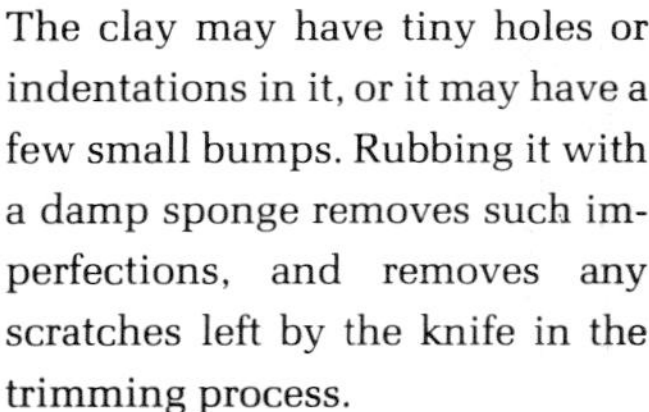

The clay may have tiny holes or indentations in it, or it may have a few small bumps. Rubbing it with a damp sponge removes such imperfections, and removes any scratches left by the knife in the trimming process.

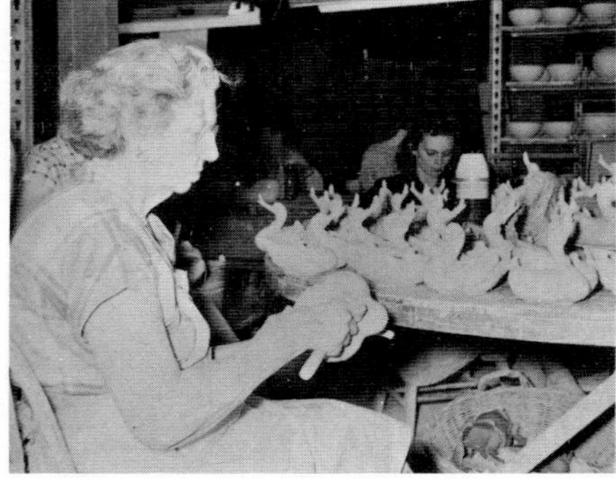

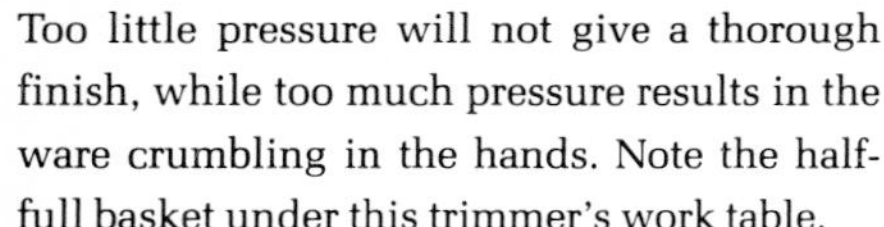

Too little pressure will not give a thorough finish, while too much pressure results in the ware crumbling in the hands. Note the half-full basket under this trimmer's work table.

The base of this ware is being sponged one last time before it moves on this rotating table to the person who will dip it in the glaze.

A tremendous volume of kitchenware was manufactured in the 1950's, a constant companion to the art ware lines being produced. Many of these items in solid high gloss colors were dipped in enormous crocks full of glaze. This continues to be a necessary part of production in today's plant. This is also true of solid colors with foam edge. In this method, the item is first dipped in glaze, then the top edge is coated with a contrasting color. During the firing process the last coat of glaze slowly melts and "runs" down the sides of the ware over the first coat, making its own decoration.

Tinters were still employed for some of the art lines of this period, and hand decorating continued to be an operation of the plant until approximately 1960.

The newly equipped plant made it possible to better meet the demands of manufacturing on a large volume basis.

Hull proclaimed the theory of "security in diversification," and produced at least three new and different patterns each year to cultivate profitable sales. Many designs can be recognized in the previous photos — Woodland, Parchment and Pine, Floral and other kitchenware items, all in production at the same time.

Woodland, which had been introduced prior to destruction of the Hull plant, was again surfacing. Emergence of matte Woodland proved that the delicate soft-bodied pastels of Dawn Rose and Harvest Yellow could not be successfully duplicated. The post-1950 matte finished production was more than an attempt, for much of this sub-standard ware has surfaced on today's market. After the matte trials, Woodland entered the market in classy high gloss two-tones which were made in abundance.

Other items in modern shapes and finishes were soon to follow one after another; but initially, each art line kept its own identity — through the years with Parchment and Pine, Ebb Tide, and Blossom Flite in striking high gloss finishes, to the textured delicate pastels of Serenade, Butterfly and the tinted embossed Tokay line, reminiscent of days gone by.

Parchment and Pine ewers were carefully rounded when they were trimmed, they cracked so easily. Some of Hull's items had separate pieces which were attached after the ware was molded — Ebb Tide's mermaids, and the handle on Blossom Flite's low bowl, for example.

Identical mold shapes were used in a variety of designs — some with, others without embossed motifs — and in various color schemes; from gloss to semi-matte finishes... florals to plains. The surity of past performance in sales most likely served a major factor in the repeated use of molds with added newness and updated glaze finishes. Many mold shapes without floral or decorated motifs in plain colored semi-mattes or gloss and drip trim, were manufactured specifically for the chain stores sales, and many of these items carried no Hull mark.

A short-lived line, Tropicana shared its molds with Continental. Tropicana, introduced shortly before the brilliantly colorful Continental, contained only seven shapes — far less than the varied shapes of Continental, whose main characteristic is its "run down" glaze decor.

Masks were used to decorate some of the 1950 lines. These lead masks made it easier and faster to decorate mass volumes of ware. The mask made to duplicate the designs to be decorated was held over the embossed design, then only a quick shot of color was necessary. Typical items that were masked-sprayed were the fruit and berry designs of Fiesta, and the grape lines, Tokay and Tuscany.

During the 1950's, Hull constantly produced novelty items, jardiniers, florist wares, and a wide variety of kitchenwares along with the art lines. 5,000 Piggy banks were manufactured daily during 1957-58. These consisted of small dime banks and the Corky Pigs, many of which were purchased by Jim Burns of Chicago. Hull swans have served as signets, representative of Hull wares, since the early 1950's. Some swan designs are still in production today.

PRODUCTION CHANGE

In 1960, Hull observed in California a movement towards casual living in almost every aspect of daily living, and following the known past pattern of style development (moving from West to East across the country) Hull designed ovenproof House 'n Garden serving ware — heavy ware with masculine lines, expected to withstand constant daily use both in and out of doors.

Originally, House 'n Garden serving ware was produced in Mirror Brown, trimmed in ivory foam. A few months later, Tangerine, then Green Agate and Butterscotch were added. The combination of the four colors produced a Rainbow table setting, and were thus advertised. There were more than forty companion kitchenware items to choose from in the Rainbow colors, but orders that did not specify a color choice were processed in the original Mirror Brown.

Rainbow's four colors were still being manufactured when Crestone entered the market in March, 1965. One advertisement calls it the "new and fashionable way of life, 30 beautiful items designed specifically for present day living habits in the breakfast nook, on the patio, at the T.V. or barbecue, as well as normal table service." Advertised features included: "extra deep, form fitting well in saucers of items like standard cups and the gravy boat; casserole covers having large deep rings as knobs to serve as glazed over trivets when inverted; platform type chimes providing far superior to ordinary handles*; gravy boat separate from saucer making ideal syrup pitcher; carafe holding two cups to start of neck, so no need for burned fingers; and cover fitting both 9 oz. french handled casserole and soup salad, making duplication unnecessary."

*"Platform type chimes" referred to the wide protruding rims which measure as much as 1½" on some of the larger vegetable bowls.

Crestone and Rainbow continued in production until 1967, with Mirror Brown the only survivor. Mirror Brown is still produced in massive volumes.

In the mid 1970's, Hull produced 75% casual serving ware and 25% florist ware, and is at this time manufacturing 90% casual serving ware and 10% florist ware. Hull, in its central marketing position, distributes nationwide and to Canada.

J.B. Hull served as President of the Hull firm until his death in 1978. Currently making decisions for the company is Robert W. Hull, Chairman of the Board of Directors, Henry Sulens, President, and Byron E. Hull, Vice President and Sales Manager.

COMPANY TRADEMARKS

1. 

2. 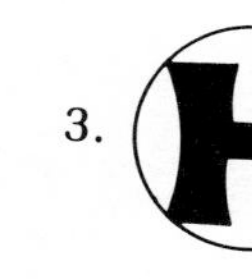

3. 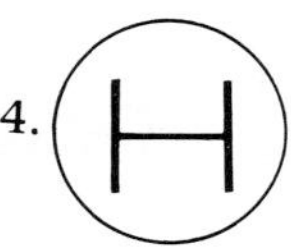

4. H

5. HULL FAIENCE
CUSHION

6. HULL TILE

7. A.E. HULL
U.S.A.

8. HULL
USA
OVEN-PROOF

9. OVEN PROOF

10. HULL
MADE
USA

11. HULL
USA

1. This ink stamp appears on porcelain wares of The Acme Pottery Company, (1903-1907,) of Crooksville, Ohio, purchased by The A.E. Hull Pottery Company in 1907.

2. 3. & 4.
In the early years, Hull did not automatically mark every item produced, some items have no trace of a marking. However, many do wear a trademark. In fact, so many, that collectors have been able to locate quite an assortment of early items without the aid of old company brochures. Hull logically began with the most simplistic motif possible — H. The bold cap H in diamond and bold cap H in circle are impressed marks for both early utilitarian and art wares, both earthenware and stoneware bodies. These marks were used from 1910 to 1935.

5. The "Hull Faience" is an impressed tile mark. Some tiles are marked "Hull Faience" only. Hull tile was produced from 1927 to 1933. The term "Cushion" referred to the type of tile with a rounded surface.

6. This is a raised tile mark, used from 1927 to 1933.

7. After their earlier years, the company trademark in nearly every instance indicated the country of origin — USA. From the early block H marks evolved this block impressed trademark used in the mid 1930's.

8. By the late 1930, this impressed block mark was used on embossed kitchenware items.

9. Although the above mark indicated that the ware of this period was oven-proof, this red and silver foil label boasted it to be heat and cold resisting.

10. This incised 1940 mark was used on novelty wares.

11. This impressed mark appeared on Hull's matte pastels, and was used from 1938 to the early 1940's.

Many of Hull's impressed trademarks were "lost" during the glazing process. A heavy glaze filling in the impressions, concealed markings totally. These obscured trademarks are not in any way related to age or production period of an item; they have only been lost under a too-thick glaze.

12. 

13. 

12. & 13. Incised markings on several circa 1940 items made no mention of Hull, but many of these items carried foil labels. 500 Series marks appear on Calla Lily items. #'s 51 through 54 appear on Thistle items, #55 on Pinecone.

14. 

14. The above lines and others manufactured from 1938 to 1947 wore this triangular seal. This seal appears in both black or maroon background with lettering in either silver or gold.

15. 

15. Seals such as this appear on Hull samples, most of which are no more than representative items of Hull production for display or salesmen. The true experimentals and trials usually carried no mark and no seal, and were scuttled long before they reached the point where the mold even carried a trademark. This particular seal is dark green and white. It also appears in a rectangular shape. Used both before and after 1950, The A.E. Hull sample seals can be dated only by dating the particular design for which it was used.

Trademarks and labels proved to be good advertising, and by 1938, The A.E. Hull Company Pottery display plaques were offered free of charge with orders totalling $20 or more.

16. HULL
USA

16. This mark is nearly identical to the one used earlier for matte art wares with the exception of its being raised rather than incised. It was used from early 1940's to mid 1940's.

17. 

18. EARLY-AMERICAN
Old Spice
SHAVING SOAP
USA
SHULTON

17. & 18. These incised trademarks appear on Shulton's Old Spice product containers manufactured by Hull from 1937 to 1944.

19. Pat. Appl'd For
LEEDS
U.S.A

19. This impressed trademark is found on pig and elephant figural liquor bottles from the Mid-1940's. "Leeds, USA" only is also a common trademark for these bottles.

20. 967
Hull Ware
Little Red Riding Hood
Patent Applied For
U.S.A.

20. This impressed Hull Ware mark appears to be an initial logo used for the Red Riding Hood kitchenware and novelty line, and is most commonly found on cookie jars, dating from the mid-1940's.

21. Hull Ware
U.S.A.

21. An additional incised trademark used for the earlier Red Riding Hood items, dating from the mid-1940's.

22. Little Red Riding Hood
Fat-Des-No- 135889
U.S.A.

22. This incised mark appears commonly on newer Red Riding Hood items, mainly cookie jars, made from the late 1940's, into the early 1950's. Nearly all Red Riding Hood items have been gold decorated and it is not unusual to find items with seals "Hand Painted Fired Ceramic Colors," indicating gold content.

23. Pat-Des-No- 135889
U.S.A.

23. The incised Pat. Des. No. mark appears on many Red Riding Hood items, the most of which date from the late 1940's into the 1950's.

24. Hull Art
U.S.A.

24. Hull's sales were fully stabilized and a great portion of the sales volume was attributed to art pottery lines. Hull chose to "advertise" the art aspect, and in the mid-1940's adopted a new Hull Art impressed logo.

25. 

25. This revised trademark called for an updated label. The round Potter-at-Wheel label was used during the mid to late 1940's and for a few of the Post 1950 wares. Although today not used in label form, the Potter-at-Wheel form appears on most company brochures. It is surprising that this trademark was not used in label form earlier, for the Potter-at-Wheel logo had been gracing Hull brochure pages since the late 1920's. It is a part of the present day Hull Company letterhead. This seal is black with silver, gold, or gray lettering.

26. 

27. U.S.A. Hull Art

28. HULL U.S.A.

29. 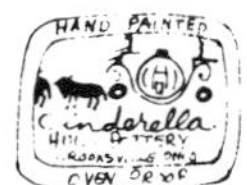

30. Hull U.S.A.

31. Hull USA

32. Hull U.S.A.

33. Hull USA

34. Hull U.S.A.

35. U.S.A. Hull Ware

36. 

37. 

38. 

39. 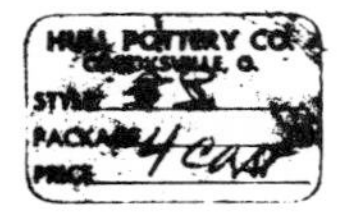

40. Grany

41. 

42. Tokay U.S.A.

43. 

26. The Rosella seal was designed and used specifically for the Rosella line in 1946. This label is brown with gold accents.

27. The next trademark to emerge on art lines was primarily the same logo, but in raised form. This mark was used from 1946 to 1950.

28. The impressed bold block Hull was used to mark Cinderella's Blossom and Bouquet kitchenware items during 1949.

29. This 1949 blue and gold label was also used for Cinderella kitchenware, indicating that it was hand painted and oven proof.

30. This beautiful flowing script mark in raised form was used in 1949 on matte Woodland, and again after the reopening of the Hull plant in 1952 on both matte and high gloss Woodland. With little variation, in both raised and impressed form, it was used during the 1950's on art lines and novelties as well as on kitchenware.

31. This small brown ink stamp mark appears on kitchenware items made just after the plant reopened in 1952.

32. This impressed, flourishing mark was used from 1952, for nearly all of the 1950 art lines and also for novelty and kitchenware items.

33. This raised trademark was also used during thé 1950's art and kitchenware lines.

34. To a greater extent the 1950 wares carried this mark in impressed form.

35. This impressed Hull Ware mark appears on Post 1950 kitchenware lines.

36. & 37. These foil labels marked wares made for chain store sales in both pre and post-1950 years. They are black with either silver or gold lettering. Granada and Mardi Gras seals were often used interchangeably for identical items.

38. This foil label was used for chain store wares made in the 1950's. Background of seal is either silver or gold with green band and gold and black lettering.

39. For identification purposes, this label was used to mark wares of the 1950's.

40. This is the signature of Granville Shafer, a gold decorator of the Zanesville area for many years. Many of his decorated items are stamped "23K Gold Guaranteed, Shafer USA, Zanesville, Ohio."

41. This impressed marking appears on the dime banks made in the late 1950's. A form of the H.P. CO mark is currently being used on House 'n Garden casual serving ware.

42. The Tokay mark is impressed on the line of the same name. This embossed grape line entered in the market in 1958.

43. The impressed Marcrest trademark was used for premium items produced by Hull in the very late 1950's. Both Heritageware and House 'n Garden casual serving ware molds were used for this production.

44. This raised block Marcrest mark appears on ashtrays made by Hull.

45. This raised block Sinclair mark was used on novelty banks made for premium items by Hull in the early 1960's.

46. This magestic logo appears in impressed form on many of Hull's novelty wares of the 1950's and 1960's which were made specifically for chain store sales.

47. & 48. The incised Coronet marks were used on chain store items in the 1960's.

49. This impressed mark appears on Hull's House 'n Garden casual serving ware manufactured since 1960.

44. MARCREST

45. SINCLAIR USA

46. REGAL

47. Coronet U.S.A.

48. Coronet U.S.A.

49. hull Oven Proof U.S.A.

50. hull U.S.A. Crestone © OVEN-PROOF

51. Imperial U.S.A.

52. planter, inc.

53. hull U.S.A.

54. hull U.S.A. crooksville, ohio

50. This impressed mark was designed and used specifically for Hull's Crestone dinnerware which entered the market in 1965.

51. The impressed Imperial logo used since 1960 marks the massive volume of florist ware items produced since that time and still in manufacture today. Many times the small case impressed "hull" appears with the script Imperial mark.

52. This incised mark was used for planters and florist ware of the 1960's.

53. This incised mark has been used since 1960 on both dinnerware and florist ware, and is still used today.

54. This black label with gold lettering has been used to mark both kitchenware and florist ware items since 1960.

LINES AND DATES OF MANUFACTURE

The extent of lines manufactured by Hull is not fully known; but the following is provided as a collector reference, for this is the point of completed research at this time.

Information is unavailable at present to verify the authenticity of line names marked with an asterisk(*.) Line names given in these instances are those preferred and used most often by collectors throughout the country.

Art Pottery: 1935. Miscelllaneous art line that included vases, jardiniers, pots and saucers. White semi-porcelain bodies glazed in matte Eggshell White, Bermuda Green, Lotus Blue, Oyster White, Autumn Brown, Egyptian Green, Maize Yellow and others, such as blended glazes.

Athena: Novelty and vase line assortment of the late 1950's. Line includes high gloss colors Lilac and Spring Green, but other solid high glass colors with or without White Lava trim were used.

Bak-Serv: 1933 Semi-porcelain banded kitchenware line.

Banded: 1920-1935. Any of the varieties of kitchenware items that have been decorated by way of color bands. Semi-porcelain, stoneware, and yellow ware bodies were available. Color bands included, but were not limited to, blue, green, red, black, brown and white, as well as luster.

Basque: 1933 No information as to color of this utility and refrigerator jar line.

Blended: 1933. High gloss brown and green blended glazes applied to planters and jardiniers.

Blossom: 1949. Ovenproof kitchenware items, white gloss finish, six-petal hand painted flower in pink or yellow with green leaves and piping. Fifteen shapes with additional items produced after 1950.

Blossom Flite: 1955. Black lattice on overall high gloss pink having charcoal gray interior, or blue lattice on overall pink with metallic green interior. Multi-colored relief spray of florals decorate this line of 15 pieces.

Blue Banded: 1929. White bodied high gloss semi-porcelain kitchenware items that included bowls, nappies, jugs, butters, custards, all with underglaze raised blue bands.

Blue Bird: 1929: Flying or perched blue bird decal used in decorating early cereal ware and salt boxes.

Blue Ribbon: Mid-1950's. White high gloss bowls, banded with green, smaller green strips either side in 5 graduated sizes.

Bouquet: 1949. Ovenproof kitchenware, white gloss finish, yellow tinted tops with hand decorated floral spray in pink, yellow and blue, in 15 shapes with additional items produced after 1950.

Bow-Knot: 1949. Embossed floral in duo-tone matte finished pastel body colors of pink and blue or turquoise and blue combination. Twenty-nine shapes.

Butterfly: 1956. Raised pastel butterfly and flower motif in a combined gloss and matte finish of white on white, or matte transparent white with turquoise inner surfaces. Twenty-five pieces.

Butters: 1920-1930. Zane Grey, ivory and yellow bodied ware with blue bands, buff body green tinted, blue Flemish, are a few butters available. Four sizes — 2, 3, 4, and 5 pound sizes.

**Calla Lilly: 1938.* Also referred to as Jack-in-Pulpit due to the embossed decor and large arrow shaped leaves. Various matte tints in duo-tone colors available.

Capri: 1961. Satin finished bowls and planters in Coral with weathered limestone effect, or Seagreen to represent sea-washed rock formations. Thirty shapes.

Cereal Ware: 1920-1930. Fifteen piece sets consisting of cannisters, spice jars, vinegar and oil cruets, and salt boxes, with underglazed decal decoration. Plain sets in semi-porcelain and stoneware bodies were manufactured in solid colors.

Checker: 1933: Semi-porcelain bowls and bowl sets offered in green or yellow.

Cinderella: 1949. Overall line name for kitchenware shapes of Blossom and Bouquet.

Chinese Red Cracquelle: 1928. Additional luster ware line, in brilliant red. At least 15 shapes offered.

Classic: 1950's. High gloss wares in transparent overall glazes of ivory or pink. Embossed florals appear on one side only. Manufactured for chain store sales. The Classic name remained a standard for chain store items; for example, a complete line of Classic jardiniers were offered.

Colored: 1935. Undecorated bake dishes offered in semi-porcelain body of transparent Lucerene Green, Maize Yellow. Colored teapots were available in a dark ivory buff semi-vitreous body glazed in opaque Lucerene Green or Burgundy Brown. Other items likely.

Combinets: 1920-1930. Semi-porcelain, metal-bailed, white glazed with raised embossed design. Other descriptions are likely.

Continental: 1959. Modern shapes in brilliant high gloss colors of Evergreen, Persimmon, and Mountain Blue, with contrasting "run." Brochure lists 28 items.

Conventional Rose: 1929. Decalcomania design used to border early cereal ware, offered in #132, Pink Double Border.

Conventional Tile: 1929. Decalcomania design used to border early cereal ware, offered in #133, Yellow Double Border.

Conventional Vine: 1929. Decalcomania design used to border early cereal ware, offered in #131, Blue Double Border.

Coronet: Late 1960's. Chain store planter and vase assortment in solid gloss colors, with or without contrasting foam edge.

Cuspidors: 1920-1930. Toilet and parlor shapes offered in semi-porcelain and dark buff bodies. Decorations included over the glaze decalcomania, transparent glazes, or color bands of gold, blue, green, maroon, and luster.

Crab Apple: 1935. Art pottery vases, jardiniers, hanging baskets, available in matte Eggshell White; matte Peacock Blue on white semi-porcelain body; hand painted flowers in rose, leaves in green on matte sun tan or buff body; or bright white on white semi-porcelain body. Catalogue lists 18 shapes.

Crestone: 1965. Ovenproof casual serving ware in high gloss turquoise, white foam edge.

Debonair: Mid-1950's. Plain shaped ovenproof kitchenware items in either solid or two-tone high gloss colors. Fifteen pieces.

Delft: 1929. Blue ship scene decal applied to early cereal ware.

Dogwood: Mid-1940's. Also known as Wild Rose. Raised hand decorated flower motif shaded in two-tone matte body colors of blue/pink, turquoise/peach, or overall peach. Twenty-two shapes.

Doric: 1928. Nested bowls with paneled design. White semi-porcelain decorated with three blue lines.

Ebb Tide: 1954. Embossed fish and sea shell designs in high gloss colors of chartreuse and wine, or shrimp and turquoise. Sixteen shapes.

Embossed: 1934. Nested bowls, green embossed. No additional information available.

Fantasy: Late 1950's. Vase and planter assortment in solid high gloss colors of pink, black, blue, and others, with or without foam edge.

Fiesta: Mid 1950's. Line name for variety of high gloss chain store items. Designs range from pieces with embossed leaves, fruits and flowers, to jardiniers in brass stands.

Flemish: 1928. Old price guide makes reference to 2, 3, and 5 pound blue Flemish butter jars. No additional information available.

Floral: 1952-53. White high gloss kitchenware line with raised yellow daisy-like flower, brown piping. Fifteen pieces.

Florist Ware: 1928. Green vases ranging from 6 to 15 inches, and jardiniers offered specifically for floral and cut flower arrangements. Thirteen items listed in brochure.

Flower Club: Early 1960's. Chain store line of planters, bowls, and swans offered in Satin White, and high gloss Jade Green and Wild Honey. Other colors are likely.

Footed: 1920-1930. Any of the varieties of kitchenware items that are footed, both yellow ware and semi-porcelain bodied, either banded, or solid transparent colors.

Garden Dishes: Early 1960's. Brochure illustrates Imperial line square and rectangular planters available in solid high gloss colors, many with faint mottled effect.

Granada: Pre and Post 1950 years. Matte finished ware with embossed florals. Base is shaded but no color detail on floral decoration. Also plain-lined deco shapes in Satin White or shaded bodies of pastel blues and pinks. Manufactured for chain store sales.

Grecian: 1929. Decalcomania design used to border cereal ware offered in #119, Blue, or #121, Gold.

Green Buff: 1933. Bowls, bowl sets, cuspidors, and butters. No additional information available.

Green Tint: 1933. Fluted, buff body, green tinted bowls, bowl sets, cuspidors, and butters. Green tinted dairy jugs were offered in 2, 3, 4, and 5 pint sizes.

Heritageware: 1958. Ovenproof kitchenware in high gloss Mint Green or Azure Blue "with a light touch of foam" edge. Heritageware shapes were decorated in other various high gloss and semi-matte finishes. These molds were also used for production of a premium line with a Marcrest marking.

Hotelware: 19201930. Semi-porcelain plain and embossed combinets, chambers, cuspidors, mugs, jugs, some decorated by over the glaze decalcomania and color bands.

House 'n Garden ware: Introduced in 1960. Refers to the Mirror Brown casual serving ware that has been produced in large volume over the past twenty years. Most shapes are still in production today.

Imperial: Massive florist ware line made since 1960, and still in production today. Arrayment of colors includes both satin and high gloss finishes, with or without foam edge. Line includes novelty planters, vases, baskets, and flower bowls.

Iris: Mid-1940's. Hand-painted embossed florals on matte tinted backgrounds of blue/rose, rose/peach, or allover peach colors. Fourteen shapes, many in graduated sizes.

Ivory: 1928. Red and blue banded ivory bodied bowls, jugs, casseroles, custards, butters.

Jardiniers: 1920-1930. Sixteen to 18 inch pedestals, and 5 to 10 inch jardiniers offered in assorted colors. No additional information available.

Just Right Kitchenware: Mid-1950's. Overall name for Floral and Vegetable kitchenware patterns. Brochure page also notes Blue Ribbon bowl nests. Other additions are very possible.

Leeds: Mid-1940's. Figural elephant and pig liquor bottles in high gloss colors of blue and pink.

Luster: 1928. Various bowls and tankard jugs of semi-porcelain white body and glaze with luster band decoration over the glaze. Decorations offered: wide red band and small blue stripes, wide ivory brown band and small blue stripes, or wide green band and small black stripes.

Lusterware: 1928. Vases, ash trays, and jardiniers, offered in luster colors of Shammy, Orange, Lavender, Slate, Emerald, Light Blue, Iridescent Dark Blue, and Golden Glow. Catalogue indicates 35 items available.

Magnolia (Gloss): 1947-48. Embossed floral decoration hand painted either blue or pink, all over transparent pink glaze. Twenty-four pieces.

Magnolia (Matte): 1946-47. Embossed hand decorated floral on matte pastels of pink and blue or dusty rose and yellow. Twenty-seven items.

Marcrest: Late 1950's. High gloss kitchenware items made for use as premiums for grocery sales. Heritageware molds were used in this production.

Mardi Gras: 1940. A line manufactured exclusively for the F.W. Woolworth Company. Included were vases and nested bowls in solid high gloss pastel colors.

Mardi Gras: Pre and Post 1950 years. Matte finished ware with embossed florals. Base is shaded but no color detail is given to floral decoration. Also plain-lined deco shapes in Satin White or shaded bodies of pastel blues and pinks. Manufactured for chain store sales, exclusively the F.W. Woolworth Co.

Mayfair: Late 1950's. Vase assortment in solid pastel high gloss finishes. At least two wall pockets are offered in this line.

Medley: Late 1950's. Vase assortment in solid high gloss pastels. Fourteen shapes.

**Nuline Bak-Serve: 1938.* Ovenproof-coldproof kitchenware in solid high gloss colors. In at least three embossed designs, marked "B," "C," and "D" series.

Nursery: 1928. Baby plates, cups, mugs, saucers, bread and milk sets are listed in catalogues. No additional information is available.

**Open Rose: Mid-1940's.* Also referred to as Camellia. Hand-decorated embossed florals on shaded pastel backgrounds, or all white backgrounds. At least 43 shapes.

Orchid: 1938. Hand-decorated embossed Orchid on two-tone matte backgrounds of blue/rose, rose/cream, or allover blue. At least 17 shapes, many in graduated sizes.

Pandora: 1933. Kitchenware line available in yellow and green, included steins, salt boxes, utility jars.

Panelled: 1929. Semi-porcelain bowls, panelled design with raised blue band decoration. The panelled salt box was also advertised as octagon.

Parchment and Pine: 1952-53. High gloss artware with embossed pine sprays, decorated in realistic pine greens and browns. At least 15 shapes.

Persian: 1928. Additional luster ware line which included vases, jardiniers. At least 15 shapes offered.

Pinecone: 1938. Simplistic embossed pinecone decor on solid matte pastel colors of blue, pink, or turquoise. Only one 6½ inch vase shape known to exist.

Plain White: 1933. White glazed kitchenware, no decoration, consisting of bake sets, bowls, refrigerator jars, bean pots, etc. Some items same as those offered in Restaurantware line.

**Poppy: Mid-1940's.* Hand decorated embossed poppy decor on duo-tone backgrounds of blues and pinks, or pink/cream. In at least 12 shapes, many in graduated sizes.

Rainbow: 1928. White semi-porcelain bowls with red and yellow, red and blue, or brown and red line decoration under glaze.

Rainbow: 1960. Ovenproof casual serving ware in solid high gloss colors of Mirror Brown, Tangerine, Green Agate, and Butterscotch, all with foam edge.

Red Riding Hood: U.S. Patent number 135,889 issued for "Cookie Jar" 1943-1957. Red Riding Hood character molded into kitchen and novelty wares. Blanks were sent to Royal China Company in Chicago for appropriate detailing. Various floral decals were applied, items usually trimmed in gold.

Regal: Late 1950's. Chain store line of novelty planters, flower bowls and vases in assorted high gloss colors.

Restaurantware: 1935. Restaurant ware items in transparent ivory semi-porcelain body, no decoration.

Rosella: 1946. Embossed wild rose floral, hand-decorated underglaze in colors of coral or ivory. Sixteen shapes, plus at least three lamp bases.

**Royal: Mid 1950's.* Woodland, Ebb Tide, Butterfly, Imperial and other line molds decorated in high gloss pink or turquoise colors with overall white spattered affect. Manufactured for chain store sales.

Rub-Off: Mid-1960's. Experimental ware in high gloss solid colors with embossed designs that have been "skinned" after ware was dipped. Imperial line molds used.

Salt Boxes: A variety of salt boxes were offered in Hull's early years — solid colors, banded semi-porcelain, Zane Grey, Pandora, decaled and stamped motifs. Available in round, square, panelled, or octagonal shapes.

Serenade: 1957. Textured exterior in solid matte Regency Blue with Sunlight Yellow gloss interior, Shell Pink with Pearl Gray gloss interior, or Jonquil Yellow with Willow Green gloss interior were colors offered in this bough and chickadee line. Twenty-four pieces.

Shamrock: 1928. Fancy shaped yellow ware bowls and yellow ware with brown bands. No additional information available.

Shulton: 1937-1944. Bottles and shaving mugs manufactured exclusively for Shulton's Old Spice products. Cream glazed bodies with fired on illustrations of sailing vessels in blue.

Spiral: Early 1960. Jardinier bowls and pedestals, along with vases all with swirled spiral effect. Items offered were available in Satin White, Moss Green gloss and Mahagony gloss with white flow.

Square Cereal Sets: 1929. Semi-porcelain canisters, spice jars, salt boxes, and cruets offered in overall white glaze with seven different decalcomania decorations. Fifteen items to the set.

Square Footed: 1935. Dark ivory buff semi-vitreous square footed kitchenware with transparent Popcorn Yellow glaze and wide Colonial Blue stripe with one Shell Bloom Pink pin stripe on each size. Square footed kitchenware items were also offerd in solid glazes of turquoise and yellow. Additional stripe decors and solid colors are likely.

Square Rim: 1920-1930. Any of the varieties of kitchenware items that were square rimmed in shape. Bodies range from dark ivory semi-vitreous buff, to yellow ware, to the square rim ivory, in assorted banded decors, solid transparent glazes, or air brush blends.

Sueno: 1938. Company Sueno brochure page illustrates Calla Lilly, Tulip, Thistle, and Pinecone designs. Most likely an overall name for chain store sales.

Sunglow: 1952. Also referred to as Pansy or Pansy and Butterfly. Novelty and vase assortment line in high gloss solid backgrounds of pink or yellow, with raised floral and sometimes floral and butterfly decoration. Many Bow-Knot molds were used in this production.

Teapots: 1935. Semi-vitreous dark ivory buff body with opaque Lucerne Green or Burgundy Brown glaze, no decoration. Also offered in semi-porcelain bodies in transparent yellow and green. Other colors are likely.

Thistle: 1938. Raised thistle on solid background matte finishes of pink, blue, or turquoise, in four known vase shapes.

Tile: 1927-1933. A very fine grade of tile was manufactured, with special orders accepted. Floor and wall tile, with coordinated accessories were offered. A large variety of colors, including pastels and black were available in matte, gloss, and stipled finishes.

Toiletware: Semi-porcelain combinets, chambers, cuspidors, mugs, and jugs, some decorated by over the glaze decalcomania and color bands, some plain, some with embossed detail. Items were marketed during many of Hull's early years.

Tokay: 1958. Embossed leaf and grape decor in high gloss colors of Milk White and Forest Green, or spray tinted Light Green and Sweet Pink. Eighteen pieces.

Tropicana: 1959. High gloss; striking white background with colorful Caribbean figures, edged in Tropic Green. Seven shapes.

Tulip: 1928. Semi-porcelain white body and glaze with tulip decal over the glaze. Six size tankard jugs offered.

Tulip: 1938. Hand-painted tulip decoration with shaded blue bases with pink, cream or blue tops. Fifteen shapes offered in graduated sizes.

Tuscany: 1960. Embossed leaf and grape decor in high gloss Milk White with Forest Green or Sweet Pink and Gray-Green colors. Eighteen pieces.

Urn Vases: Mid-1960's. Imperial line planters in graduated sizes, offered in various high gloss colors.

Vegetable Pattern: Mid-1950's. Embossed vegetable patterned kitchenware in high gloss solid colors of Yellow, Coral, and Green. Fifteen shapes.

Victorian: 1974. Heavily embossed florist ware line, most often footed. Available in gloss Olive with Willow Green trim, gloss Green with Turquoise trim or allover Satin White.

Water Lily: 1948. Hand decorated florals in two duo-tone color combinations — Walnut/Apricot and Turquoise/Sweet Pink. Twenty-eight shapes.

Wildflower: (Number Series.) Mid-1940's. Matte finished artware with tinted backgrounds of blue/pink or russet/pink. Raised hand-decorated floral in yellow, pink, and white, which very closely resembles the floral spray of Wildflower, "W" Series. Several of the Wildflower molds are identical, but this series most often has more intricate shapes and fancier handles.

Wildflower: ("W" Series.) 1946-47. Hand-decorated floral spray of Trillium, Mission and Bluebell in two-tone pastel body shades of pink/blue and yellow/dusty rose. Twenty-two shapes.

Woodland: (Matte.) 1949 and 1952-3. Pre-1950 items are noted for their matte finished, hand-decorated florals in Dawn Rose and Harvest Yellow body pastels. Post 1950 Woodland included a sub-standard matte finish, imitating the pre-1950 mattes, and several two-toned high gloss finishes. Thirty shapes, earlier matte finished wares. Brochure indicates 21 shapes available in two-tone finishes.

Woodland (Two-Tone:) 1953. Floral embossed artware in high gloss colors of chartreuse with dark green accents and interiors, dark green with blue, and rose with chartreuse. Twenty-one shapes.

Yellow Ware: Any of the varieties of early wares manufactured in durable bright glossy glazes, either plain or banded, yellow ware bodies. Items offered included jugs, butters, casseroles, custard cups, nested bowls, and other kitchenware.

Zane Grey: 1928. High quality durable kitchenware manufactured in same basic shapes as blue banded ware of semi-porcelain. This grey-bodied ware was more economical for the trade. Blue band decoration under glaze appears on kitchenware items such as jars, bowls, nappies, jugs, butters, custards, and food containers up to 6 gallon capacity.

NUMBERING SYSTEMS

Mold identification and size numbers nearly always accompanied the Hull trademark. However, these numbers have no significant value beyond that of identification purposes. Numbering systems were used primarily for the convenience of company salesmen and workers inside the plant, and are most helpful to those of us the Hull Company didn't count on... the collector.

In most instances, the first letter or number indicates mold identification. Remaining markings refer to height for vertical items such as vases, baskets, etc., or width for console bowls and other horizontal shapes. Capacities are included in markings on many of Hull's utilitarian wares.

Early Hull utility and art wares had varied numbering systems which are somewhat difficult to follow. Identical items were produced in different clay bodies, decorated differently; some carried the same mold numbers, some did not. Little is known as to the full extent of Hull's earliest lines, research is still in progress. The incomplete listings provided are presented to aid the collector in accurate identification of older stoneware and semi-porcelain items. In later years, assignment of a separate numbering system for each individual design or pattern of ware manufactured proved to be easier for all concerned.

The 1940's numbering systems were kept fairly separate and individual from one to another, although several basic ideas were shared and some items were even duplicated — same mold shape, but different floral pattern and numbering system. Kitchenware lines appear to be most alike in numbering systems. Many identically shaped post-1950 kitchenware lines are but ten digits apart on numbering systems.

In order to measure the extent of Hull's massive arrayment of wares, the following lists are provided. Please keep in mind this listing is not complete and is definitely not the final word in Hull. The Hull collector is little surprised by the diversity of styles and forms displayed by the Hull Pottery firm. Always discoveries will be made, and this is what keeps the collector interested. This listing will exclude animal planters and novelty lines made after 1950, as there seems to be no consistent standard marking system. It will also exclude the Imperial florist ware line because it is so extensive, and not particularly sought after since Imperial is still being manufactured today. (However, for identification and dating purposes, Imperial brochure pages will be added later, due to the fact that many items included in late production are being marketed to collectors as older wares. Such items include the various sizes of single swans, double swans, urn vases, etc.)

BAK-SERVE

No. 100	Bowls: 4-12 inch
No. 106	Bake Dishes: 4-9 inch
No. 107	Jugs: 42's — ½ pint, 36's — 1½ pint, 30's — 1 quart, and 18's — 2 quart
No. 110	3-lb. Refrigerator Jar and Cover
No. 111	Salt Box
No. 113	7½″ Casserole, Cover and Plate
No. 114	2's Custard Cup
No. 118	Spice Jar and Cover
No. 119	2-quart Bean Pot and Cover
No. 120	Salt Shaker
No. 121	2-lb. Range Jar and Cover

BANDED

No. 4	Custard Cups: Size No. 1 and No. 2
No. 5	Jugs: 48's — ¾ pint, 42's — 1 pint, 36's — 1½ pint, 30's — 2½ pint, 24's — 4 pint, 18's — 5 pint
No. 7	Butters: 2-lb. — 6⅝″, 3-lb. — 7¼″, 4-lb. — 7⅞″
No. 12	Bowls: 5-12 inch
No. 14	Bowls: 4-15 inch
No. 18	Bowls: 4-13 inch
No. 23	Nappies: 4-9 inch
No. 30	Bowls: 5-10 inch
No. 33	Casseroles: 6-8 inch
No. 36	Bake Dishes: 5-9 inch
No. 41	Nappies: 4-9 inch
No. 101	Bowls: 4-8 inch
No. 421	Bowls: 4-15 inch
No. 440	Jugs: 48's, 42's, 36's, 30's, 24's, and 18's
No. 450	Butters: 2, 3, and 4 lb.
No. 453	Casserole: 7 inch
No. 460	Custard cups: Size No. 1 and No. 2
No. 701	Bowls: 4-15 inch
No. 705	Bowls: 5-12 inch

BASQUE

No. 402	3-Pt. Utility Jar and Cover
No. 406	1-Quart Beater Jug
No. 428	Bowls: 5-10 inch
No. 451	3-Lb. Refrigerator Jar and Cover

BLOSSOM

No. 20	5½″, 7½″, and 9½″ Mixing Bowls
No. 21	7½″ and 8½″ Covered Casseroles
No. 22	64-Oz. Beverage Pitcher
No. 24	32-Oz. Covered Grease Jar
No. 25	Salt and Pepper Shakers
No. 26	42-Oz. Teapot
No. 27	4½″ Covered Sugar
No. 28	4½″ Creamer
No. 29	16-Oz. Pitcher
No. 29	32-Oz. Pitcher
No. 30	Cookie Jar
	9½″ Square Serving Dish

BLOSSOM FLITE

T-1	6″ Honey Jug
T-2	6″ Basket
T-3	8½″ Pitcher
T-4	8½″ Basket
T-5	None noted on brochure
T-6	10½″ Cornucopia
T-7	10½″ Handled Vase
T-8	8¼″×9¼″ Low Basket
T-9	10″ Low Bowl
T-10	16½″×6¾″ Console Bowl
T-11	Candleholder (3¼″)
T-12	10½″ Planter Flower Bowl
T-13	13½″ Pitcher Vase
T-14	8″ Teapot
T-15	Creamer
T-16	Covered Sugar

BLUE RIBBON

No. 1	Bowls: 5, 6, 7, 8, and 9 inch

BOUQUET

No. 20	5½″, 7½″, and 9½″ Mixing Bowls
No. 21	7½″ and 8½″ Covered Casseroles
No. 22	64-Oz. Beverage Pitcher
No. 24	32-Oz. Covered Grease Jar
No. 25	Salt and Pepper Shakers
No. 26	42-Oz. Teapot
No. 27	4½″ Covered Sugar

No. 28 4½" Creamer
No. 29 16-Oz. Pitcher
No. 29 32-Oz. Pitcher
No. 30 Cookie Jar
9½" Square Serving Dish

BOW-KNOT
B-1 5½" Ewer
B-2 5" Vase
B-3 6½" Vase
B-4 6½" Vase
B-5 7½" Cornucopia
B-6 6½" Flower Pot/Attached Saucer
B-7 8½" Vase
B-8 8½" Vase
B-9 8½" Vase
B-10 10½" Vase
B-11 10½" Vase
B-12 10½" Basket
B-13 13" Double Cornucopia
B-14 12½" Vase
B-15 13½" Ewer
B-16 13½" Console Bowl
B-17 3½" Candleholder
B-18 5¾" Jardinier
B-20 6" Teapot
B-21 4" Creamer
B-22 4" Covered Sugar
B-23
B-24 6" Cup/Saucer Wall Pocket
B-25 6½" Basket
B-26 6" Pitcher Wall Pocket
B-27 8" Whisk Broom Wall Pocket
B-28 10" Plate Wall Plaque
B-29 12" Basket
Unmarked 6½" Iron Wall Pocket
Unmarked Square Cup/Saucer Wall Pocket

BUTTERFLY
B1 6¼" Pitcher-Shaped Bud Vase
B2 6½" Cornucopia
B3 7" Heart-Shaped Ash Tray
B4 6¼"Bon Bon Dish
B5 6" Jardinier
B6 5½" Urn Candy Dish
B7 9¾" Flower Dish
B8 12¾" Window Box
B9 9" Vase
B10 7" Vase
B11 8¾" Pitcher Vase
B12 10½" Cornucopia
B13 8" Basket
B14 10½" Vase
B15 13½" Pitcher Vase
B16 10½" Fruit Bowl
B17 10½" Basket
B18 Teapot
B19 Creamer
B20 Covered Sugar
B21 Console Bowl
B22 Candleholder
B23 11½" Serving Tray
B25 16" Lavabo

CALLA LILY
500/32 10" Bowl
500/33 7" Vase
500/33 8" Vase
502/33 6½" Vase
506 10" Ewer
520/33 8" Vase
530/33 5" Vase
530/33 7" Vase
540/33 6" Vase
550/33 7½" Vase
560/33 10" Vase
560/33 13" Vase
570/33 8" Cornucopia
590/33 13" Console Bowl
Unmarked 2¼" Candleholder

CAPRI
C14 4" Pillow Vase
C15 5¾" Oval Pedestaled Vase
C21 3" Baby Swan Planter
C23 8½"×7"×6" Large Swan Planter
C28 9¾" Vase
C29 12" Vase
C38 6¾" Basket
C44 4¼" Round Flower Bowl
C45 4¼"×6" Ribbed Flower Bowl
C46 4½"×8" Scalloped Flower Bowl
C47 5¼"×8" Ftd. Round Flower Bowl
C47C Above Bowl with Cover/Bon Bon Bowl
C48 12¼"×5½" Leaf Basket
C49 5¾" Lion Head Urn Vase
C50 9" Lion Head Urn Vase
C51 None noted on brochure page
C52 10"×7½" Ash Tray
C57 14½" Open Front Vase
C48 13¾" Vase
C59 15" Vase
C62 5½" Compote
C62C 8½" Candy Dish w/Cover
C63 14" Caladium Leaf
C64 10" Open Front Vase
C67 4" Square Footed Planter
C68 8½" Rectangular Flower Dish
C80 Llama Planter
C81 Twin Swan Planter
C87 12" Pine Cone Pitcher
C314 Flying Duck Planter
C525 6½" Pitcher Vase

CEREAL WARE
Square Cereal Sets:
Canisters
Tea
Sugar
Rice
Flour
Cereal
Coffee
Spices
Cinnamon
Mustard
Ginger
Nutmeg
Pepper
Allspice
Salt Box
Vinegar Cruet
Oil Cruet

Cereal sets offered in the following decorations:
No. 119 Blue Grecian Border
No. 121 Gold Grecian Border
No. 131 Blue Double Border Conventional Vine
No. 132 Pink Double Border Conventional Rose
No. 133 Yellow Double Border Conventional Tile
No. 136 Flying Blue Bird
No. 150 Delft Ship Scene

No. 880 Cereal Ware was marketed in the same items listed above, with the exception of the vinegar and oil cruets. One jar may indicate "Spice" instead of "Allspice."

CHECKER
No. 17 Bowls: 5, 6, 7, 8, 9, and 10 inch.

CLASSIC
4 6" Vase
5 6" Vase
6 6" Ewer

The Classic name remained a standard for chain store items, such as flower pots, jardiniers, and jardiniers in metal stands.

CHINESE RED CRACQUELLE
505 8" Vase
505 10" Vase
505 12" Vase
513 6" Vase
513 8" Vase
513 10" Vase
513 12" Vase
514 5½" Vase
515 10" Vase
516 8" Vase
517 7" Vase
518 14" Lamp Vase
520 7" Vase
520 9" Vase

COLORED
40/5 Teapots: 30's, 24's, and 12's
250/6 6" Bake Dish
250/7 7" Bake Dish

CONTINENTAL
A1 8" Ash Tray
A3 12" Rectangular Ash Tray
A20 10" Ash Tray w/Pen
A40 13" Oval Ash Tray w/Pen
C28 9¾" Vase
C29 12" Vase
C51 15½"×4¾" Flower Dish
C52 10"×7½" Ash Tray
C53 8½" Vase
C54 12½" Vase
C55 12¾" Basket
C56 12½" Pitcher Vase
C57 14½" Open Front Vase
C58 13¾" Vase
C59 15" Vase
C60 15" Pedestaled Vase
C61 10" Dual Purpose: Vase/Candleholder
C62 5½"×6¾" Footed Compote or Planter

C63 14″ Caladium Leaf
C64 10″ Open Front Vase
C65 None noted on brochure
C66 9½″ Bud Vase
C67 4″ Square Footed Planter/Candleholder
C68 8½″×4½″ Rectangular Footed Planter
C69 9¼″ Open Footed Flower Bowl
C70 13¼″ Consolette

CRAB APPLE
600/33 8″ Vase
610/33 7″ Vase
620/33 8″ Vase
630/33 7″ Vase
640/33 3″ Vase
640/33 4″ Vase
640/33 5″ Vase
640/33 6″ Vase
650/33 5″ Vase
660/33 5″ Vase
670/30 4″ Jardinier
670/30 6½″ Jardinier
670/30 8″ Jardinier
670/31 7″ Hanging Basket
680/31 6″ Hanging Basket
680/35 6″ Pot and Saucer
680/30 6″ Jardinier
690/32 8½″ Flower Bowl

CRESTONE
300 10¼″ Dinner Plate
301 7½″ Salad or Dessert Plate
302 9-Oz. Coffee Mug
303 6″ Fruit
304 6½″ Bread and Butter Plate
305 2-Cup Carafe w/Cover
306 32-Oz. Open Baker
307 32-Oz. Casserole w/Cover
308 9-Oz. Individual Casserole w/Cover
310 10-Oz. Gravy Boat/Syrup
311 6½″ Saucer for Gravy Boat/Syrup
312 Two-Piece Gravy Boat Set
313 9-Oz. French Handled Casserole
314 6-Oz. Custard Cup
315 3¾″ Salt Shaker
316 3¾″ Pepper Shaker
317 Shaker Set
318 8-Oz. Creamer
319 8-Oz. Covered Sugar
320 Sugar and Creamer Set
321 14¼″×10¼″×2¼″ Chip 'n Dip Leaf
322 8-Cup Coffee Server
325 38-Oz. Beverage Pitcher
326 14-Oz. Beverage Stein
327 9-Oz. French Handled Casserole w/Cover
329 7-Oz. Cup
330 5⅞″ Saucer
331 9⅜″ Luncheon Plate
345 9¾″ Salad or Vegetable Bowl
346 Salad Set (above bowl with wooden utensils)
349 5-Cup Teapot
351 Mustard/Jam Jar
361 Quarter-Lb. Butter Dish
369 9-Oz. Onion Soup/Salad Bowl

CUSPIDORS
No. 17 Hotel shape, gold lines
No. 19 Parlor shape, Mahogany finish, gold line
No. 20 Hotel shape, Mahogany finish, gold line
No. 21 Parlor shape, gold lines
No. 23 Parlor shape, green lines
No. 25 Parlor shape, Blue Bird decal
No. 26 Hotel shape, green lines
No. 27 Parlor shape, Rose decal
No. 30 Hotel shape, blue lines
No. 32 Parlor shape, maroon lines
No. 33 Hotel shape, maroon lines
No. 52 Embossed parlor shape, white semi-porcelain, green tint
No. 96 Hotel shape, luster bands
No. 97 Parlor shape, luster bands
No. 98 Low Parlor shape, white w/color bands
No. 99 Parlor shape, blue lines
No. 471 Parlor shape, brown and green blended glaze
No. 784 Parlor shape, buff and green tinted

DEBONAIR
01 3-Piece Mix Set
02 Covered Casserole
04 Salt Shaker
05 Pepper Shaker
06 Pitcher
07 Individual Covered Casserole
08 Covered Cookie Jar
010 Cereal/Salad Bowl
013 Coffee/Tea w/Cover
014 Creamer
015 Covered Sugar
016 Mug
017 Partioned Dutch Oven w/Cover

DOGWOOD
501 7½″ Basket
502 6½″ Vase
503 8½″ Vase
504 8½″ Vase
505 6½″ Ewer (actually measures 8½″)
506 11½″ Ewer
507 6½″ Teapot
508 10½″ Window Box
509 6½″ Vase
510 10½″ Vase
511 11½″ Console Bowl
512 4″ Candleholder
513 6½″ Vase
514 4″ Jardinier
515 8½″ Vase
516 4¾″ Vase
517 4¾″ Vase
518
519 13½″ Ewer
520 4¾″ Ewer
521 7″ Low Bowl
522 4″ Corncucopia

DORIC
No. 20 Bowls: 5, 6, 7, 8, 9, and 10 inch

EBB TIDE
E-1 7″ Bud Vase
E-2 7″ Twin Fish Vase
E-3 7½″ Cornucopia
E-4 8¼″ Pitcher Vase
E-5 9⅛″ Basket
E-6 9¼″ Angel Fish Vase
E-7 11″ Fish Vase
E-8 Ash Tray w/Mermaid
E-9 11¾″ Cornucopia
E-10 14″ Pitcher Vase
E-11 16½″×8¾″ Basket
E-12 15¾″×9″ Console Bowl
E-13 2½″ Candleholder
E-14 Teapot
E-15 Creamer
E-16 Covered Sugar

EMBOSSED
No. 430 Shoulder Bowls: 4-14 inch

FLEMISH
No. 620 Butter Jars: 2, 3, and 5 pound

FLORAL
No. 40 5″ Bowl
No. 40 7″ Bowl
No. 40 9″ Bowl
No. 41 9″ Lipped Mixing Bowl
No. 42 7½″ Covered Casserole
No. 43 5¾″ Covered Grease Jar
No. 44 3½″ Salt and Pepper
No. 46 1-Quart Pitcher
No. 47 French Handled Casserole w/Cover
No. 48 8¾″ Cookie Jar
No. 49 10″ Salad Bowl
No. 50 6″ Cereal Bowl

FLORISTWARE
511 6″ Vase
511 8″ Vase
511 10″ Vase
511 12″ Vase
511 15″ Vase
521 6″ Vase
521 8″ Vase
521 10″ Vase
521 12″ Vase
522 5″ Vase
523 3″ Jardinier
524 3″ Jardinier
524 5″ Jardinier

FOOTED
No. 23 Covered Casserole
No. 23 Casserole Plate
No. 24 Custard
No. 25 2-Lb. Butter
No. 25 3-Lb. Butter
No. 25 Nappies: 6 and 7 inch
No. 26 Bowls: 7, 8½, and 10 inch
No. 27 Jugs: 42's — ½-Pint, 36's — 1½-Pint, and 30's — 1-Quart
No. 700 Bowls: 5-15 inch

GRANADA
31 10″ Ewer
32 8″ Basket
47 9″ Vase
48 9″ Vase
49 9″ Vase

65 8″ Basket
66 10″ Ewer
215 9″ Vase
216 9″ Vase

GREEN BUFF
No. 425 Bowls: 5, 6, 7, 8, 9, and 10 inch

GREEN TINT
No. 426 Bowls: 5, 6, 7, 8, 9, and 10 inch
No. 763 Bowls: 5, 6, 7, 8, 9, and 10 inch
No. 775 Dairy Jugs: 2-Pint to 5-Pint

HERITAGEWARE
A-1 Bowls: 6½, 7½, and 8½ inch
A-2 9″ Covered Casserole
A-3 5¾″ Range Jar
A-4 3½″ Salt Shaker
A-5 3½″ Pepper Shaker
A-6 28-Oz. Pitcher
A-7 8-Oz. Pitcher
A-8 9-Oz. Mug
A-9 10″ Salad Bowl
A-14 6¼″ Oil Bottle w/Stopper
A-15 6¼″ Vinegar Bottle w/Stopper
A-18 9¼″ Cookie Jar

HOTELWARE
No. 1 Covered Combinet
No. 4 Hall Boy Jug
No. 5 Covered Chamber
No. 5 Open Chamber
No. 52 St. Dennis Bowl
No. 53 Chili Bowl
No. 54 Oyster Bowl
No. 55 Coffee Mug
Also offered: Parlor Plain white cuspidor/ Hotel plain white cuspidor

IRIS
401 5″ Ewer
401 8″ Ewer
401 13½″ Ewer
402 4¾″ Vase
402 7″ Vase
402 8½″ Vase
403 4¾″ Vase
403 7″ Vase
403 8½″ Vase
403 10½″ Vase
404 4¾″ Vase
404 7″ Vase
404 8½″ Vase
404 10½″ Vase
405 4¾″ Vase
405 7″ Vase
405 8½″ Vase
405 10½″ Vase
406 4¾″ Vase
406 7″ Vase
406 8½″ Vase
407 4¾″ Vase
407 7″ Vase
407 8½″ Vase
408 7″ Basket
409 12″ Console Bowl
410 7½″ Bud Vase
411 5″ Candleholder
412 4″ Rose Bowl
412 7″ Rose Bowl
413 5½″ Jardinier
413 9″ Jardinier
414 10½″ Vase
414 16″ Vase

LUSTER
No. 9 Tankard Jugs: 48's — ¾-Pint, 42's — 1-Pint, 36's — 1½-Pint, 30's — 2½-Pint, 24's — 4-Pint, and 18's — 5-Pint
No. 114 Bowls: 4-10 inch

LUSTERWARE
505 8″ Vase
505 10″ Vase
505 12″ Vase
507 9″ Wall Vase
508 9″ Wall Vase
510 6″ Bud Vase
510 8″ Bud Vase
510 10″ Bud Vase
513 6″ Vase
513 8″ Vase
513 10″ Vase
513 12″ Vase
514 5″ Vase
515 10″ Vase
516 8″ Vase
517 7″ Vase
519 6″ Vase
519 8″ Vase
519 10″ Vase
520 7″ Vase
520 9″ Vase
521 6″ Vase
521 8″ Vase
521 10″ Vase
521 12″ Vase
522 5″ Vase
523 3″ Vase
524 3″ Bowl
524 5″ Bowl
534 5″ Jardinier
534 6″ Jardinier
562 6″ Bulb Bowl
562 7″ Bulb Bowl
584 Round Ash Tray
585 Square Ash Tray

MAGNOLIA (GLOSS)
H-1 5½″ Vase
H-2 5½″ Vase
H-3 5½″ Vase
H-4 6½″ Vase
H-5 6½″ Vase
H-6 6¼″ Vase
H-7 6½″ Vase
H-8 8½″ Vase
H-9 8½″ Vase
H-10 8½″ Cornucopia
H-11 8½″ Ewer
H-12 10½″ Vase
H-13 10½″ Vase
H-14 10½″ Basket
H-15 12″ Double Cornucopia
H-16 12½″ Vase
H-17 12½″ Vase
H-18 12½″ Vase
H-19 13½″ Ewer
H-20 6½″ Teapot
H-21 3¾″ Creamer
H-22 3¾″ Covered Sugar
H-23 13″ Console Bowl
H-24 4″ Candleholder

MAGNOLIA (MATTE)
1 8½″ Vase
2 8½″ Vase
3 8½″ Vase
4 6¼″ Vase
5 7″ Ewer
6 12″ Double Cornucopia
7 8½″ Vase
8 10½″ Vase
9 10½″ Vase
10 10½″ Basket
11 6¼″ Vase
12 6¼″ Vase
13 4¾″ Vase
14 4¾″ Ewer
15 6¼″ Vase
16 15″ Vase
17 12¼″ Vase
18 13½″ Ewer
19 8½″ Cornucopia
20 15″ Vase
21 12½″ Vase
22 12½″ Vase
23 6½″ Teapot
24 3¾″ Creamer
25 3¾″ Open Sugar
26 12½″ Console Bowl
27 4″ Candleholder

MARDI GRAS, 1940
No. 90 Mixing Bowls: 5¼-10¼ inch
No. 91 Spanish Pots: 3¾, 4¾, 6, 7, 8¼, and 9½ inch
No. 92 Jardiniers: 7 and 8 inch
No. 93 Italian Pots: 6¾, 7½, and 8½ inch
No. 94 Flower Vases: 6, 8, and 10 inch

MARDI GRAS
31 10″ Ewer
32 8″ Basket
47 9″ Vase
48 9″ Vase
49 9″ Vase
65 8″ Basket
66 10″ Ewer
215 9″ Vase
216 9″ Vase

MOTTLED
No. 13 Bowls: 4-10 inch

NULINE BAK-SERVE
No. 1 Bowls: 5, 6, 7, 8, and 9 inch
No. 5 Teapot
No. 6 Deep Bowls: 4½-8½ inch
No. 7 Pitchers: 1 and 2-Quart
No. 13 7½″ Covered Casserole
No. 14 Custard
No. 19 Covered Bean Pots: 4½,-6½ inch
No. 20 2-Quart Cookie Jar
No. 25 Coffee Mug
No. 29 Beverage Pitchers: 1-2-Quart

NURSERY WARE
No. 300 Deep Baby Plate
No. 300 Cup and Saucer
No. 300 48's Bread and Milk Set
No. 300 42's Bread and Milk Set

No. 300 Child's Mug
No. 301 Deep Baby Plate

OPEN ROSE

101 8½" Cornucopia
102 8½" Vase
103 8½" Vase
104 10½" Mermaid Figural Planter
105 7" Ewer
106 13¼" Ewer
107 8" Basket
108 8½" Vase
110 8½" Teapot
111 5" Creamer
112 5" Open Sugar
113 6¼" Vase
114 8¼" Jardinier
115 8½" Ewer
116 12" Console Bowl
117 6½" Dove Candleholder
118 6½" Swan Vase
119 8½" Vase
120 6¼" Vase
121 6¼" Vase
122 6¼" Vase
123 6½" Vase
124 12" Vase
125 8½" Wall Pocket
126 8½" Hand Vase
127 4¾" Vase
128 4¾" Vase
129 7" Bud Vase
130 4¾" Vase
131 4¾" Vase
132 7" Hanging Basket
133 6¼" Vase
134 6¼" Vase
135 6¼" Vase
136 6¼" Vase
137 6¼" Vase
138 6¼" Vase
139 10½" "Lamp-Shaped" Vase
140 10½" Basket
141 8½" Cornucopia
142 6¼" Basket
143 8½" Basket

ORCHID

300 6½" Vase
301 4¾" Vase
301 6" Vase
301 8" Vase
301 10" Vase
302 4¾" Vase
302 6" Vase
302 8" Vase
302 10" Vase
303 4¾" Vase
303 6" Vase
303 8" Vase
303 10" Vase
304 4½" Vase
304 6" Vase
304 8½" Vase
304 10¼" Vase
305 7" Basket
306 6¾" Bud Vase
307 4¾" Vase
307 6½" Vase
307 8" Vase
307 10" Vase
308 4¾" Vase
308 6½" Vase
308 8" Vase
308 10½" Vase
309 8" Vase
310 6" Jardinier
311 13" Ewer
312 7" Low Bowl
314 13" Console Bowl
315 4" Candleholder
316 7" Bookend
317 4¾" Jardinier

PANDORA

No. 150 Bowls: 4-11 inch
No. 150-X Bowls with covers: 5-7 inch
No. 154 1-Quart Bean Pot
No. 155 Individual Bean Pot and Cover
No. 156 7" Covered Casserole
No. 160 7-Oz. Custard Cup
No. 162 Open Jugs: ½-Pint, 1-Pint, 1-Quart, and 2-Quart
No. 162-X Covered Jugs: ½-Pint and 1-Quart
No. 164 9-Oz. Handled Mug
No. 165 12-Oz. Handled Stein
No. 166 Teapots: 30's, 36's and 42's
No. 168-X 72-Oz. Utility Jar
No. 169-X 42-Oz. Utility Jar
No. 170 Open Pudding Dish
No. 171 Vase
No. 172 Vase
No. 173 Covered Salt Box

PANELLED

No. 19 Bowls: 36's — 5⅜", 30's — 6¼", 24's — 7½", 18's — 8½", 12's — 9⅝", 9's — 10⅝"

PARCHMENT AND PINE

S-1 6" Vase
S-2 8" Right and Left Cornucopia
S-3 6" Basket
S-4 10" Vase
S-5 Planter
S-6 12" Left and Right Cornucopia
S-7 13½" Ewer
S-8 16" Basket
S-9 16" Console Bowl
S-10 2¾" Candleholder
S-11 12¼" Long, Teapot
S-12 3¼" Creamer
S-13 3¼" Covered Sugar
S-14 14" Ash Tray
S-15 8" High, Teapot

PERSIAN

505 8" Vase
505 10" Vase
505 12" Vase
513 6" Vase
513 8" Vase
513 10" Vase
513 12" Vase
514 5½" Vase
515 10" Vase
516 8" Vase
517 7" Vase
518 14" Lamp Base
520 7" Vase
520 9" Vase

PINECONE

No. 55 6½" Vase

POPPY

601 9" Basket
601 12" Basket
602 6½" Bowl Planter
604 8" Cornucopia
605 4¾" Vase
605 6½" Vase
605 8½" Vase
605 10½" Vase
606 4¾" Vase
606 6½" Vase
606 8½" Vase
606 10½" Vase
607 4¾" Vase
607 6½" Vase
607 8½" Vase
607 10½" Vase
608 4¾" Jardinier
609 9" Wall Pocket
610 4¾" Ewer
610 13½" Ewer
611 4¾" Vase
611 6½" Vase
611 8½" Vase
611 10½" Vase
612 4¾" Vase
612 6½" Vase
612 8½" Vase
612 10½" Vase

RAINBOW, 1928

No. 15 Bowls: 42's — 4-inch, 36's — 5-inch, 30's — 6-inch, 24's — 7-inch, 18's — 8-inch, and 12's — 9-inch.

RAINBOW

At least forty items of the House 'n Garden Casual Serving Ware line was offered in Rainbow Colors. The following are those listed by original brochure pages.

*536 6" Mixing Bowl
*537 7" Mixing Bowl
*538 8" Mixing Bowl with Pouring Spout
*539 Above 3-Piece Mixing Bowl Set
*540 12"×7½" Serv-All Leaf Dish
590 7¼"×4¾" Individual Leaf Dish
591 12¼"×9" Leaf Chip 'n Dip
592 Two-Tier Tid Bit Tray

*Mixing Bowls and Serv-All Trays were marketed only in Mirror Brown and Tangerine.

Luncheon sets consisted of 12 pieces:

4 8½" Plates
4 6-Oz. Cups
4 5½" Saucers

Dinnerware sets consisted of 12 pieces:

4 10½" Plates
4 9-Oz. Mugs
4 6½" Soup/Salad Bowls

RED RIDING HOOD

4½" Marmalade Jar with Spoon
5¼" Mustard Jar with Spoon
5½" Mustard Jar with Spoon, Underneath Saucer
6½" Pitcher

8″ Milk Pitcher
Butterdish
3¼″ Salt and Pepper (standing)
5½″ Salt and Pepper (standing)
5½″ Salt and Pepper (squatting)
Cream and Sugar — Side Opening
Cream and Sugar — Spout at Top Head
At least 2 different 9″ Teapots
3-Section Baby Plate
8½″Covered Jar
9″ Covered Jar
13″ Cookie Jar
11¾″ Handled Casserole
6-Piece Canister Set, 9½″ Tall. Sugar, Flour, Cereal, Rice, Coffee and Tea.
6-Piece Spice Set, 4¾″ Tall. Nutmeg, Cinnamon, Allspice, Cloves, Ginger and Pepper.
5½″ Match Holder
9″ String Holder
9″ Wall Plaque
7″ Bank
9″ Wall Bank
Lamp
Advertising Plaque 11¾″×6½″
S13 13¼″ Pitcher Vase

RESTAURANTWARE

190/22 8-Oz. Chili Bowl
190/23 12-Oz. Oyster Bowl
190/24 8-Oz. St. Dennis Bowl
190/24 12-Oz. St. Dennis Bowl
190/25 8-Oz. Coffee Mug

ROSELLA

R-1 5″ Vase
R-2 5″ Vase
R-3 5½″ Open Sugar
R-4 5½″ Creamer
R-5 6½″ Vase
R-6 6½″ Vase
R-7 6½″ Vase
R-7 9½″ Ewer
R-8 6½″ Vase
R-9 6½″ Left and Right Ewer
R-10 6½″ Wall Pocket
R-11 7″ Left and Right Ewer
R-12 7″ Basket
R-13 8½″ Left and Right Corncucopia
R-14 8½″ Vase
R-15 8½″ Vase

ROSELLA LAMPS

Lamp with 5″ pottery section, same as R-2-5″ Vase shape with brass fittings, unmarked.
11″ Lamp marked L 3, handled.
10¾″ Lamp, unmarked, handled.

SALT BOXES

No. 11 Round, Blue Band
No. 12 Round, Gold Band
No. 13 Octagon, Delft
No. 14 Octagon, Gold Line
No. 15 Octagon, Blue Line
No. 15 Octagon, Blue Asterisk
No. 16 Octagon, Flying Blue Bird
No. 67 Octagon, Stamped Asterisk
No. 119 Square, Blue Grecian
No. 121 Square, Gold Grecian
No. 135 Square, Perched Blue Bird
No. 136 Square, Flying Blue Bird
No. 203 Round, Flying Blue Bird
No. 206 Round, Delft

SERENADE

S1 6½″ Bud Vase
S2 6½″ Pitcher Vase
S3 5¾″×5″ Urn
S3C Above Urn with Cover, 8¼″×5″ Covered Candy Dish
S4 7¼″×5¼″ Puritan Vase
S5 6¾″ Bon Bon Basket
S6 8½″ Flared Vase
S7 8½″ Pedestal Vase
S8 8½″ Pitcher Vase
S9 12½″×6″×4″ Window Box
S10 11″ Cornucopia
S11 10½″ Rectangular Vase
S12 14″ Long Stem Vase
S13 13¼″ Pitcher Vase
S14 12″×11½″ Basket
S15 11½″×10″×7″ Footed Fruit/Console Bowl
S16 6½″ Candleholder
S17 6-Cup Teapot
S18 3½″ Creamer
S19 3½″ Covered Sugar
*S20 9″ Covered Casserole
S21 1½-Quart Beverage Pitcher
S22 8-Oz. Mug
S23 13″×10½″ Ash Tray
*Marketed with or without Brass Warmer.

SHAMROCK

No. 712 Bowls: 42's — 4-inch, 36's — 5-inch, 30's — 6-inch, 24's — 7-inch, 18's — 8-inch, 12's — 9-inch, and 9's — 10-inch.

SQUARE FOOTED

22/1 Bowls: 5, 7, 8, and 11 inch
22/2 Bowls: 5-14 inch
22/6 Bake Dishes: 6, 7, and 8 inch
22/7 Jugs: 1-Pint, 1-Quart
22/12 Pie Plates: 9 and 10 inch
22/13 Covered Casseroles: 7-8 inch
22/14 3″ Custard Cup
22/19 Covered Bean Pots: 5-7 inch
22/20 One-Gallon Cookie Jar

SQUARE RIM

No. 16 Bowls: 42's — 4-inch, 36's — 5-inch, 30's — 6-inch, 24's — 7-inch, 18's — 8-inch, and 12's — 9-inch.
21/2 Bowls: 4-12 inch.
23/2 Bowls: 5-12 inch.
24/2 Bowls: 4-12 inch.
No. 424 Bowls: 4-14 inch.

SUNGLOW

50 5½″ Bowl
50 7½″ Bowl
50 9½″ Bowl
51 7½″ Covered Casserole
52 24-Oz. Pitcher
53 Covered Grease Jar
54 Shakers
55 7½″ Beverage Pitcher
80 Cup/Saucer Wall Pocket
81 Pitcher Wall Pocket
82 Whisk Broom Wall Pocket
84 6½″ Basket
85 8¾″ Flamingo Vase
89 5½″ Vase
90 5½″ Pitcher
92 6½″ Vase
93 6½″ Vase
94 8″ Vase
95 8½″ Vase
96 8½″ Cornucopia
97 5½″ Flower Pot
98 7½″ Flower Pot
100 6½″ Flower Pot
Unmarked Iron Wall Pocket
Unmarked 6″ Bell

THISTLE

No. 51 6½″ Vase
No. 52 6½″ Vase
No. 53 6½″ Vase
No. 54 6½″ Vase

TOILETWARE

No. 1 Covered Combinet
No. 4 Hall Boy Jug
No. 5 Covered Chamber
No. 5 Open Chamber
No. 6 Hall Boy Jug
No. 10 Cuspidor, Parlor Shape
No. 10½ Cuspidor, Hotel Shape
No. 55 Coffee Mug

TOKAY

1 6½″ Cornucopia
2 6″ Vase
3 8″ Pitcher Vase
4 8¼″ Vase
5 5½″ Urn
6 8″ Basket
7 9½″ Fruit Bowl
8 10″ Vase
9 5½″×6½″ Planter
9C Above planter with cover, 7″×8½″ Covered Candy Dish
10 11″ Cornucopia
11 10½″ Moon Basket
12 12″ Spool Vase
13 12″ Pitcher Vase
14 15¾″ Consolette
15 12″ Basket
16 Teapot
17 Creamer
18 Covered Sugar

TROPICANA

51 15½″×4¾″ Flower Bowl
52 10″×7½″ Ash Tray
53 8½″ Flat-Sided Vase
54 12½″ Slender Vase
55 12¾″ Basket
56 12½″ Pitcher
57 14½″ Planter Vase

TULIP, 1928

No. 10 Tankard Jugs: 48's — ¾-Pint, 42's — 1-Pint, 36's — 1½-Pint, 30's — 2½-Pint, 24's — 4-Pint, and 18's — 5-Pint.

TULIP (SUENO)

100-33 4″ Vase
100-33 6½″ Vase
100-33 8″ Vase

100-33 10″ Vase
101-33 6½″ Vase
101-33 9″ Vase
101-33 10″ Vase
102-33 6″ Basket
103-33 6″ Vase
104-33 6″ Vase
105-33 8″ Vase
106-33 6″ Vase
107-33 6″ Vase
107-33 8″ Vase
108-33 6″ Vase
109 8″ Ewer
109-33 13″ Ewer
110-33 6″ Vase
111-33 6″ Vase
115-33 7″ Jardinier
116-33 4¾″ Flower Pot/Attached Saucer
*116-33 6″ Flower Pot/Attached Saucer
117-30 5″ Jardinier

*Brochure indicates this number is 116-35 which goes along with Hull's early system of 30 for jardiniers, 33 for vases, 35 for flower pots and saucers.

TUSCANY

1 6½″ Cornucopia
2 6″ Vase
3 8″ Pitcher Vase
4 8¼″ Vase
5 5½″ Urn
6 8″ Basket
7 9½″ Fruit Bowl
8 10″ Vase
9 5½″×6½″ Planter
9C Above planter with cover, 7″×8½″ Covered Candy Dish
10 11″ Cornucopia
11 10½″ Moon Basket
12 12″ Spool Vase
13 12″ Pitcher Vase
14 15¾″ Consolette
15 12″ Basket
16 Teapot
17 Creamer
18 Covered Sugar

VEGETABLE PATTERN KITCHENWARE

No. 20 5″ Bowl, coral
No. 20 6″ Bowl, coral
No. 20 7″ Bowl, green
No. 20 8″ Bowl, yellow
No. 20 9″ Bowl, yellow
No. 21 9″ Lipped Mixing Bowl
No. 22 7½″ Covered Casserole
No. 23 Covered Grease Jar
No. 24 Salt Shaker
No. 25 Pepper Shaker
No. 26 1-Quart Pitcher
No. 27 French Handled Covered Casserole
No. 28 Covered Cookie Jar
No. 29 10½″ Salad Bowl
No. 30 6″ Cereal Bowl

WATER LILY

L-A 8½″ Vase
L-1 5½″ Vase
L-2 5½″ Vase
L-3 5½″ Ewer
L-4 6½″ Vase
L-5 6½″ Vase
L-6 6½″ Vase
L-7 6½″ Cornucopia
L-8 8½″ Vase
L-9 8½″ Vase
L-10 9½″ Vase
*L-11 9½″ Vase
L-12 10½″ Vase
L-13 10½″ Vase
L-14 10½″ Basket
*L-15 12½″ Vase
L-16 12½″ Vase
L-17 13½″ Ewer
L-18 6″ Teapot
L-19 5″ Creamer
L-20 5″ Covered Sugar
L-21 13½″ Console Bowl
L-22 4½″ Candleholder
L-23 5½″ Jardinier
L-24 8½″ Jardinier
L-25 5½″ Flower Pot/Attached Saucer
L-26 None listed on brochure
L-27 12″ Double Cornucopia
Unmarked 7¼″ Lamp
*Identical Shape

WILDFLOWER

W-1 5½″ Vase
W-2 5½″ Ewer
W-3 5½″ Vase
W-4 6½″ Vase
W-5 6½″ Vase
W-6 7½″ Vase
W-7 7½″ Cornucopia
W-8 7½″ Vase
W-9 8½″ Vase
W-10 8½″ Cornucopia
W-11 8½″ Ewer
W-12 9½″ Vase
W-13 9½″ Vase
W-14 10½″ Vase
W-15 10½″ Vase
W-16 10½″ Basket
W-17 12¼″ Vase
W-18 12½″ Vase
W-19 13½″ Ewer
W-20 15½″ Vase
W-21 12″ Console Bowl
Unmarked Candleholder

WILDFLOWER (NUMBER SERIES)

51 8½″ Vase
52 6¼″ Vase
53 8½″ Vase (same shape as Wildflower — W-9 8½″)
55 13½″ Ewer (same shape as W-19 13½″)
56 4½″ Vase
57 4½″ Ewer
58 6¼″ Cornucopia
59 10½″ Vase
60 6¼″ Vase
61 8½″ Vase
64 4″ Jardinier
65 7″ Basket
67 8½″ Vase
69 4″ Candleholder
70 12″ Console Bowl
71 12″ Vase
72 8″ Teapot
73 4¾″ Creamer
74 4¾″ Sugar
75 8½″ Vase
78 8½″ Vase

WOODLAND

W1 5½″ Vase
W2 5½″ Cornucopia
W3 5½″ Ewer
W4 6½″ Vase
W5 6¼″ Cornucopia
W6 6½″ Ewer
W7 5½″ Jardinier
W8 7½″ Vase
W9 8¾″ Basket
W10 11″ Cornucopia
W11 5¾″ Flower Pot/Attached Saucer
W12 7½″ Hanging Jardinier
W13 7½″ Wall Pocket
W14 10″ Window Box
W15 8½″ Double Bud Vase
W16 8½″ Vase
W17 7½″ Vase
W18 10½″ Vase
W19 10½″ Window Box
W20 Nothing noted on brochure page
W21 9½″ Jardinier
W22 10½″ Basket
W23 14″×9¾″ Double Cornucopia
W24 13½″ Ewer
W25 12½″ Vase
W26 Teapot
W27 Creamer
W28 Covered Sugar
W29 14″ Console Bowl
W30 3½″ Candleholder
W31 5¾″ Hanging Flower Pot/Attached Saucer

ZANE GREY

No. 400 Jars: (covers sold separately) ½-Gallon, 1-Gallon, 1½-Gallon, 2-Gallon, 3-Gallon, 4-Gallon, 5-Gallon, and 6-Gallon.
No. 420 Bowls: 42's — 4⅛″, 36's — 5⅛″, 30's — 6¼″, 24's — 7¼″, 18's — 8¼″, 12's — 9⅛″, 9's — 10″, 6's — 11⅛″, 4's — 12¼″, 3's — 13⅜″, 2's — 14¾″, and 1's — 15¼″.
No. 430 Nappies: 42's — 4¼″, 36's — 5¼″, 30's — 6¼″, 24's — 7¼″, 18's — 8½″, and 12's — 9⅜″.
No. 440 Jugs: 48's — ¾-Pint, 42's — 1-Pint, 36's — 1½-Pint, 30's — 2½-Pint, 24's — 4-Pint, and 18's — 5-Pint.
No. 450 Butter Jars: 2-Lb — 6⅝″, 3-Lb. — 7¼″, and 4-Lb. — 7⅞″.
No. 460 Custard Cups: No. 1 and No. 2 Sizes.
No. 470 Cuspidor, Parlor Shape
No. 480 Salt Box

MISCELLANEOUS KITCHENWARE, 1935

The following numbers correspond to a plain white kitchen line similar to restaurantware, some shapes are identical.

No. 50	Bowls: 5-12 inch
No. 50-X	Covered Bowls: 5, 6, and 7 inch
No. 52	St. Dennis Bowl
No. 53	Chili Bowl
No. 54	30's Oyster Bowl
No. 55	Coffee Mug
No. 56	Bake Set Bowls: 5-9 inch
No. 57	Jugs: 42's — ½-Pint, 36's — 1½-Pint, 30's — 1-Quart, and 18's — 2-Quart.
No. 60	3-Lb. Refrigerator Jar and Cover
No. 64	Custard Cup
No. 65	2-Quart Covered Bean Pot
No. 67	Covered Range Jar

Shown below are numbers from a line listed as Overlap No. 75 — Yellow or Green, semi-porcelain kitchenware.

No. 75	Bowls: 5-12 inch
No. 76	Bake Dishes: 5, 6, 7, 8, and 9 inch
No. 77	Jugs: 42's — 1-Pint, 36's — 1½-Pint, 30's — 2½-Pint, and 18's — 5-Pint
No. 78	Covered Teapot
No. 79	Covered Sugar
No. 80	3-Lb. Refrigerator Jar and Cover
No. 83	7½″ Covered Casserole
No. 84	No. 2 Custard Cup
No. 85	2-Quart Covered Bean Pot
No. 87	5″ Covered Range Jar

300 Line Kitchenware, banded semi-porcelain, was offered in the following shapes.

300/1	Bowls: 5-9 inch
300/4	Deep Bowls: 4-7 inch
300/6	Bake Dishes: 4-9 inch
300/7	Jugs: ¾-Pint, 1-Pint, and 1-Quart
300/9	4″ Ramekin
300/12	Pie Plates: 9 and 10 inch
300/13	Covered Casseroles: 6-8 inch
300/14	3″ Custard Cup
300/15	French Casseroles: 4 and 5 inch
300/16	7″ Serving Plate
300/17	5″ Baked Apple
300/19	Covered Bean Pots: 3-7 inch

MISCELLANEOUS VASES, JARDINIERS, FLOWER POTS, 1935

14/33	Vases, 4¾″, 5¾″, and 6¾″
20/30	Jardiniers: 3½″-9½″
22/30	Jardiniers: 4½″-7½″
23/30	Jardiniers: 3½″-7½″
26	9″ Vase
32	8″ Vase
34/30	Jardiniers: 3½″-6½″
34/35	Flower Pots/Attached Saucers: 3½″, 4½″, 5½″, and 6½″
35/30	Jardiniers: 3¾″-7¾″
35/35	Flower Pots/Attached Saucers: 3½″, 4½″, 5½″ and 6½″
36/30	Jardiniers: 3½″-7½″
39	9″ Vase
49/33	Vases: 5″, 6″, and 7″
51/33	Vases: 5″, 6″, and 7″
52/33	Vases: 5″, 6″, and 7″
83/30	3½″ Jardinier
120/33	5½″ Vase
124	Bulb Bowls: 6 and 8 inch
125	Vases: 7½″and 9½″
132	Jardiniers: 6 and 8 inch
140/33	Vases: 5-12 inch
200/30	Jardiniers: 3-9 inch
220/30	Jardiniers: 4½″-7½″
310/30	7″ Jardinier
364/30	Jardiniers: 5-10 inch
364	Pedestals: 16 and 18 inch
400/35	6½″ Pot and Saucer
460/33	7″ Vase
470/33	6″ Vase
480/33	5½″ Vase
534/35	Flower Pots/Saucers: 3-6 inch
535/30	Jardiniers: 6-10 inch
536/30	Jardiniers: 5-10 inch
538	8″ Flower Pot, no saucer
539	6½″ Flower Pot/Attached Saucer
540	6½″ Flower Pot/Attached Saucer
543/30	Jardiniers: 5½″ and 7½″
544/30	Jardiniers: 4½″, 5½″, and 6½″
544/35	Flower Pots/Saucers, 3-6 inch
546/30	Jardiniers: 3-7 inch
546/35	7½″ Flower Pot, no saucer
550/30	7½″ Jardinier
551/30	7½″ Jardinier
560/33	6″ Vase
562	5½″ Flower Bowl
563	9″ Flower Bowl
660/33	8″ Vase
836/30	Jardinier
850	Square Pot/Saucer
865	8″ Flower Bowl

PLATE 1

Top left:

1. LUSTERWARE Candleholder, unmarked, 3″ (1928)
2. ACME POTTERY Plate, eagle stamp, 11″ (1903-1907)
3. LUSTERWARE Pitcher, unmarked, 4″ (1928)

PLATE 2

Top right:

1. LUSTERWARE Vase, unmarked, 3½″ (1928)
2. LUSTERWARE Bud Vase, unmarked, 8″ (1928)

PLATE 3

NOVELTY — Early to Mid-1940's

Row 1:

1. Bear, unmarked, 1½″
2. Owl Bank, unmarked, 3¾″
3. Rabbit, unmarked, 5½″
4. Frog Bank, unmarked, 3¾″
5. Kitten, unmarked, 1½″

Row 2:

1. Rabbit, unmarked, 2¾″
2. Rabbit, unmarked, 2¾″
3. Swing Band Tuba Player, unmarked 5¾″
4. Kitten, unmarked, 1½″
5. Swing Band Accordionist, unmarked, 6″
6. Rabbit, unmarked, 2¾″
7. Rabbit, unmarked, 2¾″

This ad taken from Blackwell Wieland Company's 1940 Catalogue illustrates the five-piece Swing Band set which was marketed through their company for $3.50 per set. The set includes band leader, drummer, accordinionist, flutist, and tuba player, all of which are ivory finished with gold trim and hand-painted features.

Plate 1

Plate 2

Plate 3

EARLY ART (1920's)

PLATE 4

Row 1:

1. Stoneware Vase, unmarked, 5½″
2. Stoneware Vase, 39 Ⓗ 8″
3. Stoneware Jardinier, Ⓗ, 4″

Row 2:

1. Stoneware Vase, 40 Ⓗ 7″
2. Semi-Porcelain Vase, 660/33-8″
3. Stoneware Vase, 40 Ⓗ 7″

Row 3:

1. Semi-Porcelain Vase, Ⓗ, 4½″
2. Stoneware Vase, 32 Ⓗ 8″
3. Stoneware Vase, 32 Ⓗ 8″
4. Stoneware Pitcher, 27 Ⓗ 30, 6½″

Row 4:

1. Semi-Porcelain Jardinier, 546 Ⓗ 7.″
2. Stoneware Vase, 26 Ⓗ 8″
3. Stoneware Vase, 32 Ⓗ 8″
4. Stoneware Jardinier, Ⓗ, 6½″

Below: Original Advertising Material

Plate 4

PLATE 5

TILE (1927-1933)

Square Tiles measure 4¼″ × 4¼″
Border Tiles measure 2⅞″ × 6″

PLATE 6

1. Stoneware Vase, unmarked, 5″
2. Stoneware Vase, unmarked, 5″

PLATE 7

EARLY UTILITY (1920's)

Row 1:

1. Pitcher, 107 Ⓗ 30, 4¾″
2. Bowl, 106 Ⓗ 6″
3. Semi-Porcelain Pitcher, Ⓗ, 4¼″

Row 2:

1. Bowl, 106 Ⓗ 5″
2. Salt Box, Ⓗ 111, 6″
3. Pitcher, 107 Ⓗ 42, 3¾″
4. Custard, Ⓗ 60, 2½″

Row 3:

1. Flower Pot/Separate Saucer, 538 Ⓗ 4″
2. Sugar Canister, block H in diamond, 6½″
3. Vinegar, unmarked, 6½″
4. Pepper, block H in diamond, 3½″
5. Spice Jar, block H in diamond, 3½″

Right: Original Advertising Material.

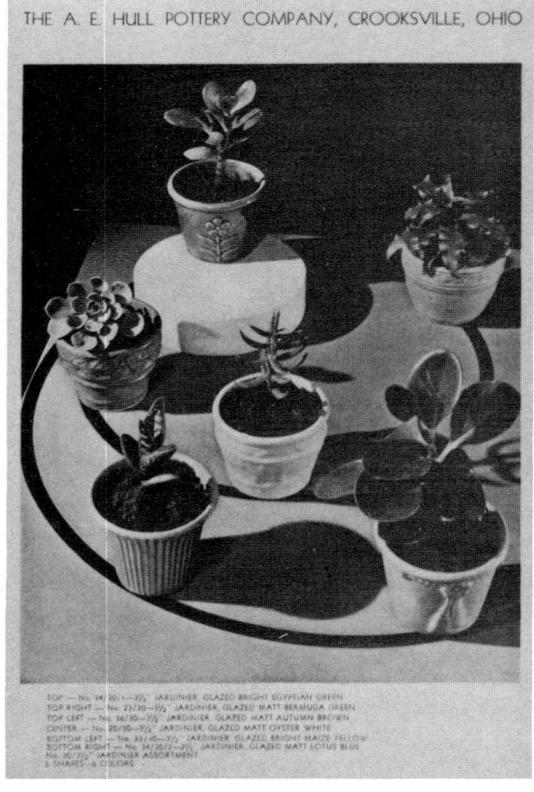

THE A. E. HULL POTTERY COMPANY, CROOKSVILLE, OHIO
TOP — No. 34/30/1—3½" JARDINIER, GLAZED BRIGHT EGYPTIAN GREEN
TOP RIGHT — No. 23/30—3½" JARDINIER, GLAZED MATT BERMUDA GREEN
TOP LEFT — No. 36/30—3½" JARDINIER, GLAZED MATT AUTUMN BROWN
CENTER — No. 20/30—3½" JARDINIER, GLAZED MATT OYSTER WHITE
BOTTOM LEFT — No. 83/30—3½" JARDINIER, GLAZED BRIGHT MAIZE YELLOW
BOTTOM RIGHT — No. 34/30/2—3½" JARDINIER, GLAZED MATT LOTUS BLUE
No. 30/3½" JARDINIER ASSORTMENT
5 SHAPES—6 COLORS

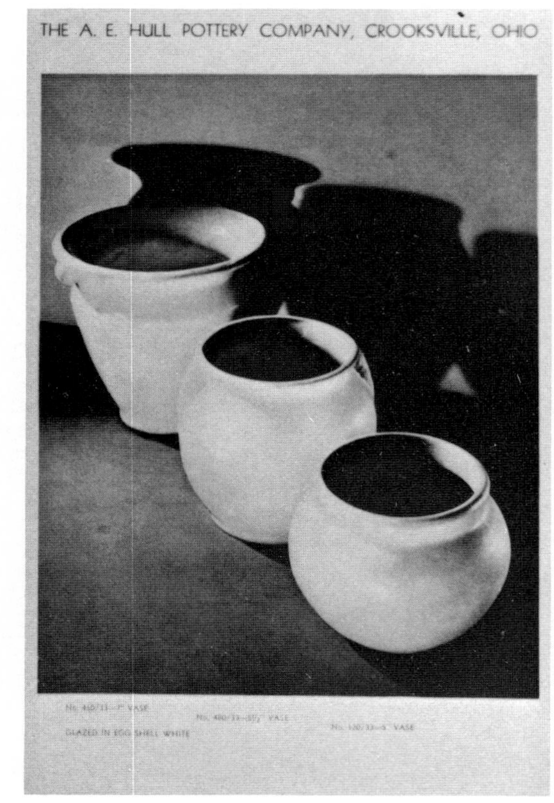

THE A. E. HULL POTTERY COMPANY, CROOKSVILLE, OHIO
GLAZED IN EGG SHELL WHITE

Plate 5

Plate 6

Plate 7

PLATE 8

EARLY UTILITY (1920's)

(All stoneware with the exception of the banded items on Row 3 which are semi-porcelain.)

Row 1:
1. Mug, Ⓗ, 4½″
2. American Legion Stein, 498 Ⓗ, 6½″
3. Tankard, 492 Ⓗ, 9½″
4. Stein, 499 Ⓗ, 6½″
5. Mug, 494 Ⓗ, 4¼″, embossed scene with "Rhein Stein, Burg, Cochem, Stolzenfels"

Row 2:
1. Mug, 265 Ⓗ, 4½″, embossed "Happy Days Are Here Again"
2. Pretzel Jar, Ⓗ, 9½″
3. Pretzel Jar, Ⓗ, 9½″ This "Sunday" item was hand-decorated by Sylvanus Burdette (Mose) Wilson
4. Mug, 497 Ⓗ, embossed "Happy Days Are Here Again," 5″
5. Mug, Ⓗ, embossed "Chocolate Soldier" 3¾″

Row 3:
1. Covered Casserole, 113 Ⓗ, 7½″
2. Bowl, 25 Ⓗ 7″
3. Bowl, 421 Ⓗ 7″
4. Bowl, 100 Ⓗ 8″

Row 4:
1. Bowl, 421 Ⓗ 10″
2. Nested Bowls: 428 Ⓗ 5″, 6″, 7″, 8″, and 9″
3. Bowl, 30 Ⓗ 7″

A 1934 A.E. Hull Pottery Company Net Price List reflects the following rates for several of the items shown in Plate 8.

Item Number:	
#491-16 oz. Stein	.90 Per Dozen
#492-18 oz. Stein	1.20 Per Dozen
#493-16 oz. Stein	.90 Per Dozen
#494-16 oz. Mug	1.20 Per Dozen
#264- 8 oz. Stein	.84 Per Dozen
#265-12 oz. Mug	.90 Per Dozen
#492- 5 Pint Tankard	3.72 Per Dozen
#492- 3 Quart Pretzel Jar	3.72 Per Dozen
#492- 7 Piece Pretzel Set	1.02 Each
#499-16 oz. Stein	.90 Per Dozen

Plate 8

UTILITY

Plate 9

PLATE 9 (1920's)

Row 1, Top:

1. Bowl, unmarked, 8″, rust colored

Row 2:

1. Banded Jug, unmarked, 6″, cream with pink and blue underglazed bands
2. Jardinier, 546 Ⓗ 3″, blended
3. Covered Bean Pot, 219-6″, turquoise glazed

Row 3, Bottom:

1. Flower Pot, Ⓗ, 4″, green glazed
2. Covered Bean Pot, 219-5″, turquoise glazed

PLATE 10

Row 1:

1. Banded Bowl, unmarked, 7″
2. Banded Bowl, E-1-10″
3. Banded Bowl, unmarked, 7″

Row 2: NULINE BAK-SERVE (1940)

1. Pitcher, C-29, 7″
2. Pitcher, B-29, 8½″
3. Pitcher, B-7 1 Qt., 6″

Row 3: NULINE BAK-SERVE (1940)

1. Custard, B-14, 2¾″
2. Covered Casserole, D-13-7½″
3. Cookie Jar, D-20 2 Qt., 8″
4. Covered Bean Pot, B-19-5½″
5. Mug, C-25, 3½″

Row 4: (1940)

1. MARDI GRAS Mixing Bowl, unmarked, 10¼″
2. MARDI GRAS Vase, unmarked, 6″
3. MARDI GRAS Vase, unmarked, 6″
4. Nested Bowls: NULINE BAK-SERVE B-1-5″, 6″, 7″, 8″, and 9″

At least three embossed designs appear on Nuline Bak-Serve shapes: "B" Series — diamond quilt; "C" Series — a fish-scale pattern; and "D" Series — a drape and panel design.

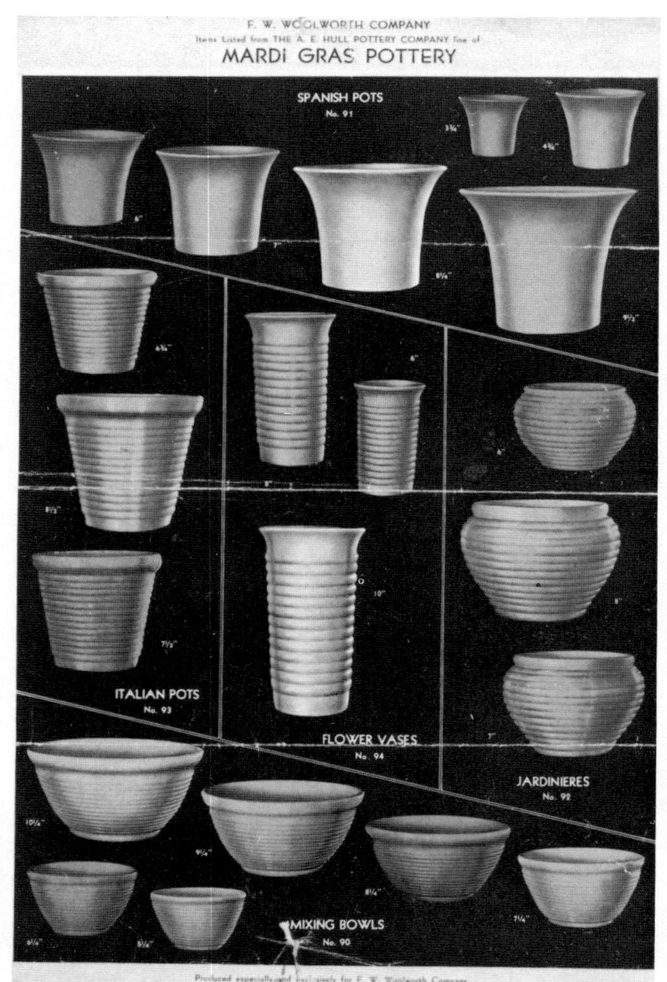

Plate 10

CALLA LILY (1938)

Also referred to as Jack-in-Pulpit

PLATE 11
Row 1:
1. Bowl, 500/32-10″

Row 2:
1. Vase, 502/33-6½″, reverse side shown
2. Console Bowl, 590/33, 4″×13″

PLATE 12
Row 1:
1. Vase, 540/33-6″
2. Cornucopia, 570/33-8″
3. Vase, 530/33-5″, *reverse side shown*

Row 2:
1. Candleholder, unmarked, 2¼″
2. Vase, 500/33-8″
3. Vase, 530/33-7″
4. Candleholder, unmarked, 2¼″

Row 3:
1. Vase, 520/33-8″
2. Vase, 560/33-13″
3. Ewer, 506-10″
4. Vase, 550/33-7½″

Plate 11

Plate 12

SUENO TUPLIP (1938)

PLATE 13
1. Vase, 107-33-8″
2. Vase, 100-33-10″

PLATE 14
Row 1:
1. Vase, 106-33-6″
2. Vase, 108-33-6″
3. Vase, 107-33-6″

Row 2:
1. *Bud Vase, 104-33-6″
2. Vase, 100-33-6½″
3. Basket, 102-33-6″
4. Vase, 111-33-6″

Row 3:
1. Vase, 110-33-6″
2. Jardinier, 115-33-7″
3. Flower Pot/Attached Saucer, 116-33-6″
4. Flower Pot/Attached Saucer, 116-33-4¼″

Row 4:
1. Vase, 101-33-9″
2. Ewer, 109-33-13″
3. Ewer, 109-8″
4. Vase, 103-33-6″

*Laced handles are shown on brochure.

Plate 13

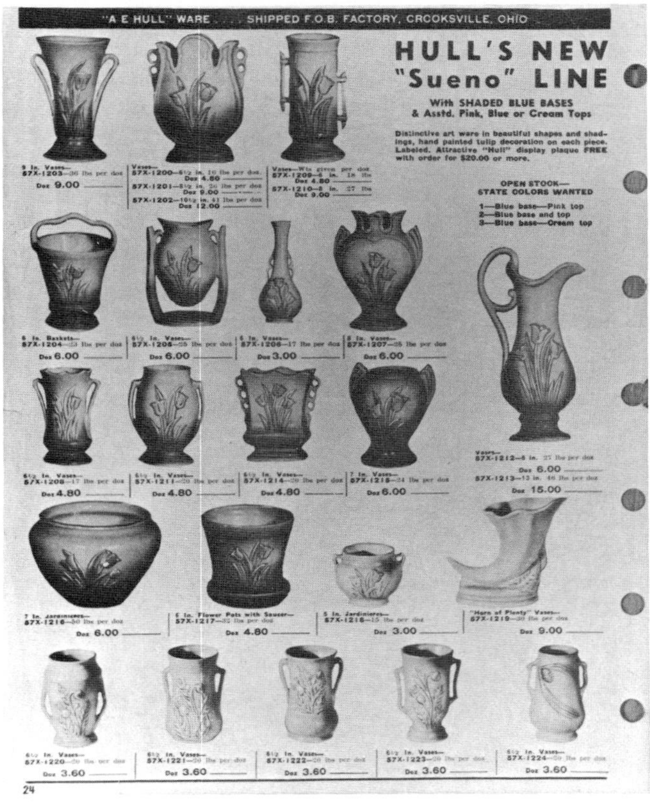

"A E HULL" WARE . . . SHIPPED F.O.B. FACTORY, CROOKSVILLE, OHIO

HULL'S NEW "Sueno" LINE

With SHADED BLUE BASES & Asstd. Pink, Blue or Cream Tops

Distinctive art ware in beautiful shapes and shadings, hand painted tulip decoration on each piece. Labeled. Attractive "Hull" display plaque FREE with order for $20.00 or more.

OPEN STOCK— STATE COLORS WANTED

1—Blue base—Pink top
2—Blue base and top
3—Blue base—Cream top

9 In. Vases— 57X-1203—30 lbs per doz Doz 9.00

Vases— 57X-1200—6½ in. 16 lbs per doz. Doz 4.80
57X-1201—8½ in. 25 lbs per doz Doz 9.00
57X-1202—10½ in. 41 lbs per doz Doz 12.00

Vases—Wts given per doz 57X-1209—6 in. 18 lbs Doz 4.80
57X-1210—8 in. 27 lbs Doz 9.00

6 In. Baskets— 57X-1204—23 lbs per doz Doz 6.00

6½ In. Vases— 57X-1205—25 lbs per doz Doz 6.00

6 In. Vases— 57X-1206—17 lbs per doz Doz 3.00

8 In. Vases— 57X-1207—35 lbs per doz Doz 6.00

Vases— 57X-1212—8 in. 27 lbs per doz Doz 6.00
57X-1213—13 in. 46 lbs per doz Doz 15.00

6½ In. Vases— 57X-1208—17 lbs per doz Doz 4.80

6½ In. Vases— 57X-1211—20 lbs per doz Doz 4.80

6½ In. Vases— 57X-1214—20 lbs per doz Doz 4.80

7 In. Vases— 57X-1215—24 lbs per doz Doz 6.00

7 In. Jardinieres— 57X-1216—30 lbs per doz Doz 6.00

6 In. Flower Pots with Saucer— 57X-1217—32 lbs per doz Doz 4.80

5 In. Jardinieres— 57X-1218—15 lbs per doz Doz 3.00

"Horn of Plenty" Vases— 57X-1219—30 lbs per doz Doz 9.00

6½ In. Vases— 57X-1220—20 lbs per doz Doz 3.60

6½ In. Vases— 57X-1221—20 lbs per doz Doz 3.60

6½ In. Vases— 57X-1222—20 lbs per doz Doz 3.60

6½ In. Vases— 57X-1223—20 lbs per doz Doz 3.60

6½ In. Vases— 57X-1224—20 lbs per doz Doz 3.60

24

Plate 14

ORCHID (1938)

PLATE 15
1. Bookends, 316-7″
2. Basket, 305-7″

PLATE 16
1. Jardinier, 310-6″
2. Console Bowl, 314-13″

PLATE 17
Row 1:
1. Vase, 308-4¼″
2. Vase, 302-6″
3. Vase, 308-6″
4. Vase, 303-4¾″

Row 2:
1. Jardinier, 317-4¾″
2. Vase, 307-4¾″
3. Bud Vase, 306-6¾″
4. Low Bowl, 312-7″

Row 3:
1. Vase, 304-6″
2. Candleholder, 315, 4″
3. Lamp Base, unmarked, 10″
4. Candleholder, 315, 4″
5. Vase, 307-6½″

Row 4:
1. Vase, 301-10″
2. Vase, 304-10¼″
3. Ewer, 311-13″

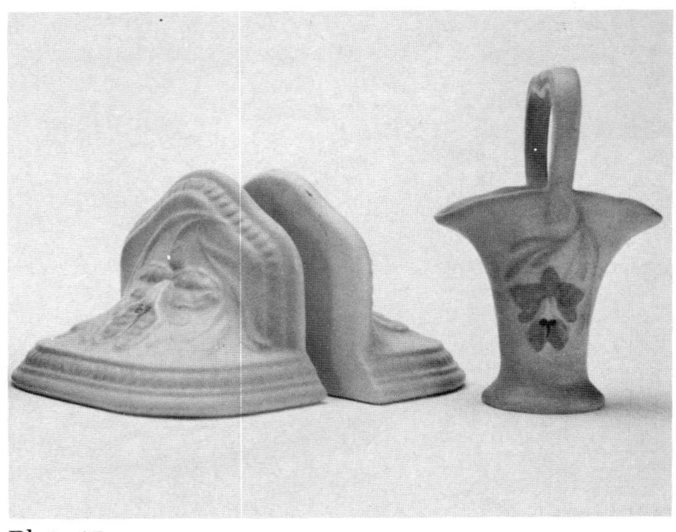

Plate 15

Plate 16

Plate 17

IRIS (Mid-1940's)

PLATE 18

Row 1:

1. Vase, 402-7″
2. Vase, 406-8½″
3. Bud Vase, 410-7½″
4. Vase, 403-7″

Row 2:

1. Rose Bowl, 412-7″
2. Vase, 407-8½″
3. Vase, 404-8½″
4. Basket, 408-7″

Row 3:

1. Vase, 402-8½″
2. Vase, 404-10½″
3. Ewer, 401-13½″
4. Vase, 414-10½″

Dec. No. 1 — Blue Bottom and Rose Top
Dec. No. 2 — Peach Bottom and Top
Dec. No. 3 — Rose Bottom and Peach Top

Original wholesale prices for Iris were as follows:

Item	*Per Dozen*
Ewer, 8″	$15.00
Ewer, 13″	$45.00
Vase, 4¾″	$ 7.50
Vase, 7″	$15.00
Vase, 8½″	$22.50
Vase, 9″	$22.50
Vase, 10½″	$37.50
Vase, 16″	$60.00
Basket	$18.75
Console Bowl	$45.00
Candleholder	$ 9.00
Bud Vase	$12.00
Rose Bowl, 4″	$ 7.50
Rose Bowl, 7″	$16.50
Jardinier, 5½″	$ 9.00
Jardinier, 9″	$22.50

Plate 18

PLATE 19

IRIS (Mid-1940's)

Row 1:

1. Vase, 403-4¾″
2. Vase, 404-4¾″
3. Advertising Plaque, 5″×11″ (1938)
4. Vase, 407-4¾″
5. Vase, 406-4¾″

Row 2:

1. Jardinier, 413-5½″
2. Ewer, 401-8″
3. Ewer, 401-5″
4. Rose Bowl, 412-4″

Row 3:

1. Candleholder, 411-5″
2. Console Bowl, 409-12″
3. Candleholder, 411-5″
4. Jardinier, 413-9″

THISTLE AND PINECONE (1938)

Row 4:

1. THISTLE Vase, #52-6½″
2. THISTLE Vase, #53-6½″
3. THISTLE Vase, #54-6½″
4. THISTLE Vase, #51-6½″
5. PINECONE Vase, #55-6½″

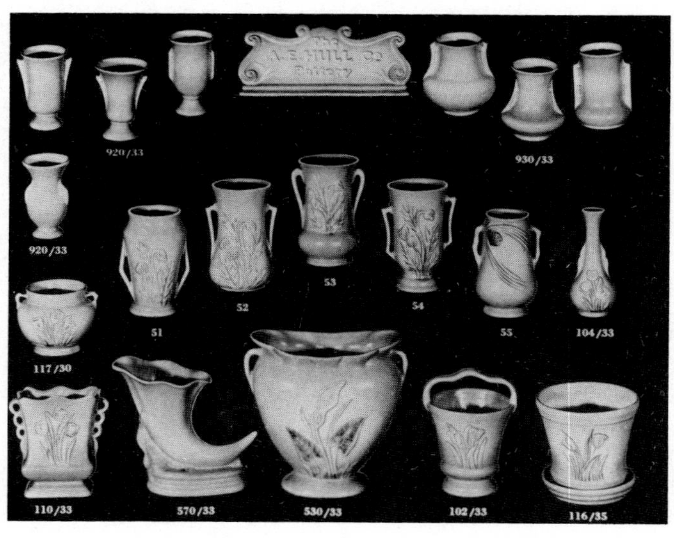

Plate 19

DOGWOOD (Mid-1940's)

PLATE 20

Row 1:

1. Cornucopia, 522, 3¾″
2. Low Bowl, 521-7″
3. Window Box, 508-10½″
4. Jardinier, 514-4″

Row 2:

1. Basket, 501-7½″
2. Candleholder, 512, 3¾″
3. Console Bowl, 511-11½″
4. Candleholder, 512, 3¾″

Row 3:

1. Ewer, 520-4¾″
2. Vase, 516-4¾″
3. Vase, 509-6½″
4. Ewer, 505-6½″ (8½″)
5. Vase, 502-6½″
6. Vase, 517-4¾″

Row 4:

1. Vase, 510-10½″
2. Ewer, 519-13½″
3. Ewer, 516-11½″
4. Vase, 513-6½″

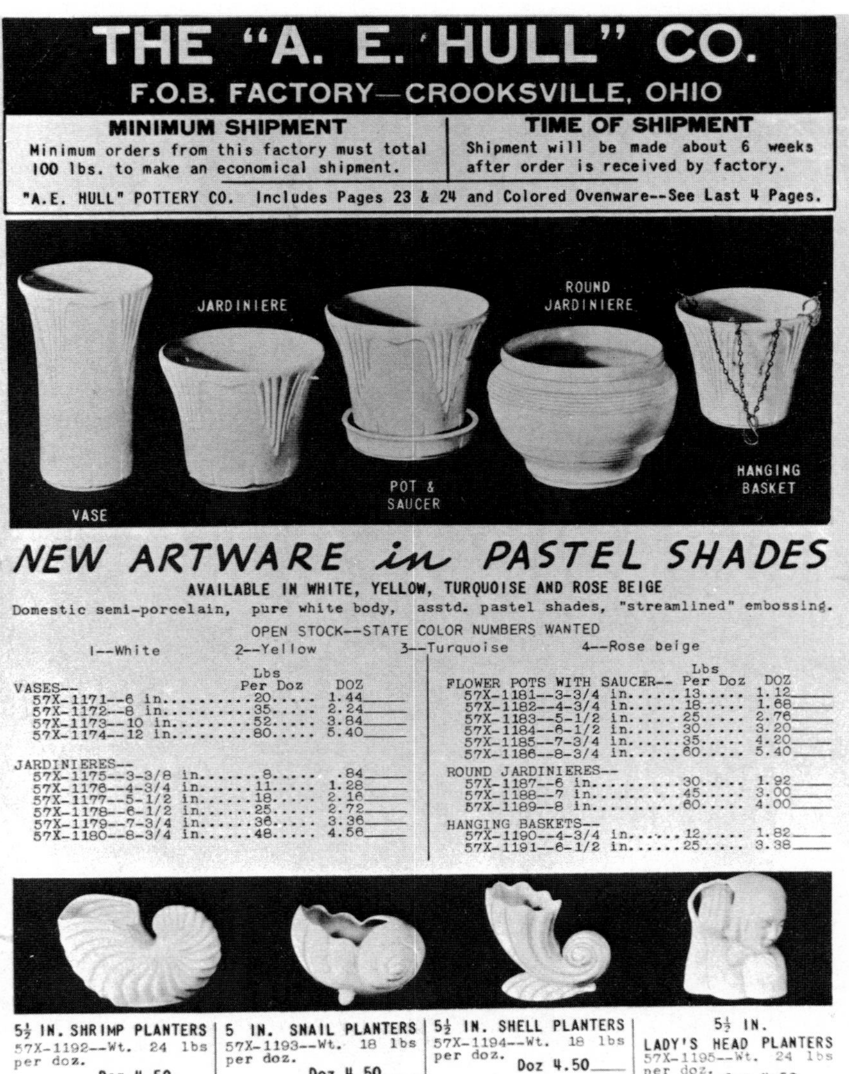

THE "A. E. HULL" CO.

F.O.B. FACTORY—CROOKSVILLE, OHIO

MINIMUM SHIPMENT	TIME OF SHIPMENT
Minimum orders from this factory must total 100 lbs. to make an economical shipment.	Shipment will be made about 6 weeks after order is received by factory.

"A.E. HULL" POTTERY CO. Includes Pages 23 & 24 and Colored Ovenware--See Last 4 Pages.

VASE
JARDINIERE
POT & SAUCER
ROUND JARDINIERE
HANGING BASKET

NEW ARTWARE *in* PASTEL SHADES

AVAILABLE IN WHITE, YELLOW, TURQUOISE AND ROSE BEIGE

Domestic semi-porcelain, pure white body, asstd. pastel shades, "streamlined" embossing.

OPEN STOCK--STATE COLOR NUMBERS WANTED

1--White 2--Yellow 3--Turquoise 4--Rose beige

	Lbs Per Doz	DOZ
VASES--		
57X-1171--6 in.	20	1.44
57X-1172--8 in.	35	2.24
57X-1173--10 in.	52	3.84
57X-1174--12 in.	80	5.40
JARDINIERES--		
57X-1175--3-3/8 in.	8	.84
57X-1176--4-3/4 in.	11	1.28
57X-1177--5-1/2 in.	18	2.16
57X-1178--6-1/2 in.	25	2.72
57X-1179--7-3/4 in.	36	3.36
57X-1180--8-3/4 in.	48	4.56

	Lbs Per Doz	DOZ
FLOWER POTS WITH SAUCER--		
57X-1181--3-3/4 in.	13	1.12
57X-1182--4-3/4 in.	18	1.68
57X-1183--5-1/2 in.	25	2.76
57X-1184--6-1/2 in.	30	3.20
57X-1185--7-3/4 in.	35	4.20
57X-1186--8-3/4 in.	60	5.40
ROUND JARDINIERES--		
57X-1187--6 in.	30	1.92
57X-1188--7 in.	45	3.00
57X-1189--8 in.	60	4.00
HANGING BASKETS--		
57X-1190--4-3/4 in.	12	1.82
57X-1191--6-1/2 in.	25	3.38

5½ IN. SHRIMP PLANTERS	5 IN. SNAIL PLANTERS	5½ IN. SHELL PLANTERS	5½ IN. LADY'S HEAD PLANTERS
57X-1192--Wt. 24 lbs per doz. Doz 4.50	57X-1193--Wt. 18 lbs per doz. Doz 4.50	57X-1194--Wt. 18 lbs per doz. Doz 4.50	57X-1195--Wt. 24 lbs per doz. Doz 4.50

Plate 20

POPPY (Mid-1940's)

PLATE 21

1. Planter, 602-6½″
2. Basket, 601-12″

PLATE 22

Row 1:

1. Vase, 607-6½″
2. Basket, 601-9″
3. Vase, 612-6½″

Row 2:

1. Lamp Base, unnamed design, unmarked, 9″
2. Ewer, 610-4¾″
3. Vase, 607-8½″

Row 3:

1. Vase, 606-10½″
2. Ewer, 610-13½″
3. Wall Pocket, 609-9″

Plate 21

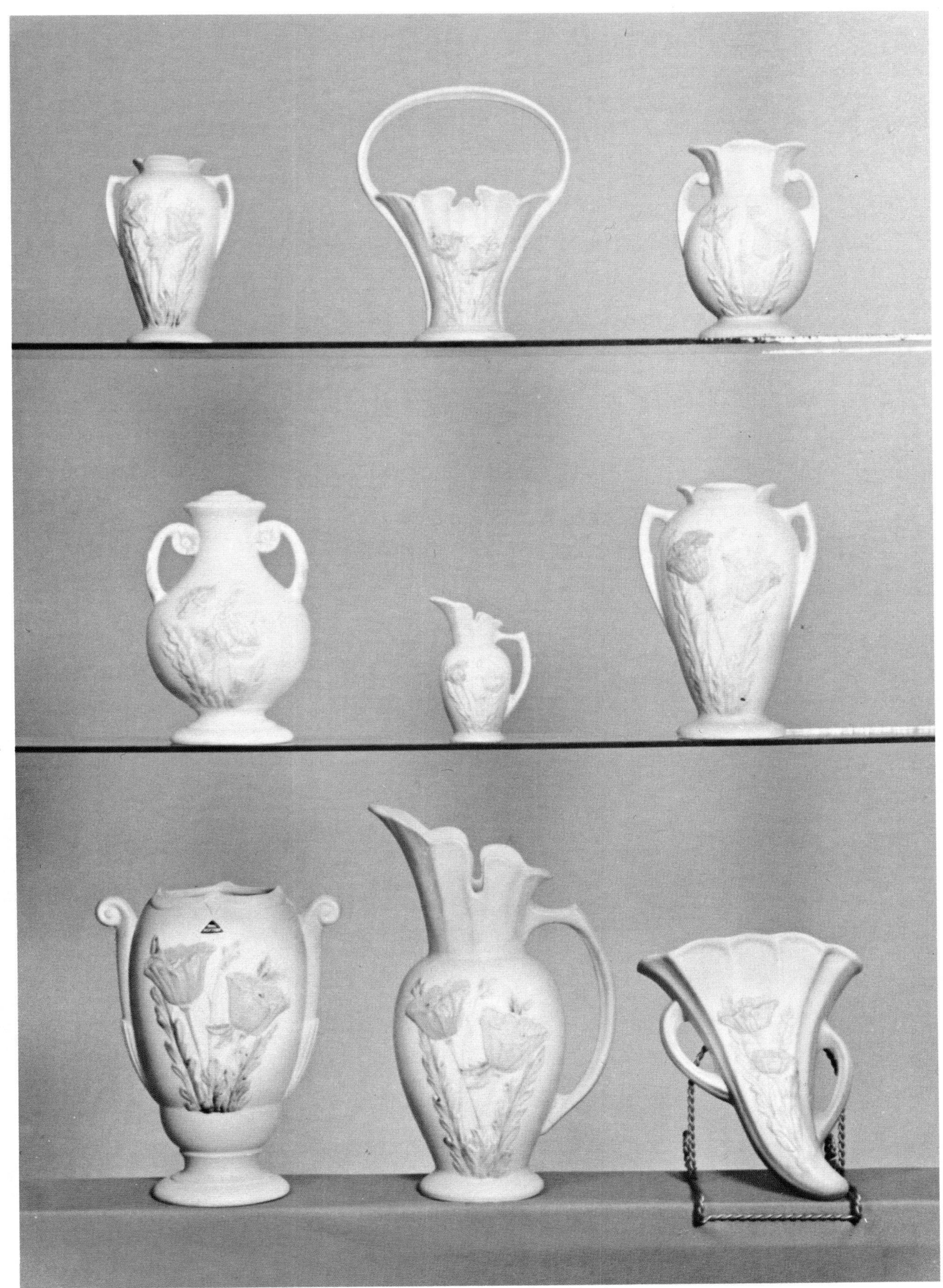

Plate 22

PLATE 23 (Mid-1940's)

Row 1, Rear

1. POPPY Vase, 605-8½″
2. DOGWOOD Teapot, 507-6½″
3. OPEN ROSE Wall Pocket, 125-8½″

Row 2, Front

1. TULIP Jardinier, 117-30-5″ (1938)
2. Vase, unmarked, 4″, may be Hull, similar to those shown in brochure page (1938) Oyster White satin finish.

PLATE 24

OPEN ROSE (Mid-1940's)

Row 1:

1. Vase, 123-6½″
2. Mermaid/Shell Planter, 104-10½″
3. Hanging Basket, 132-7″

Row 2:

1. Vase, 118-6½″
2. Vase, 135-6¼″
3. Ewer, 115-8½″
4. Vase, 138-6¼″
5. Vase, 134-6¼″

Row 3:

1. Cornucopia, 101-8½″
2. Vase, 130-4¾″
3. Vase, 102-8½″
4. Ewer, 128-4¾″
5. Vase, 141-8½″

Row 4:

1. Vase, 121-6¼″
2. Basket, 107-8″
3. Ewer, 106-13¼″
4. Ewer, 105-7″
5. Vase, 131-4¾″

Plate 23

Plate 24

OPEN ROSE (Mid-1940's)

PLATE 25

1. Bud Vase, 129-7″
2. "Lamp-Shaped" Vase, 139-10½″
3. Vase, 103-8½″

PLATE 26

Row 1:

1. Creamer, 111-5″
2. Teapot, 110-8½″
3. Open Sugar, 112-5″
4. Basket, 142-6¼″

Row 2:

1. Candleholder, 117-6½″
2. Console Bowl, 116-12″
3. Candleholder, 117-6½″

Row 3:

1. Low Bowl, 113-7″
2. Vase, 126-8½″
3. Vase, 108-8½″
4. Vase, 136-6¼″

Row 4:

1. Basket, 140-10½″
2. Jardinier, 114-8¼″
3. Vase, 143-8½″

Open Rose is a line with much variance in mold designs. Extensive planning was no doubt necessary, for each item possesses its own individual style. However, these shapes, unique from other art lines are just part of the "package," when it comes to Open Rose.

Most misleading is Lamp-Shaped Vase, 139-10½″ — not at all a lamp, nor should it be priced as such.

Plate 25

Plate 26

NOVELTY

PLATE 27

Row 1:

1. Flower Pot, 95-4½″ (1940)
2. Shrimp Planter, 201, 5″ (1940)
3. Shell Planter, 203, 5½″ (1940)
4. Old Spice Shaving Mug, 3″ (1937-1944)

Row 2:

1. Basket Girl, 954, 8″ (Mid-1940's)
2. Dancing Girl, 955, 7″ (Mid-1940's)
3. Basket Girl, 954, 8″ (1940)

Row 3:

1. Pig Planter, #60, 5″ (Mid-1940's)
2. Rooster, 951, 7″ (Early 1940's)
3. Baby, 62, 6¼″ (Mid-1940's)
4. Lamb Planter, 965, 8″ (Mid-1940's)

Row 4:

1. Kitten Planter, 61, 7½″ (Mid-1940's)
2. Male/Female Turnabout Cat Bank, never put into production, 198, 11″ (1970)
3. Cat Figural, unmarked, 7″ (1940)

The 1940 matte finished "Basket Girl" Planters headed the long-lived production use of mold No. 954.

This design, first marketed in the matte finish with "cold color"* decorations, was used for several years thereafter; most often it is found in high gloss finishes with underglaze decorations.

* Unfired, overglaze paint.

Plate 27

MARDI GRAS/GRANADA

(With the following exception: *Row 1, #4.*)

The Hull Pottery Company was the manufacturer of many lines used specifically for chain store sales. Mardi Gras was such a line, and was produced exclusively for the F.W. Woolworth Company.

It appears as though this line name was used repeatedly through a number of production years, both pre and post-1950. Line names Mardi Gras and Granada seem to have been used interchangeably.

PLATE 28

Row 1:

1. Vase, 216-9″, (1947)
2. Vase, 49-9″, (1947)
3. Vase, 215-9″, (1947)
4. Planter, 204, 6″, (1940)

Row 2:

1. Ewer, 31-10″
2. Basket, 32-8″
3. Basket, 65-8″
4. Ewer, 66-10″

Row 3:

1. Vase, 47-9″, (1947)
2. Ewer, 31-10″, signed "Grany," Shafer Gold
3. Ewer, 63, 10½″
4. Vase, 48-9″, (1947)

"Grany" Granville Shafer, of Zanesville, Ohio, has been a decorator of pottery items for nearly 50 years. He is responsible for decorating many of the Hull items on today's market. Shafer, with very little capital, launched his own business in 1932 when he bought Hull Pottery which he decorated and fired in his own kilns. From that meager beginning, the Shafer Pottery Company now has outlets in Denver, Chicago, and other major cities for the gold decorated wares for which he is best known.

Plate 28

LITTLE RED RIDING HOOD (1943-1957)

PLATE 29

1. Teapot, unmarked, 8″
2. Pitcher, unmarked, 8″

PLATE 30

1. Undecorated shaker set, unmarked, 5½″

PLATE 31

Row 1:

1. & 2. Shaker Set, unmarked, 3¼″
3. Shaker, unmarked, 5¼″
4. Mustard with Spoon, unmarked, 5¼″
5. & 6. Partially Decorated Shaker Set, 135889, 3¼″

Row 2:

1. Handled Casserole, 135889, 11¾″, Scenes of the Big Bad Wolf, Little Red Riding Hood, Grandma and the Ax Man emboss the casserole's circumference.
2. Wall Pocket, 4¾″, not Hull, but many collectors are adding this coordinated floral to their Little Red Riding Hood items. This wall pocket was made in nearby Zanesville, Ohio, by Chic Pottery, and decorated by Arthur Wagner.

Row 3:

1. Pitcher, unmarked, 7″
2. Covered Jar, unmarked, 8½″
3. Covered Jar, unmarked, 9″
4. Bank, unmarked, 7″

Row 4:

Cookie Jars with assorted floral decals, item 3 being the newest of those pictured, please note the different shaped basket.

Plate 29

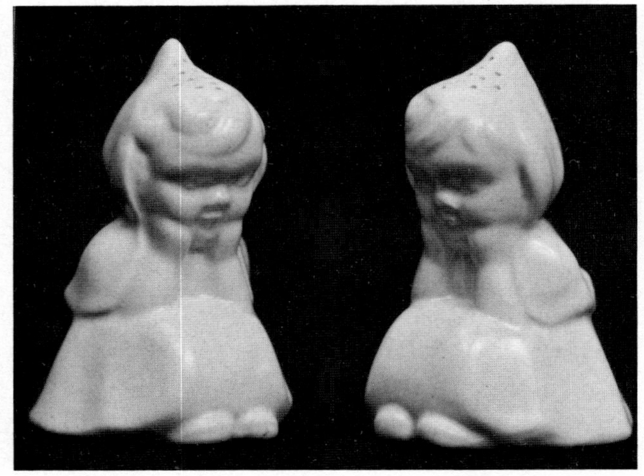

Plate 30

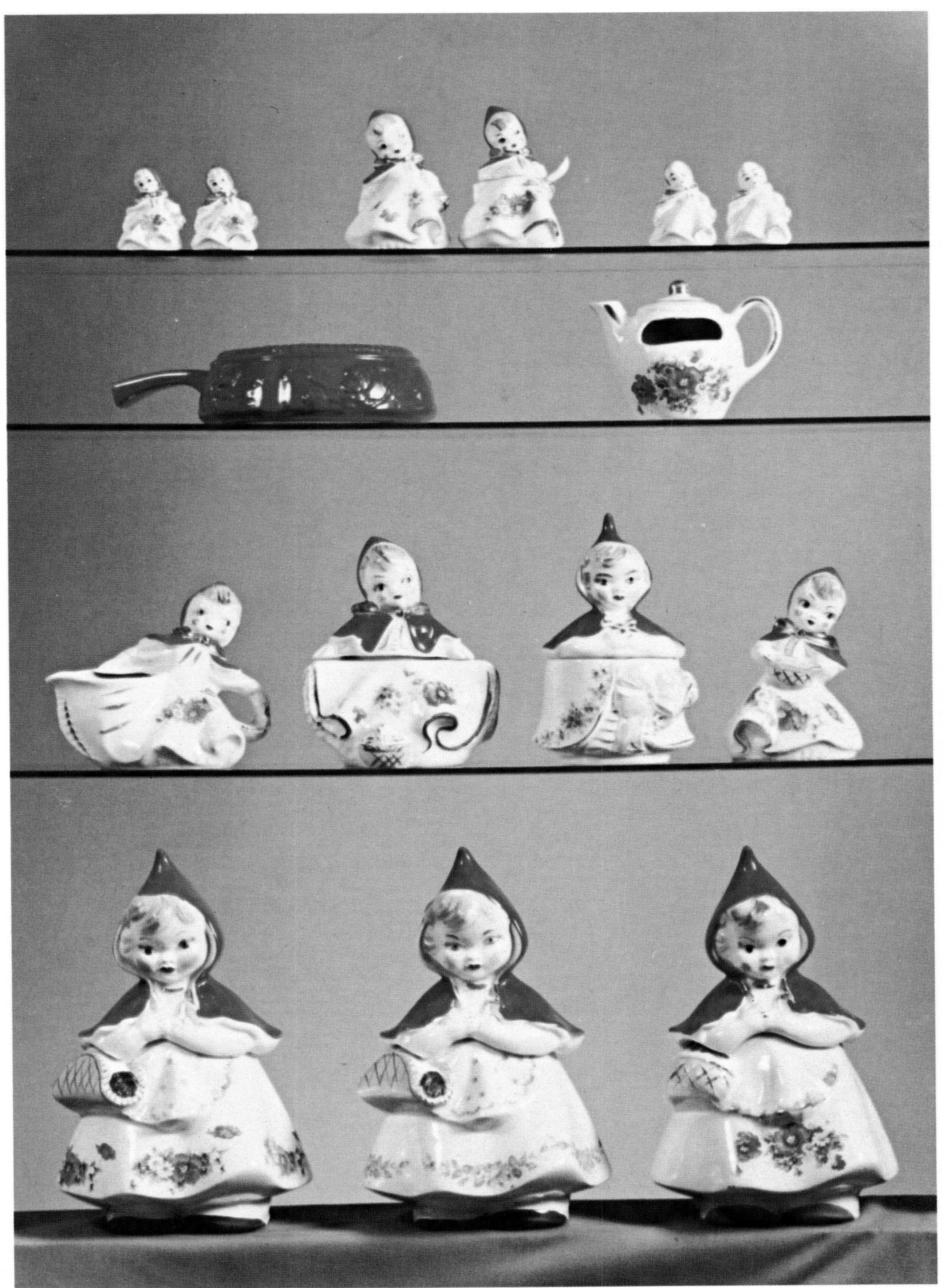

Plate 31

NOVELTIES

PLATE 32

7″ Bank made as premium item for Sinclair Oil Company. It was produced in Color 101: Matte Green. (Early 1960's)

PLATE 33

Row 1:

1. Greenware, Pig Bank, 3½″, manufactured in 1958 in solid color satin finishes
2. LEEDS Pig Liquor Bottle, 7¾″ (Mid-1940's)
3. Pig Bank, 3½″, manufactured in 1958
   Banks 1 and 3 were referred to as "dime banks" and employees of the Hull Company proved they held $75 in dimes.

Row 2:

1. Corky Pig Bank, 5″, pastel tints manufactured in 1957-58, at which time the company could produce 5,000 banks daily.
2. LEEDS Elephant Liquor Bottle, 7¾″ (Mid-1940's)
3. Corky Pig Bank, 5″, pastel tints manufactured in 1957-58, and sold to Jim Burns of Chicago. About this same period, Corky Pigs were also spray tinted dark green and pink.

Row 3:

1. Corky Pig Bank, 5″, of present-day Mirror Brown finish. The 1957 patent trademark is still in use. (1978)
2. Pig Bank, 196, 6″, of present-day Mirror Brown finish, used since 1960.
3. Pig Bank, 196, 6″, made into lamp base by Hull employee, money slot was never cut, of present-day Mirror Brown finish. (1974)
4. Pig Bank, 197, 8″, of present-day Mirror Brown finish. (1978)

Row 4:

1. Embossed Floral Pig Bank, USA, 14″, produced in 1940, cold color decor.
2. Pig Bank, unmarked, 14″, produced in 1940, underglazed decoration.

Plate 32

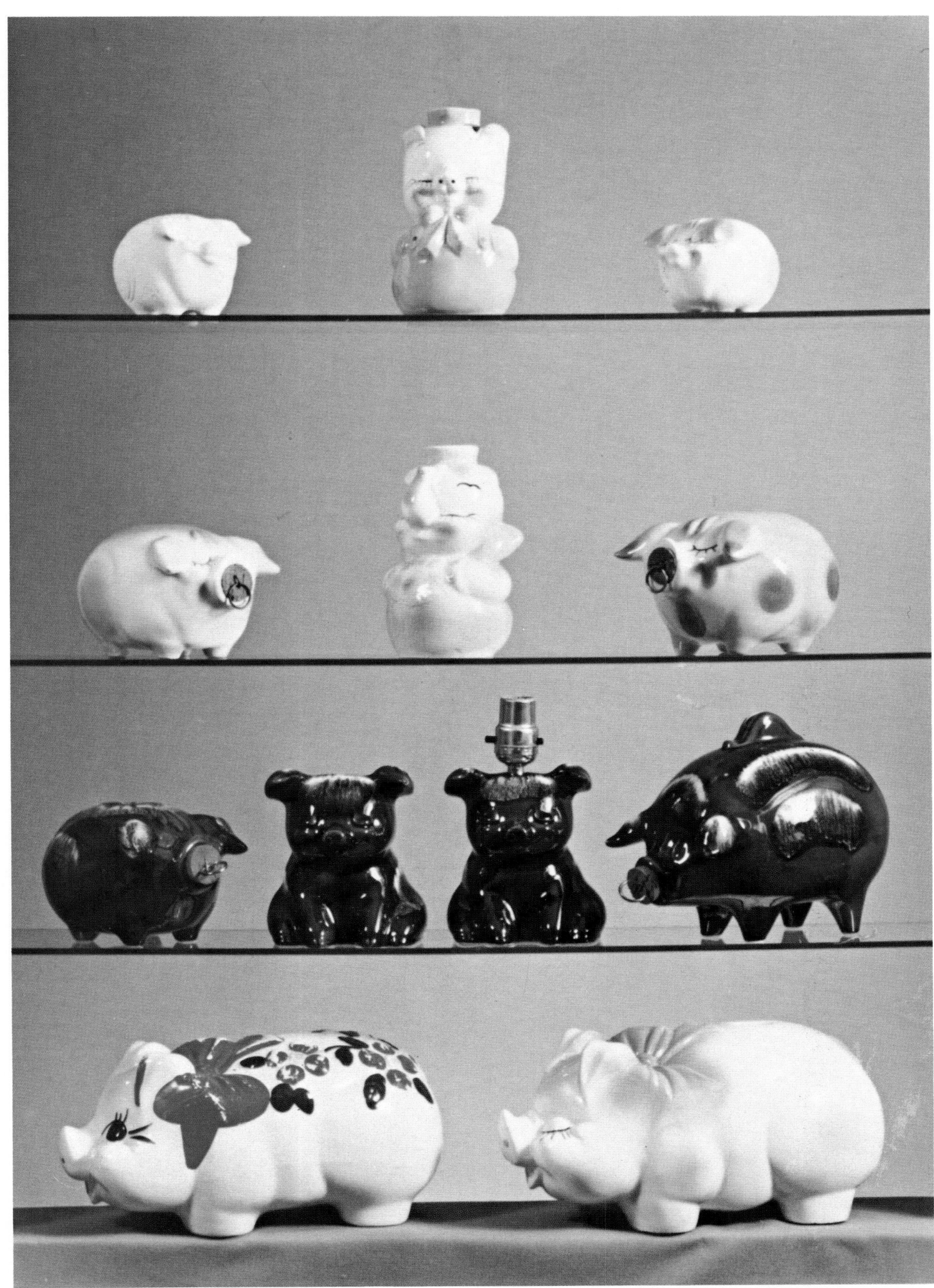

Plate 33

ROSELLA (1946)

PLATE 34
1. Vase, R-2-5″
2. Vase, R-1-5″

PLATE 35
Row 1:
1. Open Sugar, R-4-5½″
2. Vase, R-8-6½″
3. Ewer, R-9-6½″
4. Wall Pocket, R-10-6½″
5. Creamer, R-3-5½″

Row 2:
1. Vase, R-5-6½″
2. Vase, R-7-6½″
3. Basket, R-12-7″
4. Vase, R-6-6½″

Row 3:
1. Cornucopia, R-13-8½″ L
2. Ewer, R-11-7″ L
3. Ewer, R-11-7″ R
4. Cornucopia, R-13-8½″ R

Row 4:
1. Vase, R-14-8½″
2. Ewer, R-7-9½″
3. Vase, R-15-8½″

Superb achievement of the potter's wheel from Hull. Crafted to add beauty to modern American homes. The sculptured design is hand-tinted under glaze. Choice of coral or ivory, with color baked into the clay for enduring loveliness. At finer stores throughout the nation.

Ask for free ROSELLA folder showing 15 beautiful items. A. E. Hull Pottery Co., Crooksville, Ohio.

Plate 34

Plate 35

LAMPS

PLATE 36

Row 1:

1. Lamp Base, unmarked 6″, (Mid-1940's)

Row 2:

1. ROSELLA Lamp Base, L 3, 11″ (1946)
2. *Lamp Base, L 2, 13″ (Early 1940's)
3. ROSELLA Lamp Base, unmarked, 10¾″ (1946)

Row 3:

1. ROSELLA Lamp Base, unmarked, 6¾″ (1946)
2. **Woodland Lamp Base, unmarked, incised by maker, "M. Wilson," 14¾″ (1952)
3. Lamp Base, unmarked, 7¾″ (Mid-1940's)

*This lamp base has several look-alikes, so be careful when buying. Look for the wider separation from the bottom scroll work under floral decal to the top edge of the base.

**This lamp has a much larger circumference than the regular Woodland Ewer mold, therefore we can be sure that a separate mold was made for this item, and there should be several on the market for those who want to add a lamp to their collection.

In November, 1948, a specialty company offered this lamp through *Better Homes & Gardens* magazine.

Accentuate the beauty of your favorite flowers with ROSELLA vases. Distinctively designed by Hull master craftsmen; with the sculptured wild rose pattern hand-tinted under the glaze on a choice of ivory or coral body. Sixteen smart shapes at better stores everywhere . . . Rosella folder on request to A. E. Hull Pottery Co., Crooksville, Ohio.

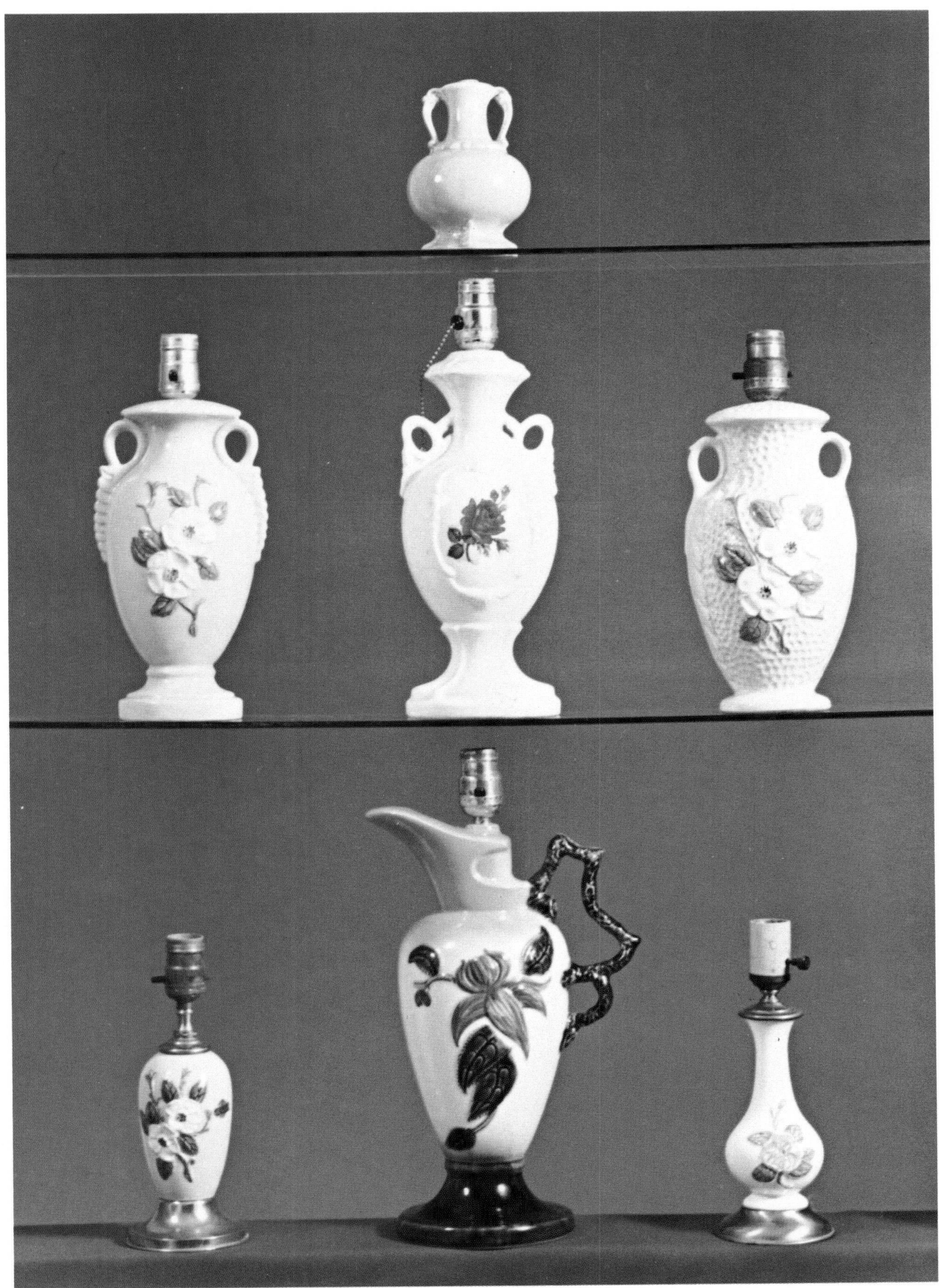

Plate 36

MAGNOLIA MATTE (1946-1947)

PLATE 37

Row 1:

1. Basket, 10-10½", not marketed in this color, this one-of-a-kind combination was decorated by an employee to suit his own taste.
2. Vase, 9-10½"
3. Basket, 10-10½"

Row 2:

1. Vase, 3-8½"
2. Vase, 17-12¼"
3. Vase 8-10½"

Row 3:

1. Vase, 20-15"
2. Lamp Base, 12½" Pottery Section
3. Vase, 16-15"

Magnolia is one of the most common Hull art lines, and you'll find the pink/blue combination outdistances the dusty rose/yellow combination in most cases. However, this should not affect price evaluation at this time, as both are common.

Plate 37

MAGNOLIA MATTE (1946-1947)

PLATE 38

Row 1:

1. Vase, 13-4¾″
2. Double Cornucopia, 6-12″
3. Ewer, 14-4¾″

Row 2:

1. Vase, 12-6¼″
2. Open Sugar, 25-3¾″
3. Teapot, 23-6½″
4. Creamer, 24-3¾″

Row 3:

1. Vase, 11-6¼″
2. Vase, 4-6¼″
3. Vase, 15-6¼″
4. Ewer, 5-7″

Row 4:

1. Vase, 21-12½″ (Tab Handles)
2. *Vase, 8-10½″
3. Vase, 21-12½″ (Open Handles)

*Gold decorators were plentiful in this Ohio region, some of which decorated entire items and then refired them for lasting beauty. Many items can be found with seals, "Hand Painted Fired Ceramic Colors" that indicate gold content.

Active area decorators of this period were: Granville "Grany" Shafer, Shafer Pottery Company, Zanesville, Ohio; Arthur Pemberton, Roseville, Ohio, and George Earl, Zanesville, Ohio, known as P.&E. Decorators; John and Edith Hilaman, J.&E. Decorators, Zanesville, Ohio; Arthur Wagner, employed by Chic Pottery, Zanesville, Ohio; Art Richards, employed by The Crooksville China Company, Crooksville, Ohio; and Bob Young, Roseville, Ohio.

By the 1950's, some gold decoration was applied to Hull wares inside the Hull plant.

Plate 38

MAGNOLIA MATTE (1946-1947)

PLATE 39

Row 1:

1. Candleholder, 27-4″
2. Console Bowl, 26-12″
3. Candleholder, 27-4″

Row 2:

1. Vase, 1-8½″
2. Vase, 22-12½″
3. Vase, 7-8½″

Row 3:

1. Vase, 2-8½″
2. Ewer, 18-13½″
3. Cornucopia, 19-8½″

Many of the Magnolia molds were used in the production of the same line with the all over transparent pink glaze as shown on Page 79. Numbering systems were changed for this updated line even though the shapes and sizes were identical.

Limited only to matte production were: Vase 13-4¾″ and Ewer 14-4¾″.

Limited only to high gloss production were: Vase H-2-5½″ and Ewer H-3-5½″.

Plate 39

MAGNOLIA GLOSS (1947-1948)

PLATE 40

Row 1:

1. Covered Sugar, H-22-3¾″
2. Teapot, H-20-6½″
3. Creamer, H-21-3¾″

Row 2:

1. Ewer, H-11-8½″
2. Vase, H-1-5½″
3. Cornucopia, H-10-8½″

Row 3:

1. Candleholder, H-24, 4″
2. Console Bowl, H-23-13″
3. Candleholder, H-24, 4″, reverse side shown

Row 4:

1. Vase, H-9-8½″
2. Ewer, H-19-13½″
3. Vase, H-16-12½″

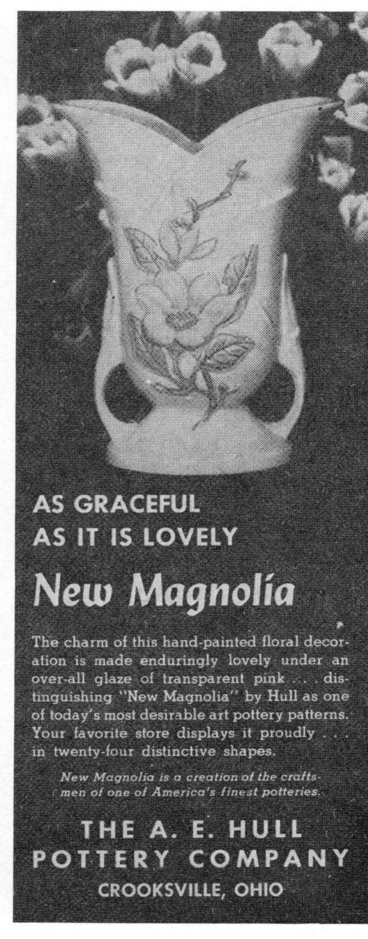

Plate 40

MAGNOLIA GLOSS (1947-1948)

PLATE 41

Row 1:

1. Vase, H-6-6½″
2. Basket, H-14-10½″
3. Vase, H-7-6½″

Row 2:

1. Vase, H-2-5½″
2. Double Cornucopia, H-15-12″
3. Ewer, H-3-5½″

Row 3:

1. Vase, H-8-8½″
2. Vase, H-17-12½″
3. Vase, H-13-10½″

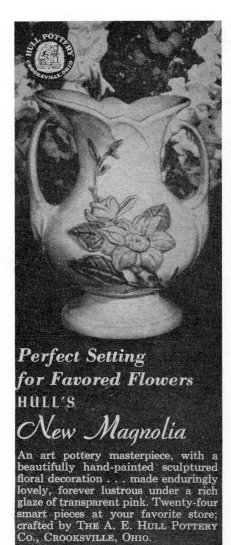

HULL POTTERY
CROOKSVILLE, OHIO
Perfect Setting
for Favored Flowers
HULL'S
New Magnolia
An art pottery masterpiece, with a beautifully hand-painted sculptured floral decoration . . . made enduringly lovely, forever lustrous under a rich glaze of transparent pink. Twenty-four smart pieces at your favorite store; crafted by THE A. E. HULL POTTERY CO., CROOKSVILLE, OHIO.

New Magnolia
Art Pottery
Patterned
By Hull
The perfect companion for your favorite flowers. The sculptured floral decoration is hand-painted in natural colors, glazed overall for enduring loveliness. There are twenty-four pieces in New Magnolia, available now at your favorite store. A creation of THE A. E. HULL POTTERY CO., CROOKSVILLE, OHIO.

Plate 41

WILDFLOWER (NUMBER SERIES) (MID-1940's)

PLATE 42

1. Vase, 78-8½″
2. Open Sugar, 74-4¾″
3. Teapot, 72-8″
4. Creamer, 73-4¾″

PLATE 43

Row 1:

1. Double Candleholder, 69-4″
2. Console Bowl, 70-12″
3. Double Candleholder, 69-4″

Row 2:

1. Cornucopia, 58-6¼″
2. Jardinier, 64-4″
3. Vase, 52-5¼″

Row 3:

1. Vase, 67-8½″
2. Vase, 51-8½″
3. Vase, 52-5¼″, reverse side shown

Row 4:

1. Vase, 59-10½″
2. Vase, 71-12″
3. Ewer, 55-13½″

Plate 42

Plate 43

WILDFLOWER (1946-1947)

PLATE 44

Row 1:

1. Vase, W-1-5½″
2. Vase, W-6-7½″
3. Cornucopia, W-10-8½″
4. Vase, W-8-7½″
5. Ewer, W-2-5½″

Row 2:

1. Vase, W-4-6½″
2. Vase, W-12-9½″
3. Vase, W-13-9½″
4. Vase, W-9-8½″

Row 3:

1. Vase, W-17-12½″
2. Lamp Base, W-17-12½″
3. Vase, W-18-12½″
4. Ewer, W-19-13½″

Wildflower

Fashionable foundations for your favorite flowers are these exquisite vases in the *Wildflower* Art Pottery line by Hull. There are 20 other equally delightful pieces, each with hand-tinted floral decoration embossed on a body of two-tone pastels. See *Wildflower* at your favorite store . . .

The A. E. HULL POTTERY CO.
Crooksville, Ohio

Plate 44

WILDFLOWER (1946-1947)

PLATE 45

1. Vase, W-20-15½″

PLATE 46

Row 1:

1. Vase, W-3-5½″, reverse side shown
2. Candleholder, unmarked
3. Console Bowl, W-21-12″
4. Candleholder, unmarked

Row 2:

1. Cornucopia, W-7-7½″
2. Vase, W-15-10½″
3. Vase, W-5-6½″

Row 3:

1. Basket, W-16-10½″
2. Vase, W-14-10½″
3. Ewer, W-11-8½″

Plate 45

This handsome console set admirably reflects the completeness of the *Wildflower* Art Pottery line by Hull. Two-tone spray tinting of the top and bottom distinguish each of the 22 pieces; each decorated front and back with exquisitely hand-painted floral group. Available at your favorite store.

Created and produced by the masterpotters of The A.E. Hull Pottery Co., Crooksville, Ohio

Wildflower

The sculptured beauty of the tasteful floral decoration . . . the exquisite delicacy of its hand-tinting and the artistry of its shapes, have made *Wildflower* the favorite of many in fine Art Pottery. 22 pieces, at better stores.

***Wildflower is a creation of the master potters of* The A. E. Hull Pottery Company, Crooksville, O.**

Plate 46

WATER LILY (1948)

PLATE 47

Row 1:

1. Cornucopia, L-7-6½″
2. Vase, L-8-8½″
3. Vase, L-6-6½″
4. Jardinier, L-23-5½″

Row 2:

1. Vase, L-13-10½″
2. Jardinier, L-24-8½″
3. Vase, L-12-10½″

Row 3:

1. Vase, L-15-12½″
2. Vase, L-2-5½″
3. Ewer, L-17-13½″
4. Ewer, L-3-5½″
5. Vase, L-16-12½″

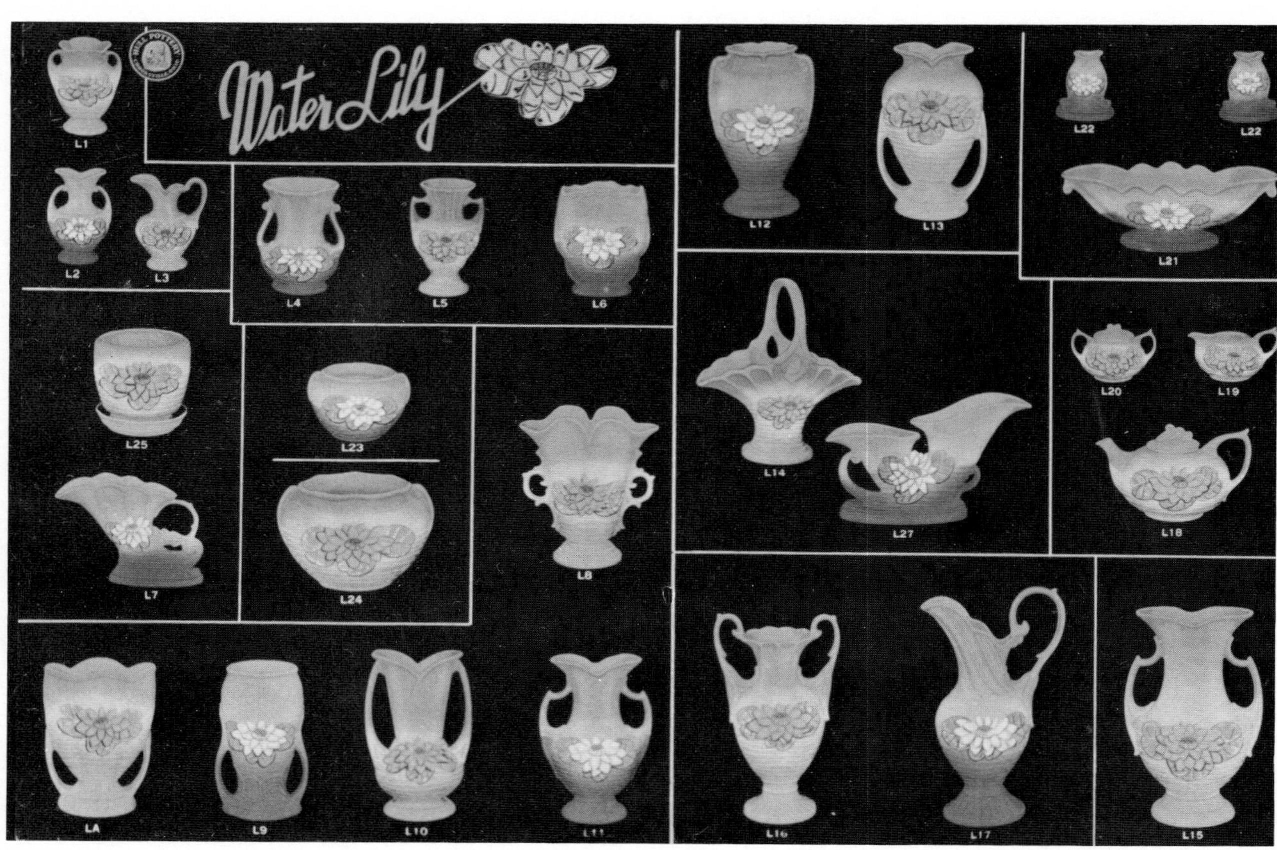

Plate 47

WATER LILY (1948)

PLATE 48

Row 1:

1. Creamer, L-19-5″
2. Teapot, L-18-6″
3. Covered Sugar, L-20-5″
4. Vase, L-1-5½″

Row 2:

1. Candleholder, L-22, 4½″
2. Console Bowl, L-21-13½″
3. Candleholder, L-22, 4½″
4. Vase, L-5-6½″

Row 3:

1. Lamp Base, unmarked, 7½″
2. Vase, L-10-9½″
3. Vase, L-11-9½″
4. Vase, L-4-6½″

Row 4:

1. Basket, L-14-10½″
2. Double Cornucopia, L-27-12″
3. Vase, L-A-8½″

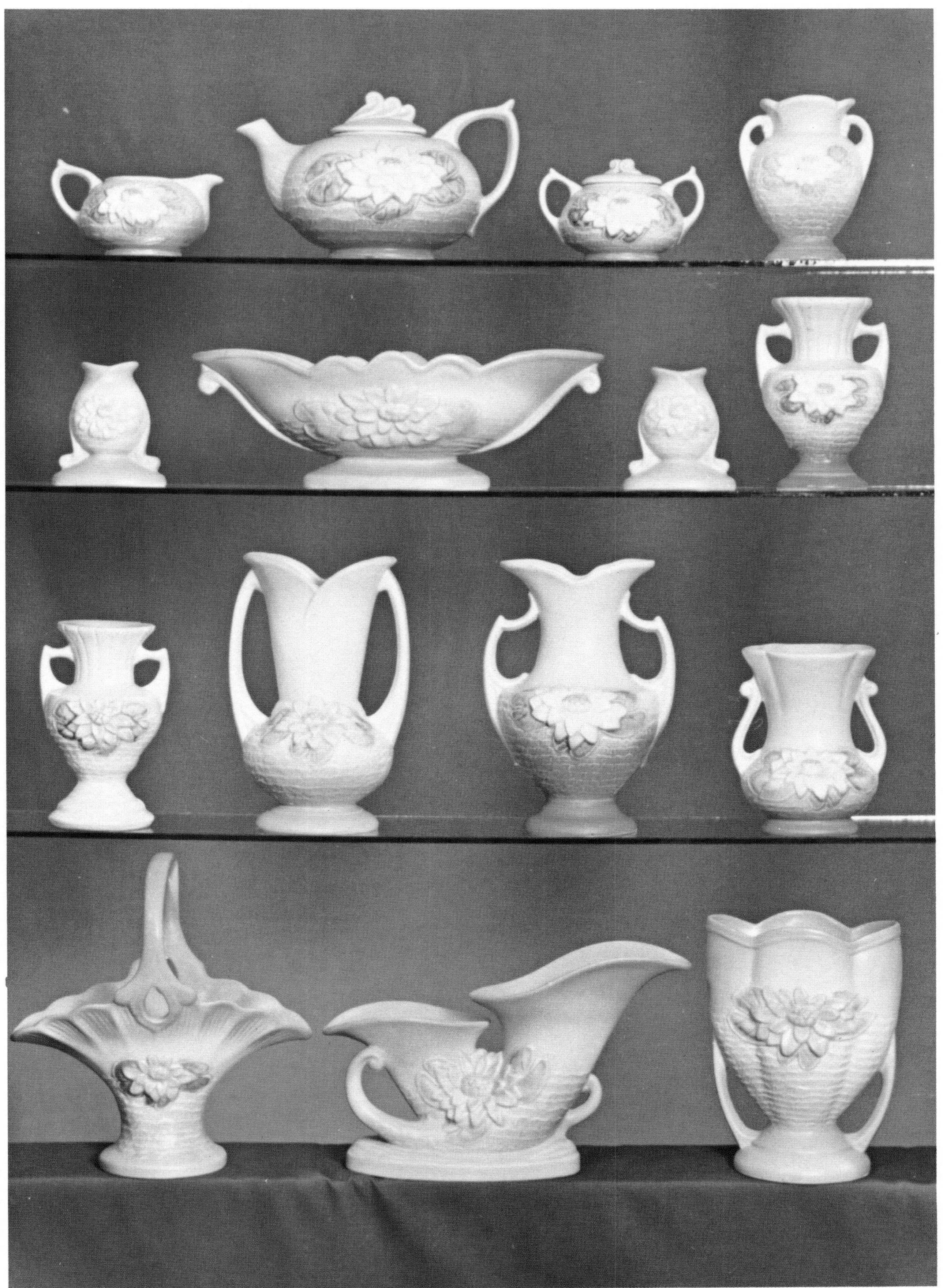

Plate 48

BOW-KNOT (1949)

(With exception of *Row 2*, items 4 & 5, and *Row 4*, item 3)

PLATE 49
1. Basket, B-29-12″

PLATE 50
Row 1:
1. Candleholder, B-17, 4″
2. Console Bowl, B-16-13½″
3. Candleholder, B-17, 4″

Row 2:
1. Cornucopia, B-5-7½″
2. Vase, B-7-8½″
3. Vase, B-9-8½″
4. Bell, unmarked, 6½″
5. Bell, unmarked, 6″

Row 3:
1. Jardinier, B-18-5¾″
2. Flower Pot/Attached Saucer, B-6-6½″
3. Vase, B-8-8½″
4. Vase, B-4-6½″
5. Basket, B-25-6½″

Row 4:
1. Vase, B-11-10½″
2. Vase, B-2-5″
3. Lamp Base, unmarked, 12¾″
4. Ewer, B-1-5½″
5. Vase, B-10-10½″

Plate 49

Plate 50

BOW-KNOT (1949)

PLATE 51

Row 1:

1. Cup/Saucer Wall Pocket, B-24-6″
2. Wall Plaque, B-28-10″
3. Pitcher Wall Pocket, B-26-6″

Row 2:

1. Iron Wall Pocket, unmarked, 6¼″
2. Teapot, B-20-6″
3. Covered Sugar, B-22-4″
4. Creamer, B-21-4″

Row 3:

1. Whisk Broom Wall Pocket, B-27-8″
2. Double Cornucopia, B-13-13″
3. Vase, B-3-6½″

Row 4:

1. Basket, B-12-10½″
2. Vase, B-14-12½″
3. Jardinier, B-19-9⅜″

Plate 51

CINDERELLA KITCHENWARE (1949) BLOSSOM AND BOUQUET

PLATE 52

Row 1:

1. BLOSSOM Casserole, minus lid, 21-7½″
2. BLOSSOM Pitcher, 29-16 Oz.

Row 2:

1. BLOSSOM Creamer, 28-4½″
2. BLOSSOM Teapot, 26-42 Oz.
3. BLOSSOM Covered Sugar, 27-4½″

Row 3:

1. BOUQUET Mixing Bowl, 20-7½″
2. BOUQUET Shaker, 25, 3½″
3. BOUQUET Grease Jar, 24-32 Oz.
4. BOUQUET Shaker, 25, 3½″

Row 4:

1. BOUQUET Pitcher, 29-32 Oz.
2. BLOSSOM Mixing Bowl, 20-9½″
3. BOUQUET Teapot, 26-42 Oz.

Row 5:

1. BOUQUET Pitcher, 22-64 Oz.
2. BOUQUET Bowl, brown ink stamp only, 9¾″
3. BLOSSOM Pitcher, 22-64 Oz.

Plate 52

WOODLAND (1949)

PLATE 53

Row 1:

1. Cornucopia, W2-5½″
2. Cornucopia, W10-11″
3. Cornucopia, W5-6½″

Row 2:

1. Ewer, W6-6½″
2. Vase, W8-7½″
3. Double Bud Vase, W15-8½″
4. Vase, W4-6½″

Row 3:

1. Vase, W17-7½″
2. Vase, W1-5½″
3. Vase, W25-12½″
4. Ewer, W3-5½″
5. Vase, W16-8½″

HULL POTTERY CROOKSVILLE, OHIO
Smart—New—Styled for You . . .
WOODLAND ARTWARE BY HULL
This lovely double horn is just one of the 30 graceful, smart pieces of Woodland—now available at your favorite store. Gay hand-painted florals, in a choice of Dawn Rose or Harvest Yellow body pastels. Styled by THE A. E. HULL POTTERY CO., CROOKSVILLE, OHIO.

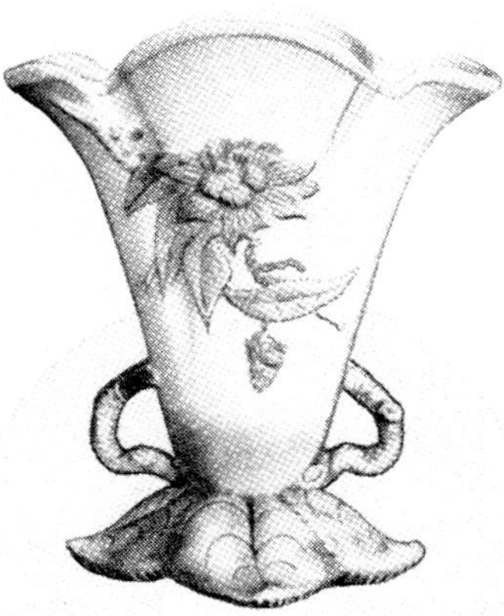

Created for You . . .
WOODLAND
ARTWARE BY HULL
This charming vase is one of the 30 graceful, smart pieces available in this new artware design . . . now at your favorite store in your choice of Dawn Rose and Harvest Yellow. Styled by THE A. E. HULL POTTERY CO., CROOKSVILLE, OHIO

Plate 53

WOODLAND (1949)

PLATE 54

Row 1:

1. Candleholder, W30, 3½″
2. Console Bowl, W29, 14″
3. Candleholder, W30, 3½″

Row 2:

1. Window Box, W14-10″
2. Wall Pocket, W13-7½″
3. Planter, W19-10½″

Row 3:

1. Jardinier, W7-5½″
2. Hanging Basket, W31-5½″
3. Hanging Basket, W12-7½″
4. Flower Pot/Attached Saucer, W11-5¾″

Row 4:

1. Double Cornucopia, W23, 14″
2. Basket, W9-8¾″
3. Basket, W22-10½″

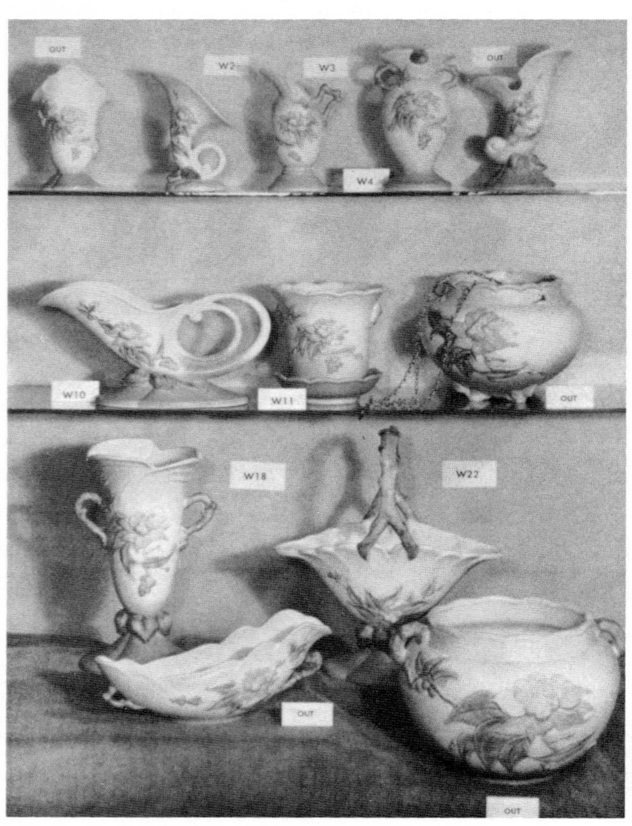

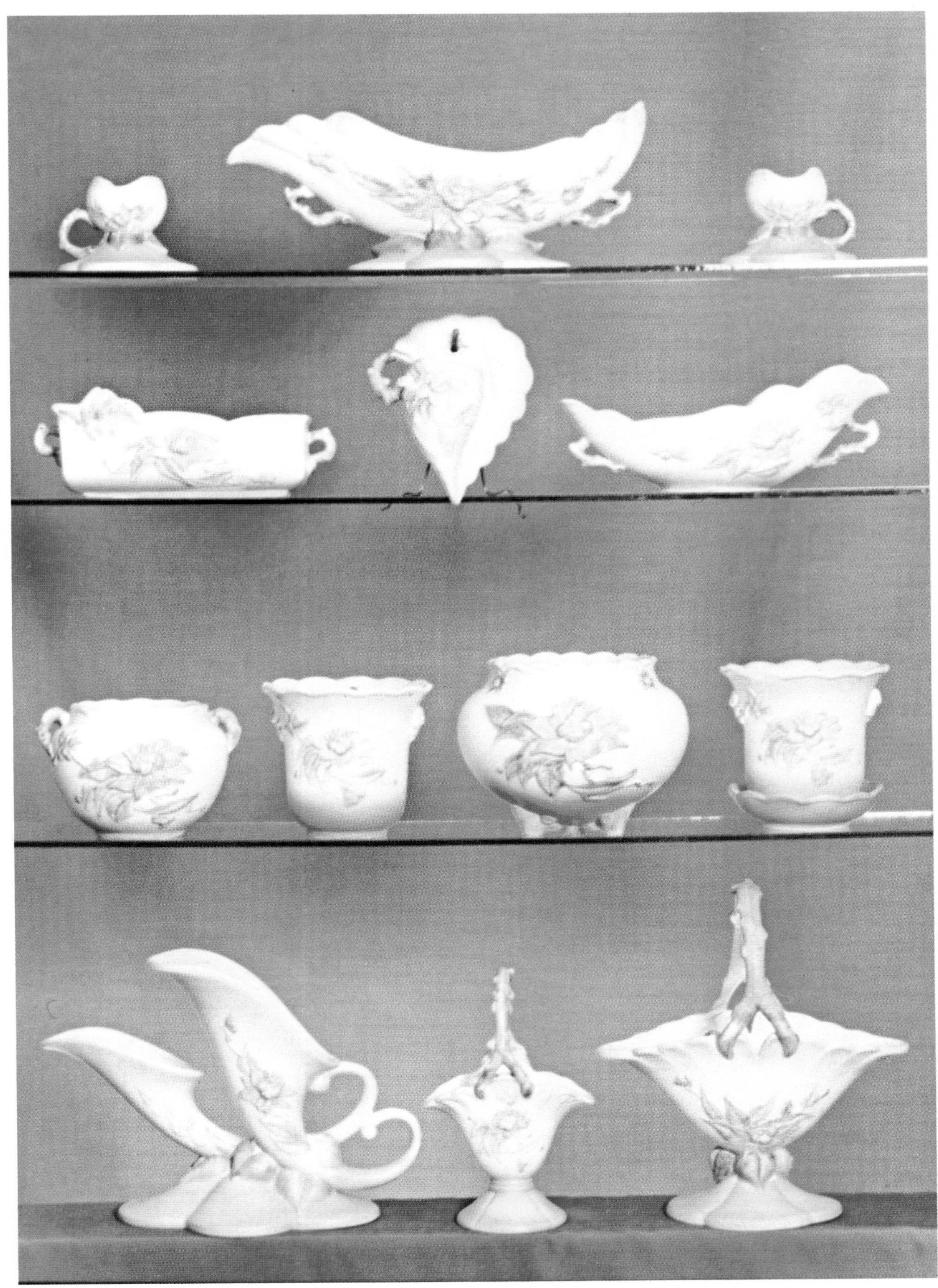

Plate 54

WOODLAND
POST-1950 MATTE AND TWO-TONES

PLATE 55

Row 1:

1. Vase, W16-8½″
2. Candleholder, W30, 3½″
3. Console Bowl, W29, 14″
4. Candleholder, W30, 3½″

Row 2:

1. Cornucopia, W10-11″, reverse side shown
2. Window Box, W14-10″
3. Cornucopia, W2-5½″
4. Basket, W9-8¾″

Row 3:

1. Flower Pot/Attached Saucer, W11-5¾″
2. Covered Sugar, W28, 3½″
3. Teapot, W26, 6½″
4. Creamer, W27, 3½″

Row 4:

1. Double Bud Vase, W15-8½″
2. Vase, W4-6½″
3. Ewer, W24-13½″
4. Ewer, W3-5½″
5. Basket, W22-10½″

In 1952, Woodland's molds were turned completely around, with handles and decor appearing on the opposite side from those used prior to the plant destruction.

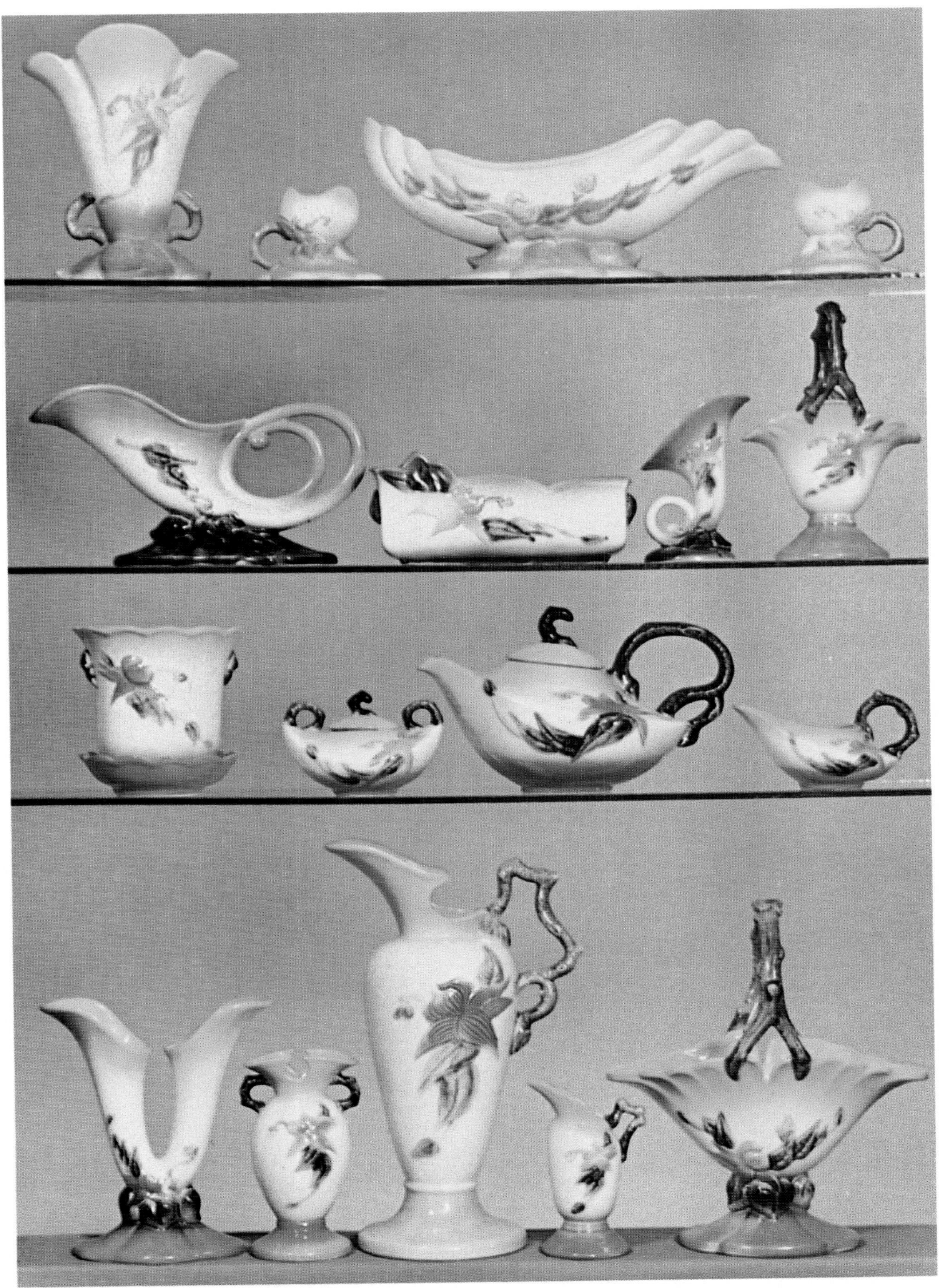

Plate 55

PARCHMENT AND PINE (1952-1953)

PLATE 56

1. Candleholder, unmarked, 5″ long
2. Console Bowl, unmarked, 16″ long
3. Candleholder, unmarked, 5″ long

PLATE 57

Teapot, unmarked, 6″, unmarketed color

PLATE 58

Row 1:

1. Cornucopia, S-2-R, 7¾″
2. Basket, S-8, 16½″ long
3. Teapot, unmarked, 6″

Row 2:

1. Ashtray, S-14, 14″
2. Ewer, S-7, 14¼″
3. Teapot, S-15, 8″

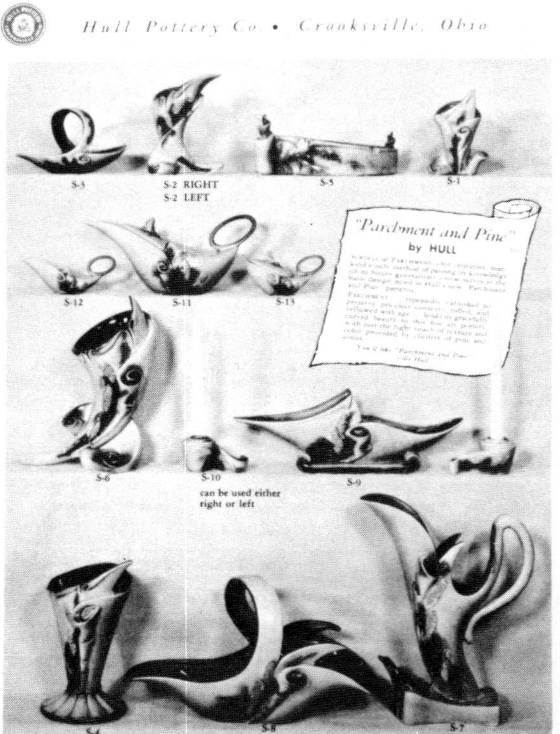

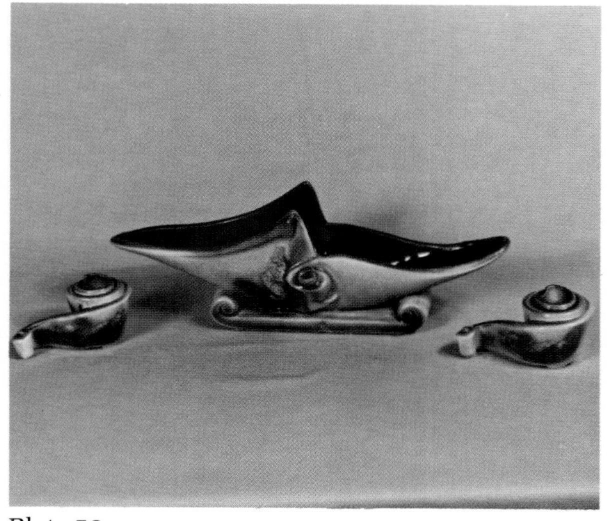

Plate 56

Plate 57

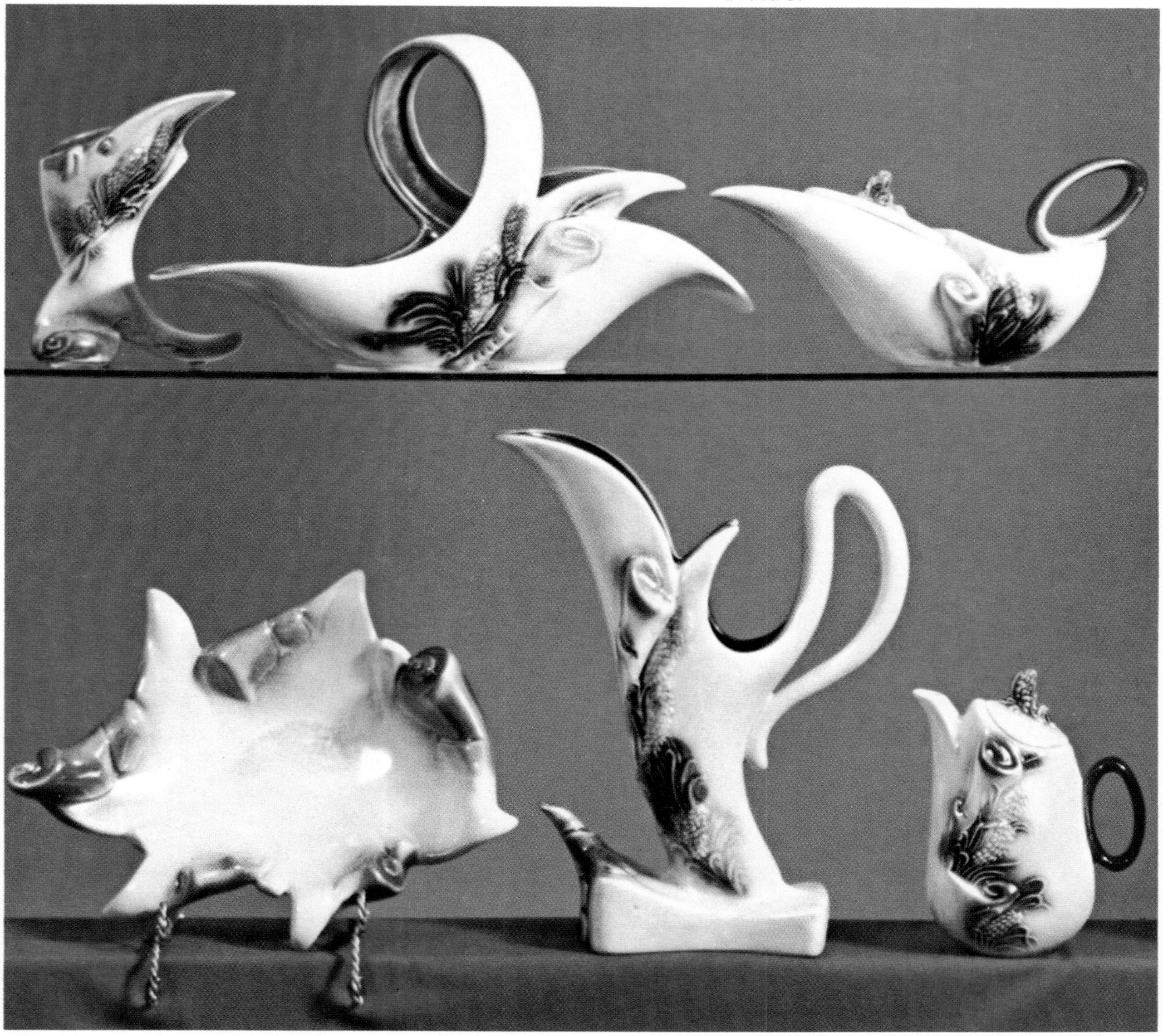

Plate 58

PLATE 59

Row 1:

1. SUNGLOW Vase, 100-6½″ (1952) Dark pink gloss
2. IMPERIAL Planter, F24, 12½″ Carnation Pink
3. Vase, 85, 8¾″ Dark pink gloss

Row 2:

1. IMPERIAL Vase, 413, 8¾″, Carnation Pink
2. Heart Planter, 19, 11¾″, Carnation Pink
3. IMPERIAL Vase, F28, 9½″, Carnation Pink

PLATE 60

SUNGLOW (1952)

Row 1:

1. Flower Pot, 97-5½″
2. Basket, 84, 6½″
3. Pitcher, 52-24 Oz.

Row 2:

1. Iron Wall Pocket, unmarked, 6″
2. Cup/Saucer Wall Pocket, 80, 6¼″
3. Ewer, 90-5½″
4. Pitcher Wall Pocket, 81, 5½″

Row 3:

1. Covered Casserole, 51-7½″
2. Shaker, 54, 2¾″
3. Grease Jar, 53, 5¼″
4. Shaker, 54, 2¾″

Row 4:

1. Vase, 89-5½″
2. Vase, 93-6½″
3. Vase, 95-8½″
4. Vase, 94-8″, reverse side shown
5. Whisk Broom Wall Pocket, 82, 8¼″

Row 5:

1. Flower Pot, 98-7½″
2. Bowl, 50-9½″
3. Pitcher, 55, 7½″

Plate 59

Plate 60

KITCHENWARE

PLATE 61

Row 1:

1. FLORAL Shaker, 44, 3½″ (1952-1953)
2. FLORAL Grease Jar, 43, 5¾″ (1952-1953)
3. FLORAL Shaker, 44, 3½″ (1952-1953)

Row 2:

1. FLORAL Salad Bowl, 49-10″ (1952-1953)
2. FLORAL Mixing Bowl, 40-5″ (1952-1953)

Row 3:

1. FLORAL Pitcher, 46, 6″ (1952-1953)
2. FLORAL Cookie Jar, 48, 8¾″ (1952-1953)
3. FLORAL Mixing Bowl, 40-9″ (1952-1953)

Row 4:

1. DEBONAIR Cookie Jar, 0-8, 8¾″ (Mid 1950's)
2. DEBONAIR Cookie Jar, 0-8, 8¾″ (Mid 1950's)
3. VEGETABLE Cookie Jar, 28, 8¾″, reverse side shown (Mid 1950's)

Row 4:

1. Banded Bowl, D-1-7½″
2. Banded Bowl, A-1-7½″
3. Banded Bowl, D-1-7½″

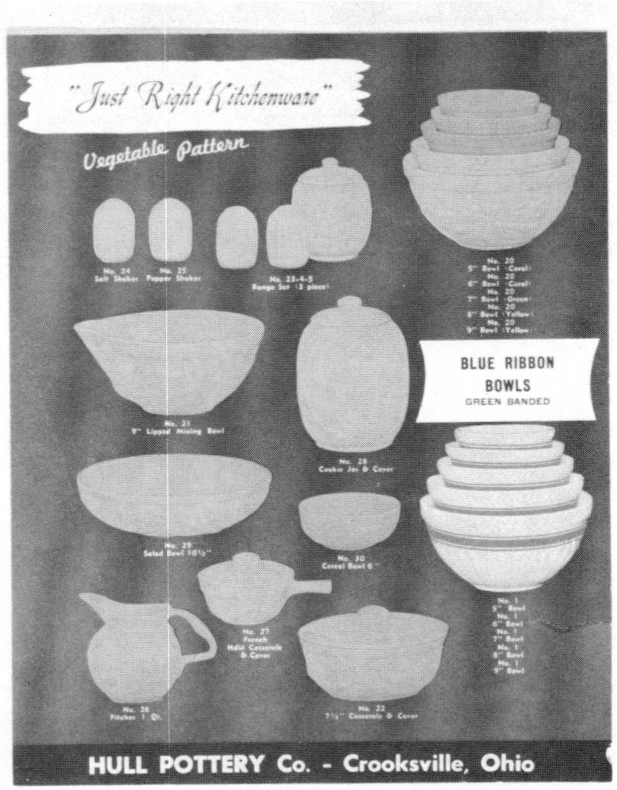

Plate 61

CRESCENT KITCHENWARE (Mid to late-1950's)
(With Exception of Row 4, Items 1 & 2)

PLATE 62

Row 1:

1. Sugar, minus lid, B-14, 4¼″
2. Teapot, B-13, 7½″
3. Creamer, B-15, 4¼″

Row 2:

1. Shaker, B-4, 3½″
2. Shaker, B-5, 3½″
3. Cookie Jar, B-8, 9½″
4. Mug, B-16, 4¼″

Row 3:

1. Bowl, B-1-9½″
2. Bowl, B-1-7½″
3. Bowl, B-1-5½″

Row 4:

1. Divided Covered Casserole, No. 35, 11½″
2. Bowl, No. 10, 8½″
3. Covered Casserole, B-2, 10″

For the cookie jar collector, this listing of Hull possibilities is included for your collecting pleasure.

Ⓗ Pretzel Jar, mid to late 1920's, buff body, embossed decor in ivory and brown, 3 quart.

No. 401 Painted Cookie Jar, 1934, no additional information available.

22/20 Square Footed kitchenware cookie jar, 1935. Buff body with wide Colonial Blue stripe with one Shell Bloom Pink stripe on each side, gallon-size.

70 Line Cookie Jar, 1935. Vitreous stoneware with hand-painted lacquer decorations in Poppy Red, Nubian Black, White and Jade Green, assorted as to Poppy, Rose, Tulip or Poinsetta, gallon-size.

NuLine Bak-Serve Cookie Jars, 1940. Three embossed styles, B-20, C-20 and D-20, 2 quart.

Little Red Riding Hood Cookie Jars, two styles, 1943 to mid-1950's.

Duck Cookie Jar, 966, mid-1940.

Blossom Cookie Jar No. 30, 1949, hand-painted underglaze.

Bouquet Cookie Jar No. 30, 1949, hand-painted underglaze.

Floral Cookie Jar No. 48, 1952-53, embossed Daisy-like flower

Crescent Cookie Jar, B-8, 1953.

Debonair Cookie Jar, 0-8, mid-1950, plain cylinder-shaped body.

Vegetable Cookie Jar No. 28, mid-1950, embossed decor glazed in solid colors.

Heritageware Cookie Jar No. 0-18, "Milk Can" shaped.

House 'n Garden Cookie Jar, 523, early 1960's to present day.

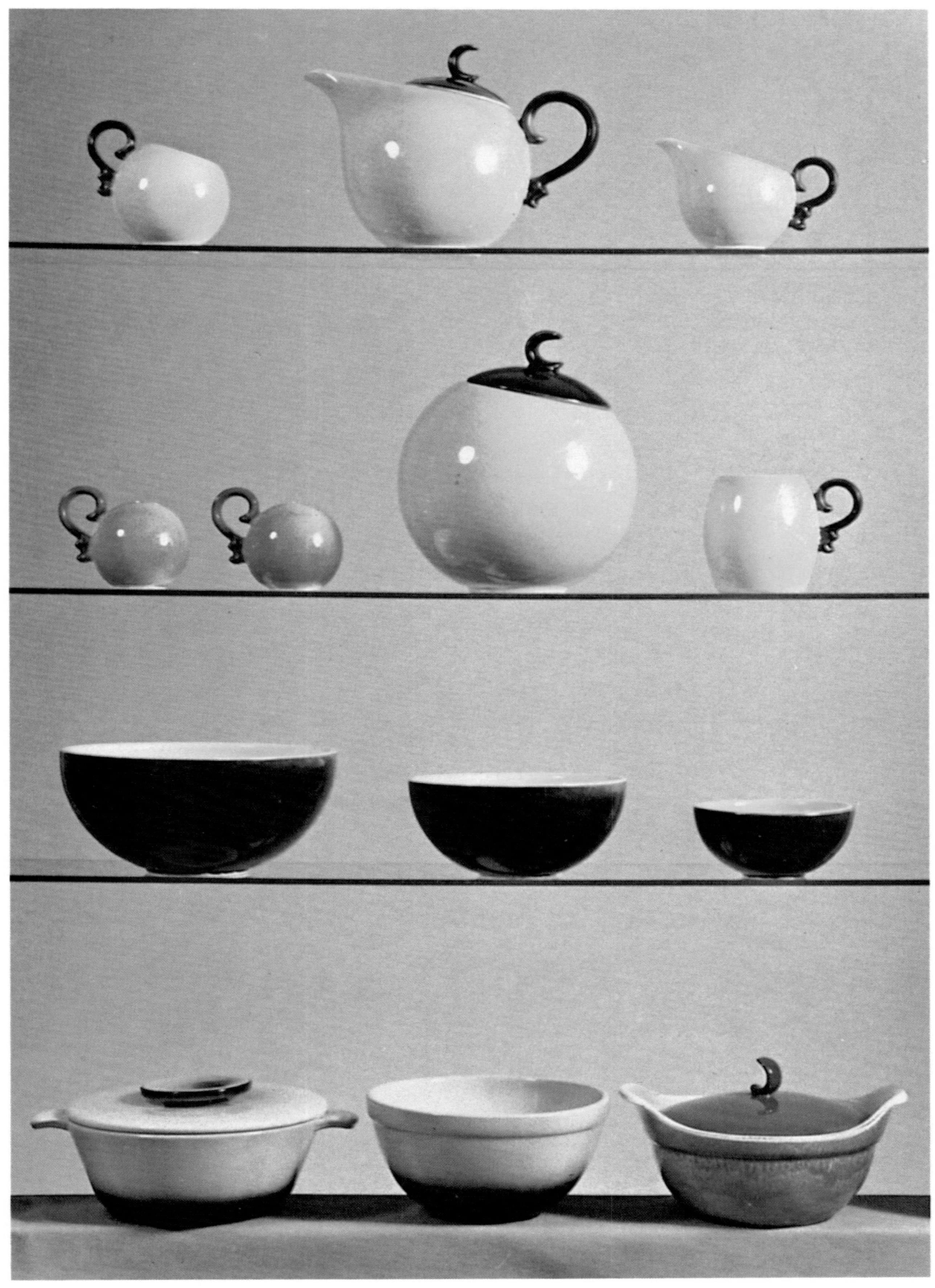

Plate 62

EBB TIDE (1954)

PLATE 63

Row 1:

1. Creamer, E-15, 4″
2. Basket, unmarked, 6¼″
3. Covered Sugar, E-16, 4″

Row 2:

1. Candleholder, E-13, 2¾″
2. Console Bowl, E-12, 15¾″
3. Candleholder, E-13, 2¾″

Row 3:

1. Basket, E-11, 16½″
2. Ewer, E-10, 14″

Plate 63

CLASSIC (1950's)

PLATE 64

Row 1:

1. Vase, 5-6″
2. Vase, 5-6″
3. Ewer, 6-6″
4. Vase, 4-6″

BLOSSOM FLITE (1955)

Row 2:

1. Candleholder T11, 3″
2. Console Bowl, T10, 16½″
3. Candleholder, T11, 3″

Row 3:

1. Basket, T2, 6″
2. Planter, 10½″
3. Teapot, T14, 8¼″

Row 4:

1. Basket, T9, 10″
2. Ewer, T13, 13½″

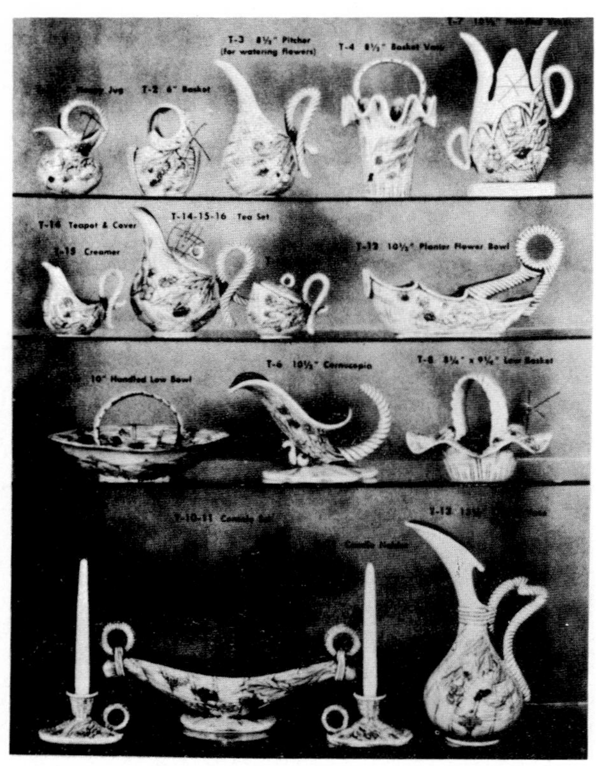

Plate 64

BUTTERFLY (1956)

PLATE 65
1. Serving Tray, B-23, 11½″, Matte White and Turquoise, gold-trimmed.

PLATE 66

Row 1:
1. Lavabo, 16″, Top B25, Base B24

Row 2:
1. Ashtray, B3, 7″
2. Ewer, B11, 8¾″

Row 3:
1. Vase, B10, 7″
2. Ewer, B15, 13½″

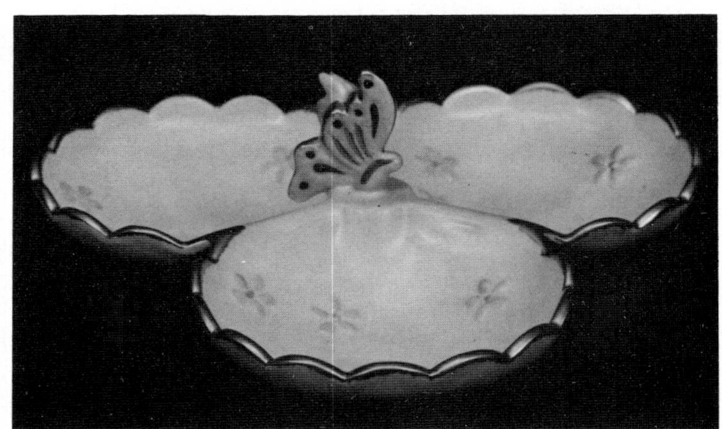

Plate 65

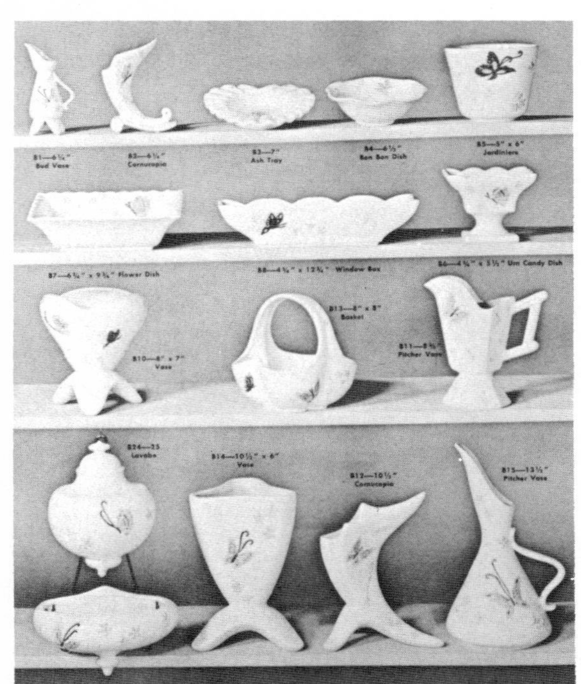

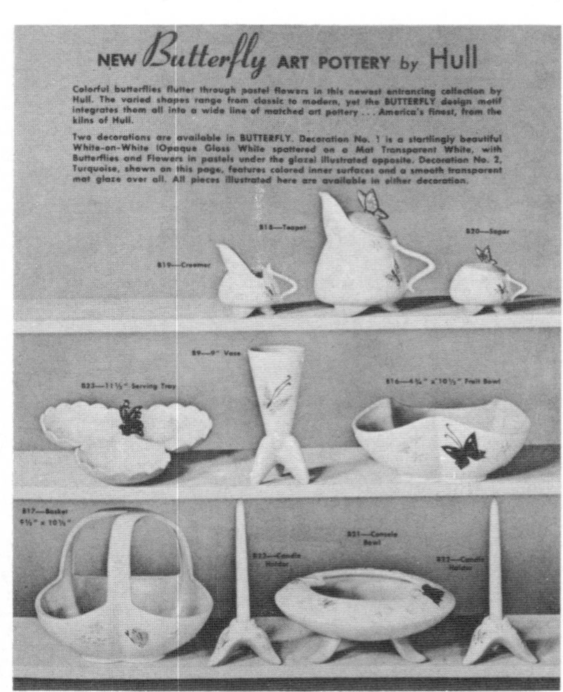

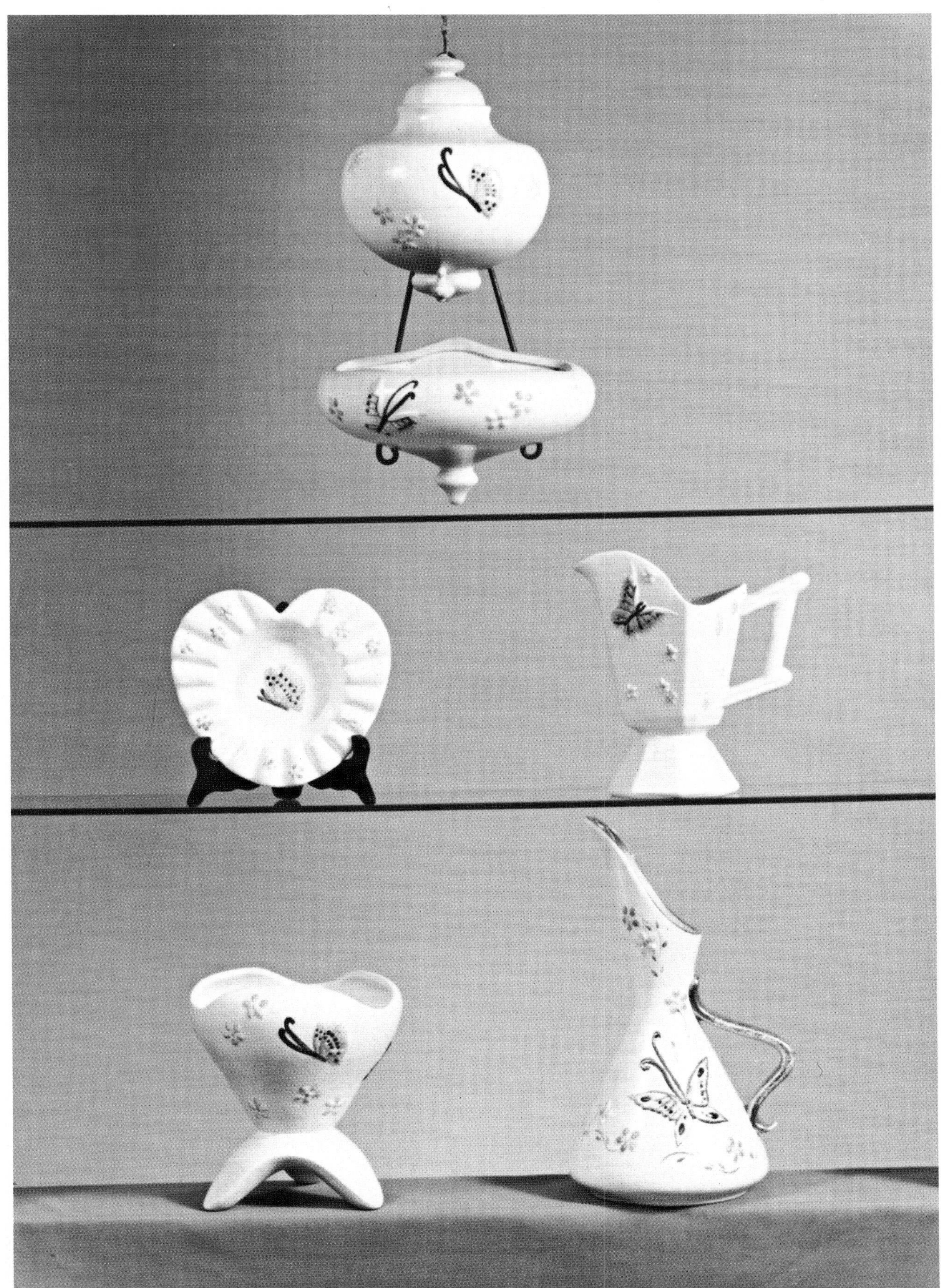

Plate 66

SERENADE (1957)

PLATE 67

1. Candleholders, S16, 6½″, Regency Blue with Sunlight Yellow interior
2. Fruit Bowl, S15, 7″ high, Regency Blue with Sunlight Yellow interior

PLATE 68

Row 1:

1. Vase, S1, 6½″
2. Ewer, S2, 6½″

Row 2:

1. Covered Sugar, S19, 3¼″
2. Teapot, S17, 5″
3. Creamer, S18, 3¼″

Row 3:

1. Vase, S4, 5¼″
2. Ashtray, S23, 13″×10½″
3. Candy Dish, S3, 8¼″

Row 4:

1. Basket, S14, 12″×11½″
2. Ewer, S13, 13¼″
3. Beverage Pitcher, S21, 10½″

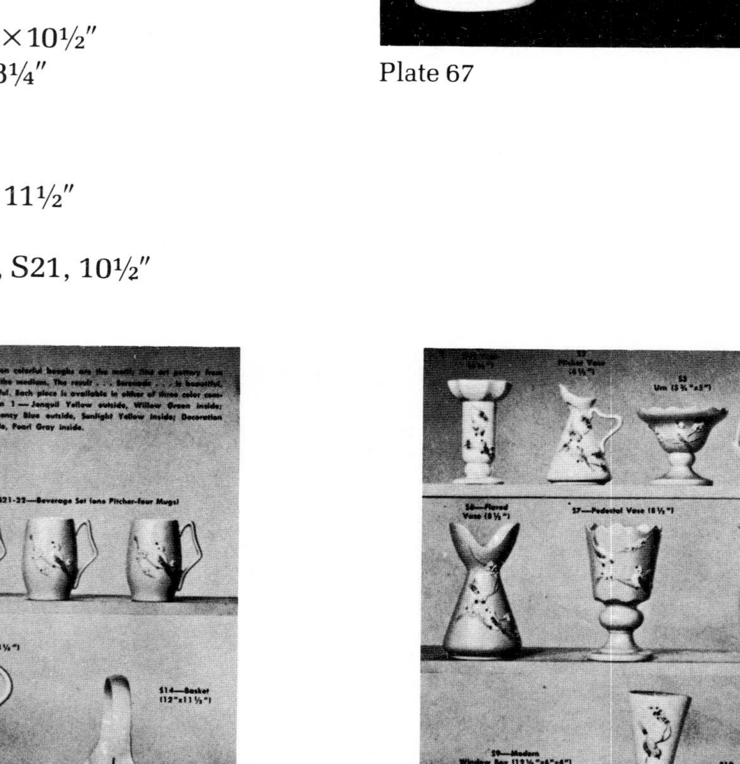

Plate 67

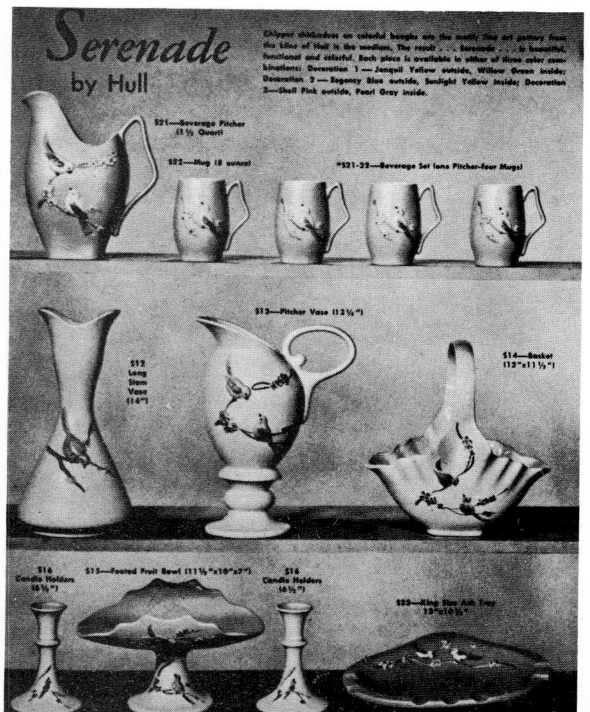

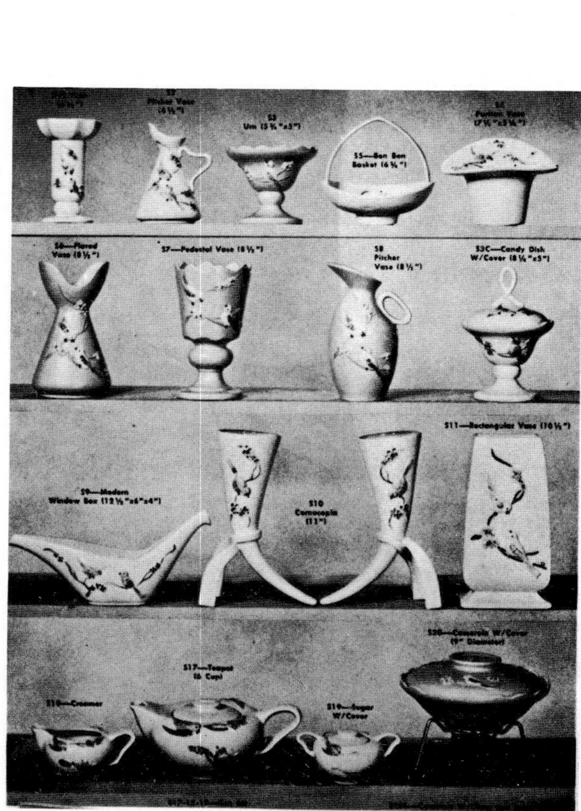

Plate 68

NOVELTY (1950's)

PLATE 69

10½″ Unmarked Flower Frog, marketed with Leaf Dish 85, dark green and maroon high gloss blends.

PLATE 70

Row 1:

1. Poodle Planter, 114, 8″
2. REGAL Planter, 124, 10″
3. Giraffe Planter, 115, 8″

Row 2:

1. Wall Pocket, 112, 10½″
2. Vase, 108, 8″
3. Planter, USA, 10½″

Row 3:

1. Bandana Duck, 76, 3½″×3½″
2. Bandana Duck, 75, 5″×7″
3. Bandana Duck, 74, 7″×9″
4. Goose Wall Pocket, 67, 6½″

Row 4:

1. Leaf Dish, 85, 13″
2. Duck Planter, 104, 9″×10½″
3. Vase, 110, 9¼″

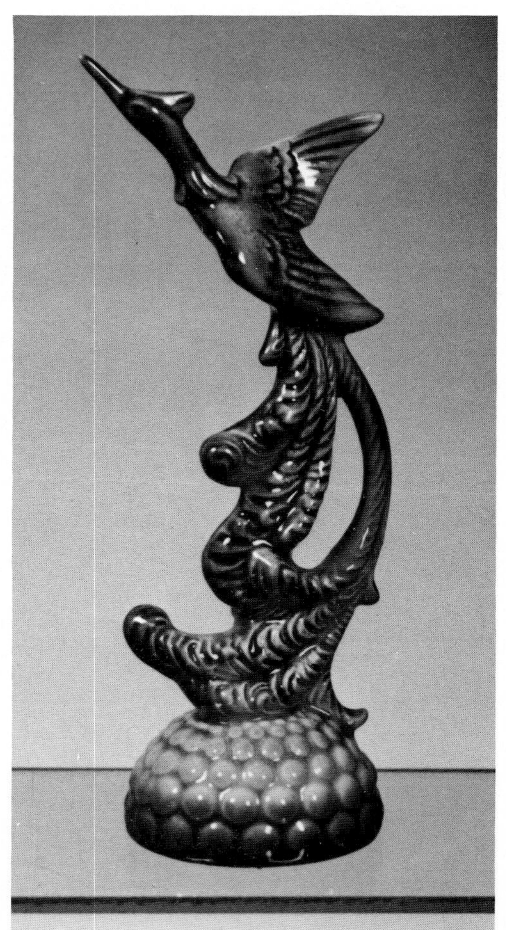

Plate 69

Plate 70

NOVELTY (1950's)

PLATE 71

Row 1:

1. Baby Shoes, unmarked, 3½", present-day production, but not marketed
2. Clown Planter, 82, 6¼"
3. Teddy Bear Planter, 811, 7"
4. Colt figurine, unmarked, 5½"

PLATE 72

Row 1:

1. Siamese Cats, 63, 5¾" tall

Row 2:

1. Love Birds, 93, 6"
2. Knight, 55, 8"
3. Bandana Duck Candleholder, 77, 3½"×3½"

Row 3:

1. Basket, 72, 8"
2. FIESTA Vase, 50, 9"
3. FIESTA Basket, 44, 6½"

Plate 71

Plate 72

NOVELTY (1950's)

PLATE 73

Row 1:

1. Parrot Planter, 60, 9½″×6″
2. Twin Geese Planter, 95, 7¼″
3. Baby Planter, 92, 5½″
4. Little Girl Planter, 90, 5½″

Row 2:

1. REGAL Parrot Planter, 313, 7¾″×12½″
2. Dog With Yarn Planter, 88, 5½″×8″
3. Pig Planter, 86, 6¾″×8″

Row 3:

1. Poodle Planter, 38, 6¼″
2. Dachshund Figural, 6″×14″
3. Kitten Planter, 37, 6¼″

Row 4:

1. Vase, 72, 8¼″
2. Goose Planter, 411, 12¼″
3. Vase, 73, 10½″
4. Pheasant Planter, 61, 6″×8″

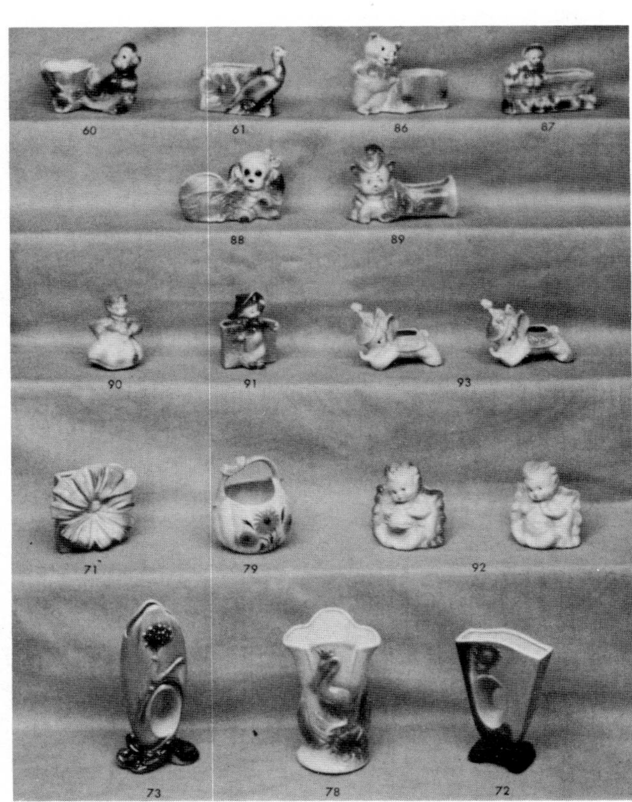

Plate 73

PLATE 74 (1950's)
Top, Left to Right:
1. Goose Bud Vase, 96, 9½", dark green and purple high gloss.
2. Cylinder Vase, 121, 4¼", dark green and maroon high gloss.

Row 2:
1. ROYAL WOODLAND Console Bowl, W29, 14½", turquoise with gray accents.
2. Wall Pocket, 120, 8", matte black with gold accents.

PLATE 75 (1950's)
Row 1:
1. ROYAL WOODLAND Wall Pocket, W13-7½"
2. ROYAL BUTTERFLY Lavabo, 16", Top, 86, Base, 87
3. ROYAL EBB TIDE Vase, unmarked, 7"

Row 2:
1. ROYAL WOODLAND Cornucopia, W10-11"
2. ROYAL IMPERIAL Window Box, 82, 12½"

Row 3:
1. ROYAL WOODLAND Basket, W9-8¾"
2. ROYAL EBB TIDE Vase, unmarked, 10¾"
3. ROYAL WOODLAND Ewer, W24-13½"
4. ROYAL IMPERIAL Jardinier, 75-7"

Plate 74

Plate 75

PLATE 76 (1950's)

Row 1:

1. Candy Dish, 158, 6¾″
2. Conch Shell, unmarked, 7¼″
3. FIESTA Jardinier, 43, 6″

Row 2:

1. Window Box, 153, 12½″
2. Window Box, 152, 13″

Row 3:

1. Planter, 71, 13″
2. Double Bud Vase, 103, 9″
3. Basket, 56, 6¼″

Row 4:

1. Vase, Woodland Blank, W18-10½″, Experimental
2. Fruit Bowl, 159, 5¼″×10¼″
3. Vase, 39, 12″

This is a photo of Gene Whitlatch and her display at the 1958 Ohio State Fair, Columbus, Ohio. All pottery shown is Hull, with the exception of small items in foreground.

Plate 76

PLATE 77 (1950's)

Row 1:

1. Urn, 44, 4½″
2. Leaf Vase, 100, 9″
3. Well Planter, 101, 7¾″

Row 2:

1. Planter, 118, 10¼″
2. FIESTA Cornucopia, 49, 8½″
3. Pillow Vase, 116, 6″

Row 3:

1. FIESTA Basket, 51, 12½″
2. Basket, unmarked, 12½″

Row 4:

1. Triple Bulb Bowls, 107, 3¼″×7″
2. Vase, 110, 9½″
3. Vase, 103, 12″
4. Triple Bulb Bowls, 3¼″×10½″

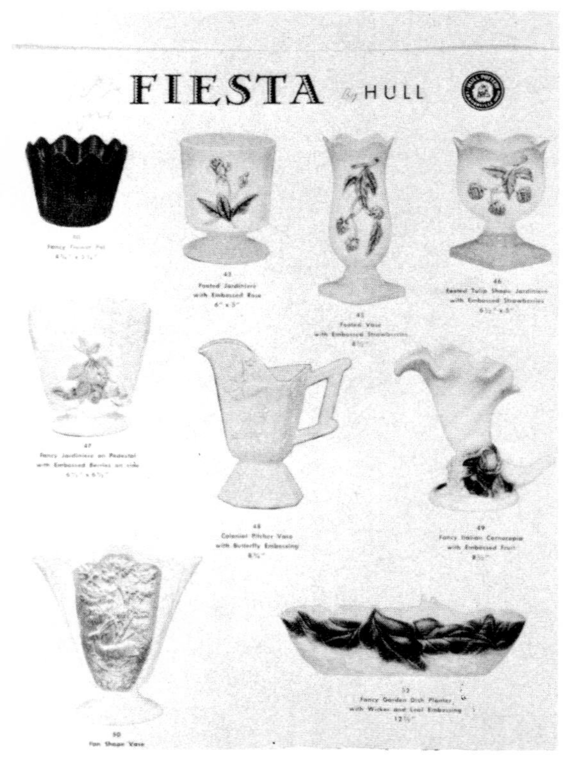

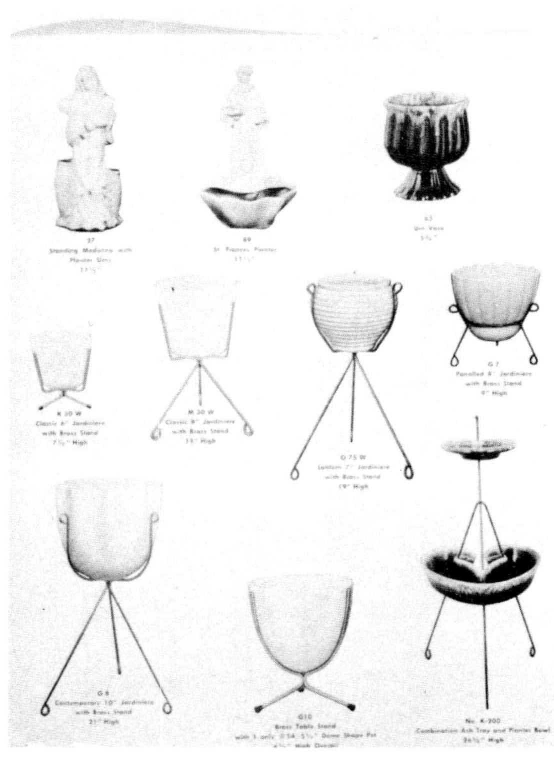

Plate 77

PLATE 78 (1950's)

Row 1:

1. FIESTA Flower Pot, 40, 4¼″
2. Basket, unmarked, 7″
3. Pedestaled Planter, 38, 4½″
4. Bowl, 29-6″

Row 2:

1. IMPERIAL Window Box, 82, 12½″
2. Flower Pot, unmarked, 3½″
3. Planter, 71, 12½″

Row 3:

1. Cornucopia, 64, 10″
2. Candy Dish, unmarked, 9″
3. Telephone Planter, 50, 9″
4. IMPERIAL Planter, unmarked, 6¾″

Row 4:

1. Heart Planter, T21, 11¼″ (Coordinates with Ashtray T20 for combination planter/ashtray in metal stand.)
2. Vase 111, 15″
3. Ashtray, T20, 7″
4. IMPERIAL Urn Vase, 454, 5″

Plate 78

TOKAY (1958)

TUSCANY (1960)

PLATE 79

Row 1:

1. Urn, 5, 5½″
2. Creamer, 17
3. Covered Sugar, 18

Row 2:

1. Cornucopia, 10, 11″
2. Ewer, 3, 8″
3. Candy Dish, 9, 7″×8½″

Row 3:

1. Vase, 8, 10″
2. Leaf Dish, 19
3. Vase, 4, 8¼″

Row 4:

1. Vase, 12, 12″
2. Basket, 11, 10½″
3. Ewer, 13, 12″

Plate 79

PLATE 80

This No. 6, 8″ basket was decorated with white "run" on Olive Green. (Early 1960's)

PLATE 81

10″ Pedestaled Vase that is similiar to Tokay/Tuscany lines. This was also used without grape motif as Imperial line Bell Vase. (Early 1960's)

PLATE 82

Tokay/Tuscany are raised, embossed designs. This pattern is an incised design, very similar, and in fact, even more beautiful than the grape lines mentioned. From all indications, it seems to have been a short-lived line of the early 1960's.

Row 1:

1. 10½″ Dinner Plate, unmarked
2. 8½″ Beverage Pitcher; marked Ovenproof, USA

Row 2:

1. Coffee Mug, unmarked, 3¼″×5″
2. Cereal, unmarked, 5¼″
3. Saucer, unmarked, 8¼″

Plate 80

Plate 81

Plate 82

PLATE 83

Row 1:

1. Leaf Bowl, 31, 8¾″
2. Bowl, Butterfly mold, unmarked, 6½″
3. Leaf Bowl, 31, 8¾″

HERITAGEWARE (1958)

MARCREST (1960)

Row 2:

1. HERITAGEWARE Vinegar Cruet, USA, 6¼″
2. HERITAGEWARE Oil Cruet, USA, 6¼″
3. HERITAGEWARE Cookie Jar, 0-18, 9¼″
4. HERITAGEWARE Grease Jar, A-3, 5¾″
5. HERITAGEWARE Shaker, 3½″
6. HERITAGEWARE Shaker, 3½″

Row 3:

1. MARCREST Mug, 3¼″
2. MARCREST Mug, 3¼″
3. MARCREST Pitcher, 7½″
4. HERITAGEWARE Mug, A-8, 3¼″
5. HERITAGEWARE Pitcher, A-7, 4½″

Row 4:

1. Pitcher, No. 22, 7¾″, Floral Blank
2. HERITAGEWARE Cookie Jar, 0-18, 9¼″
3. HERITAGEWARE Pitcher, A-6, 7″

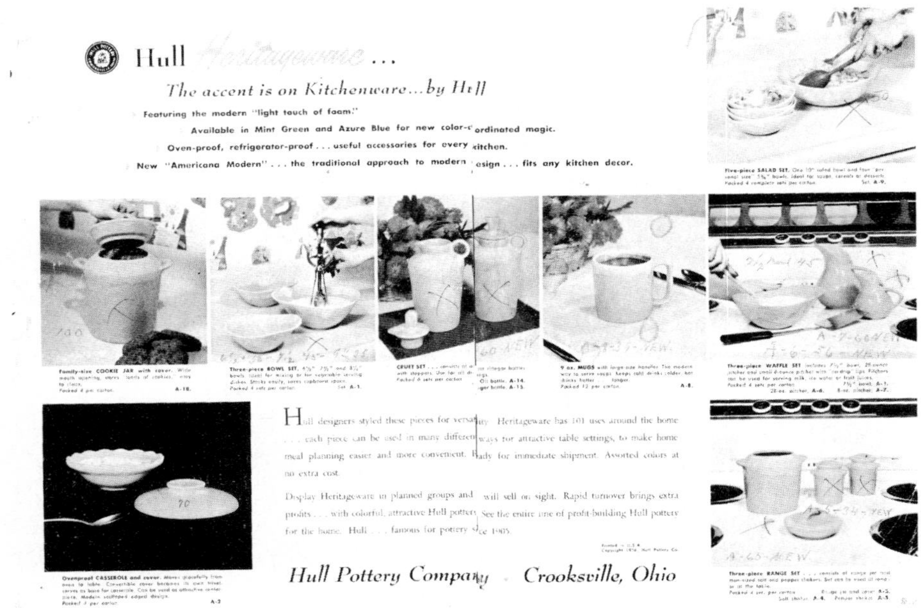

Plate 83

PLATE 84 (1959)

1. CONTINENTAL Basket, 55, 12¾″, Mountain Blue, White Haze.
2. CONTINENTAL Planter, 41, 15½″, Evergreen, White Haze.
3. TROPICANA Ewer, 56, 12½″, White high gloss edged in Tropic Green.

PLATE 85 (Early 1960's)

Row 1:

1. Ashtray, 18, 7″
2. Ashtray, 407, 11¾″
3. Ashtray, 8″

Row 2:

1. Ashtray, 18, 7″
2. Ashtray, 18, 7″
3. Ashtray, 18, 7″
4. Ashtray, 18, 7″

Row 3:

1. Leaf Dish, 86, 10″
2. RAINBOW Leaf Dish, 12¼″
3. RAINBOW Leaf Dish, 7¼″

Row 4:

1. Leaf Dish, 14″
2. IMPERIAL Leaf, 63, 14″

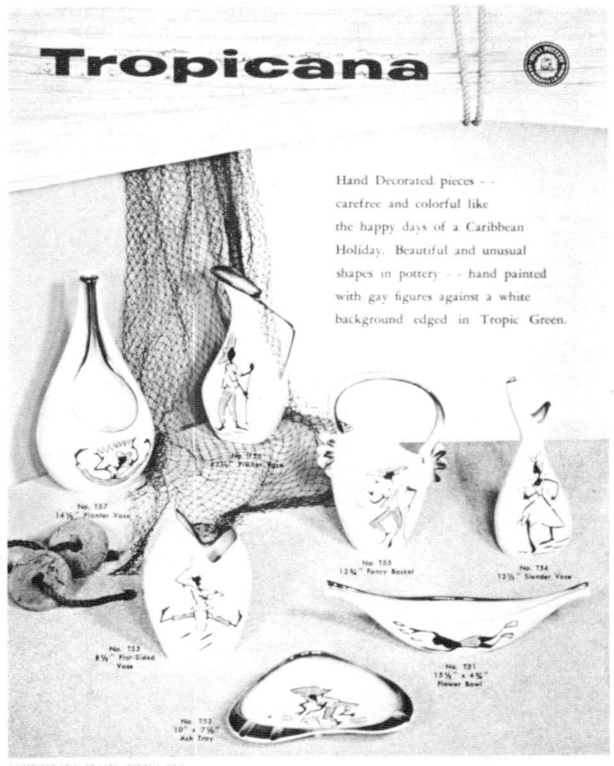

Hull Pottery Company - - Crooksville, Ohio

Plate 84

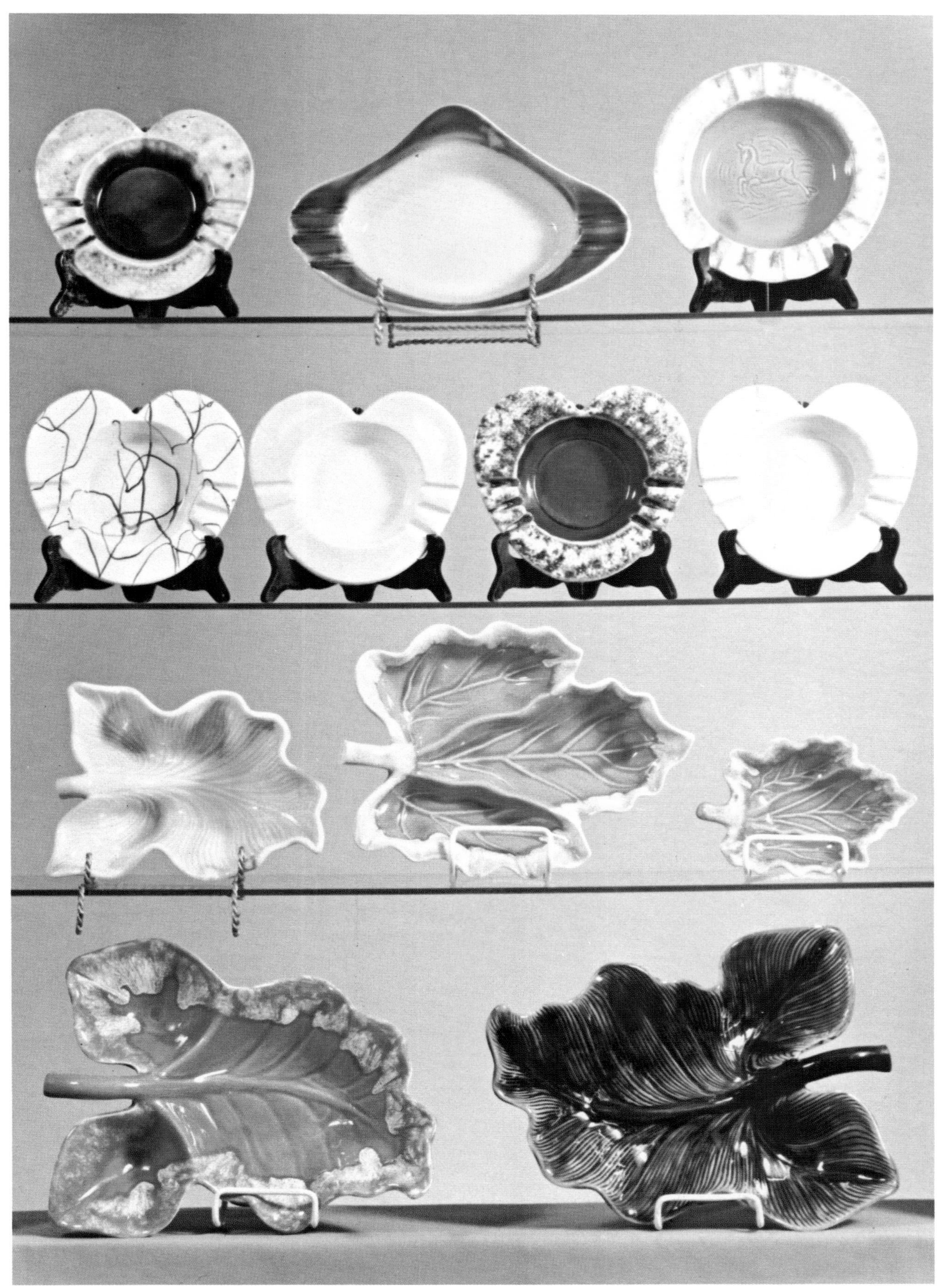

Plate 85

CONTINENTAL/TROPICANA (1959)

PLATE 86

Row 1:

1. CONTINENTAL Candleholder/Planter, unmarked, 4″
2. CONTINENTAL Bud Vase, 66, 9½″
3. CONTINENTAL Candleholder/Planter, unmarked, 4″

Row 2:

1. TROPICANA Basket, 55, 12¾″
2. TROPICANA Vase, 54, 12½″
3. CONTINENTAL Basket, 55, 12¾″

Row 3:

1. CONTINENTAL Vase, 53, 8½″
2. CONTINENTAL Vase, 57, 14½″
3. CONTINENTAL Ewer, 56, 12½″

Sophisticated, Modern Shapes In Three Delightful Decorator Colors

MOUNTAIN BLUE — Imagine twilight in the Blue Mountains modernized with stripes of white haze

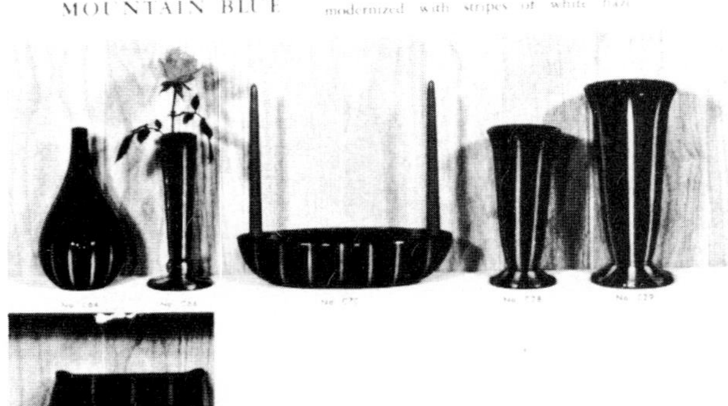

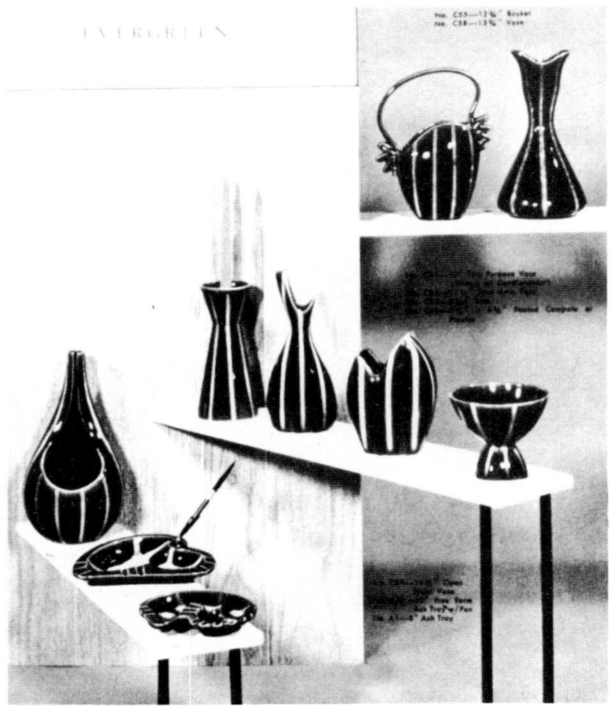

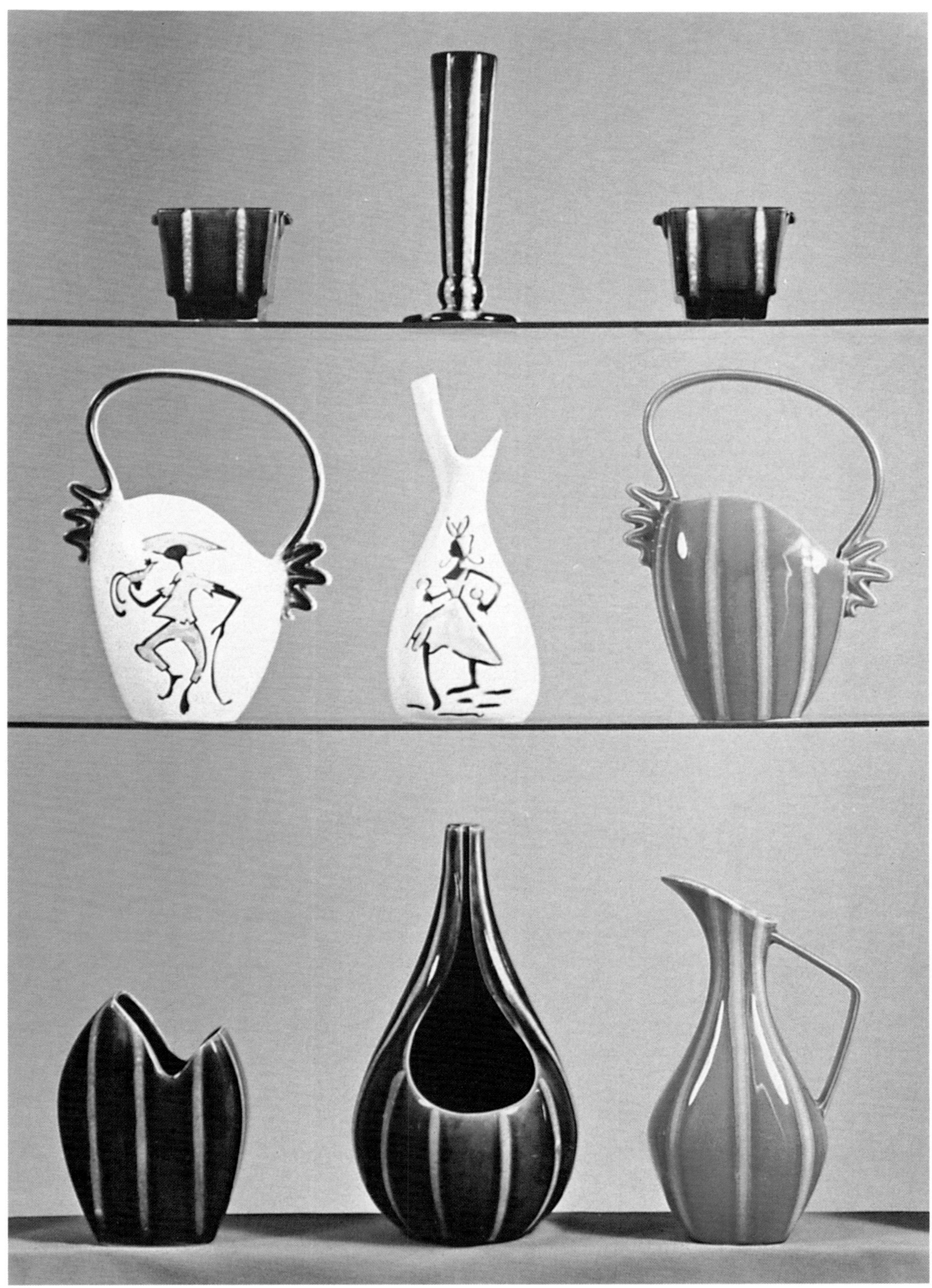

Plate 86

PLATE 87

Dark Green Glazed Marcrest Ashtray, 8½″×4½″ (Early 1960's)

PLATE 88

1. Jardinier in Brass Stand, 427, 21″ tall, Black gloss with White foam edge. (Late 1950's)
2. Ashtray/Planter Combination in Metal Stand, ashtray marked 22, planter marked 23, 26″ tall, Black gloss, Pink trace. (Mid-1950's)
3. Jardinier in Metal Stand, jardinier marked 8, 14″ tall, Spring Green with slight mottled affect. (Late-1950's)

PLATE 89 (Early 1960's)

Rows 1 & 2:

Ashtrays, 10¼″×6½″, all unmarked, all treated with different colors.

Row 3:

1. Ashtray, unmarked, 12½″
2. Ashtray, unmarked, 13″

In the mid to late 1950's, much of Hull's production centered on miscellaneous novelty planters and jardiniers many of which were marketed through the compa .n their own metal stands. Such items ranged from ash tray and planter combinations, to metal "bird cage" planters. Some jardiniers were offered in single units, while others were marketed in two and even three graduated stair-step stands.

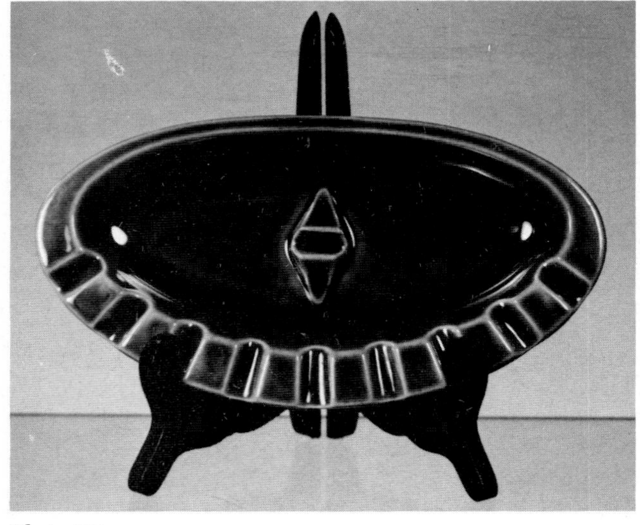

Plate 87

Plate 88

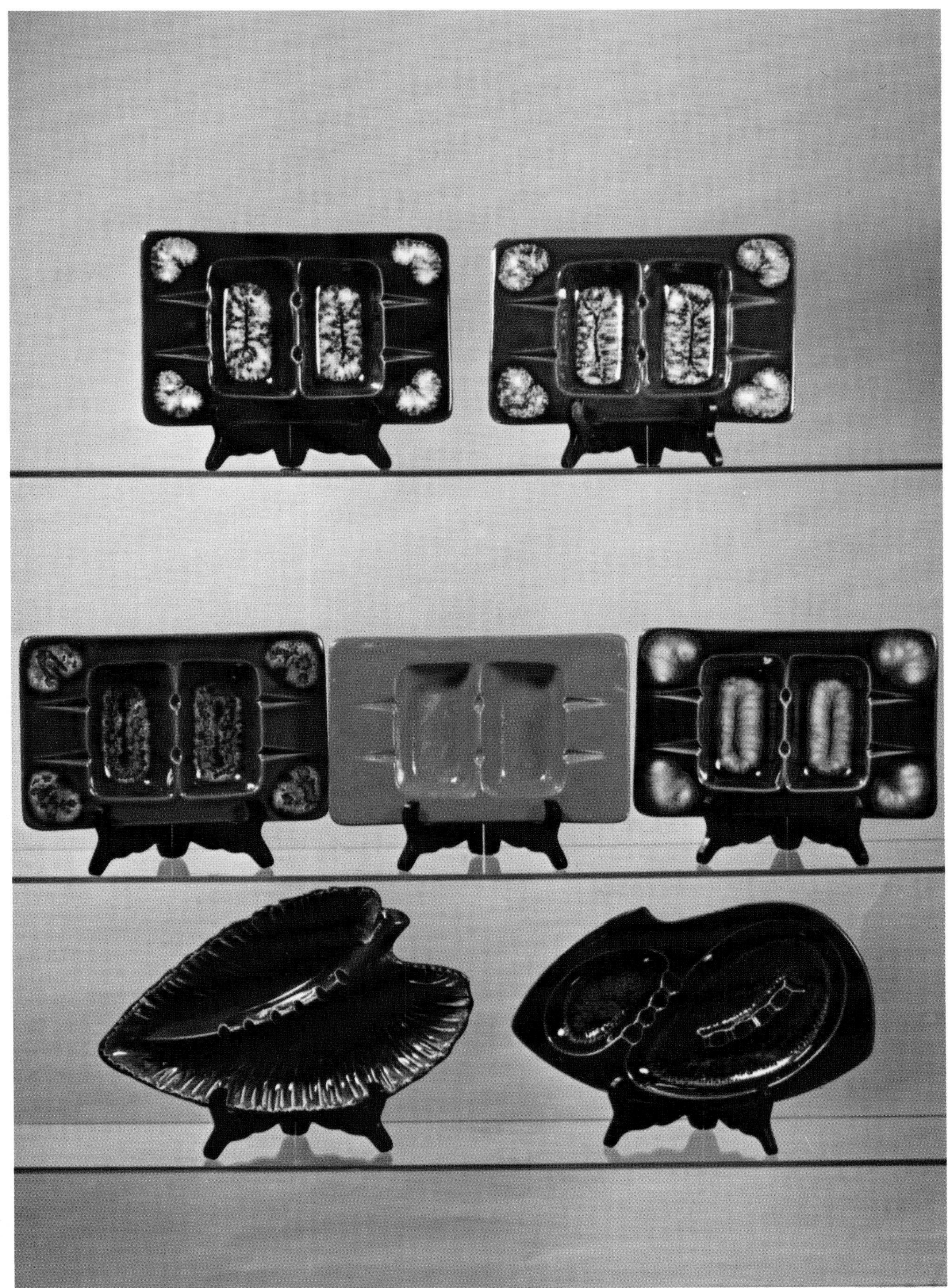

Plate 89

PLATE 90

Row 1:

Experimental glasses used for test glazes within the plant, 3½". Some dates of manufacture of these glasses can be determined through their colors. These are from the 1960's: Rainbow colors Butterscotch and Tangerine, Crestone's Turquoise; the others are most likely from Imperial color experiments.

4. Cruet, 984, 4¾"

Row 2:

1. Basket, 70, 6½" (Mid-1950's)
2. CAPRI Basket, 48, 12¼" (1961)
3. This Pedestaled planter is an experimental item, gold veining, marked 156, 5" (Late 1950's)

Row 3:

1. CAPRI Swan, 23, 8½" (1961)
2. IMPERIAL Basket, F38, 6¾" (1960's)
3. IMPERIAL Swan, 81, 10½" (1960's)

Row 4:

1. IMPERIAL Ewer, F480, 10½" (Late 1960's)
2. CAPRI Vase, 58, 13¾" (1961)
3. This is an experimental IMPERIAL Rose Vase, 11", unmarked (1960's)
4. CAPRI Urn Vase, 50, 9" (1961)

Plate 90

PLATE 91

Row 1: (1950's)

1. Swan, 80, 6″
2. Swan, 69, 8½″
3. Swan, 70, 4″
4. Swan, unmarked, 4½″

Row 2: (1960's-1970's)

1. IMPERIAL Madonna, F7, 7″
2. IMPERIAL Madonna, 81, 8¼″
3. IMPERIAL Baby Planter, F51, 5¼″

Row 3: (1960's-1970's)

1. IMPERIAL Praying Hands Planter, F475, 6″
2. IMPERIAL St. Frances Planter, 89, 11″
3. IMPERIAL Madonna, 24, 7″

Row 4: Items decorated by Granville Shafer (1970's)

1. IMPERIAL Urn, F88, 5¾″, luster gold decor
2. VICTORIAN Vase, B37, 9″
3. IMPERIAL Urn, F88, 5¾″, luster gold decor
4. IMPERIAL Urn, F34, 5″, "Daisy Chain" decor

The high gloss spray-tinted swans were made through the 1950's. Capri's satin-finished swans were a 1961 production. Several swan shapes remained on the Imperial lists through the 1960's and 1970's, offered in Satin White finish.

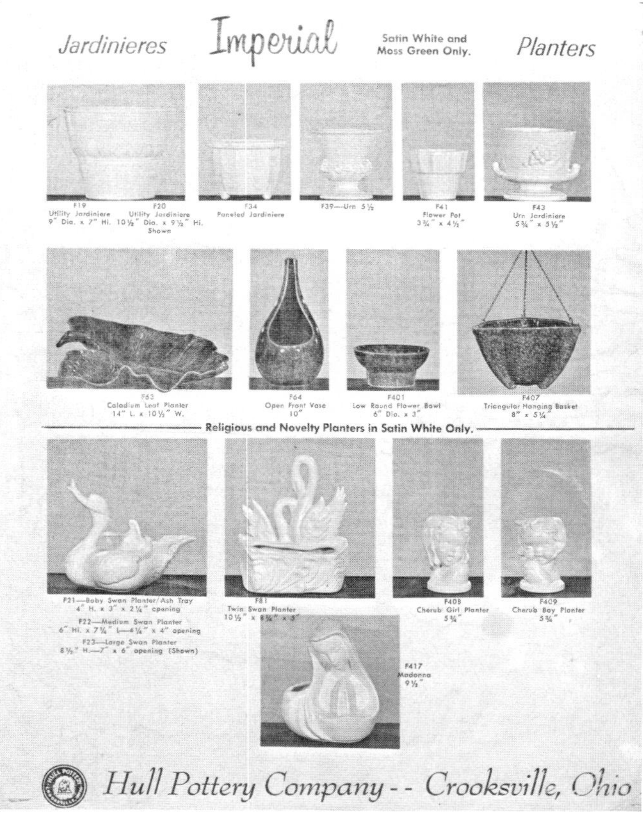

Plate 91

PLATE 92 (1960's-1970's)

Row 1:

1. REGAL Planter, 301, 3½″
2. REGAL Planter, 6½″
3. REGAL Planter, 303, 5″

Row 2:

1. MAYFAIR Mandolin Wall Pocket, 84, 7″
2. FANTASY Window Box, 74, 12½″
3. CORONET Flower Pot, 204, 4″

Row 3:

1. IMPERIAL Bowl, 117, 9″
2. IMPERIAL Bucket Planter, 94B, 6¼″
3. IMPERIAL Urn Vase, 418, 5″

Row 4:

1. PLANTER, INC., 25, 3¼″
2. CORONET Window Box, 207, 8″
3. PLANTER, INC., 25, 3¼″

Row 5:

1. MAYFAIR Vase, 83, 7¾″
2. ATHENA Wall Pocket, 611, 8½″
3. FANTASY Vase, 71, 9″
4. ATHENA Cornucopia, 608, 8½″

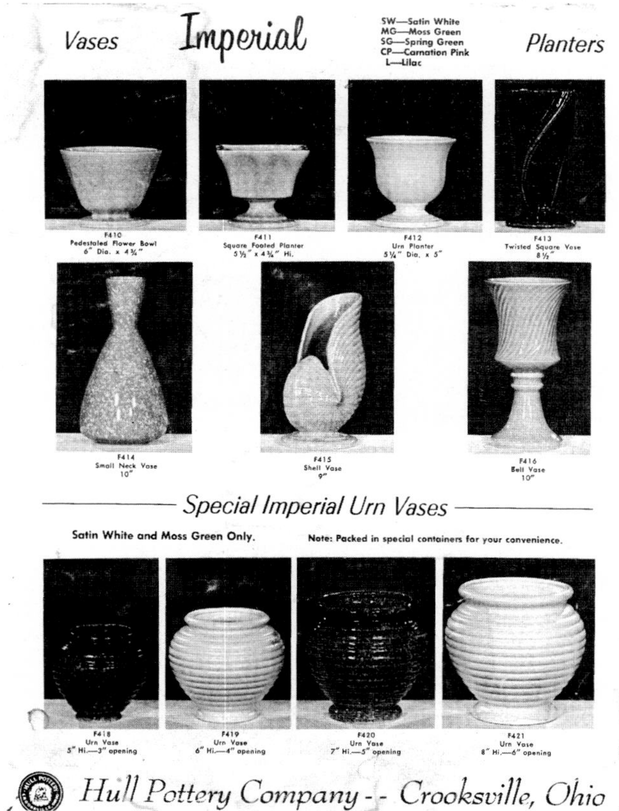

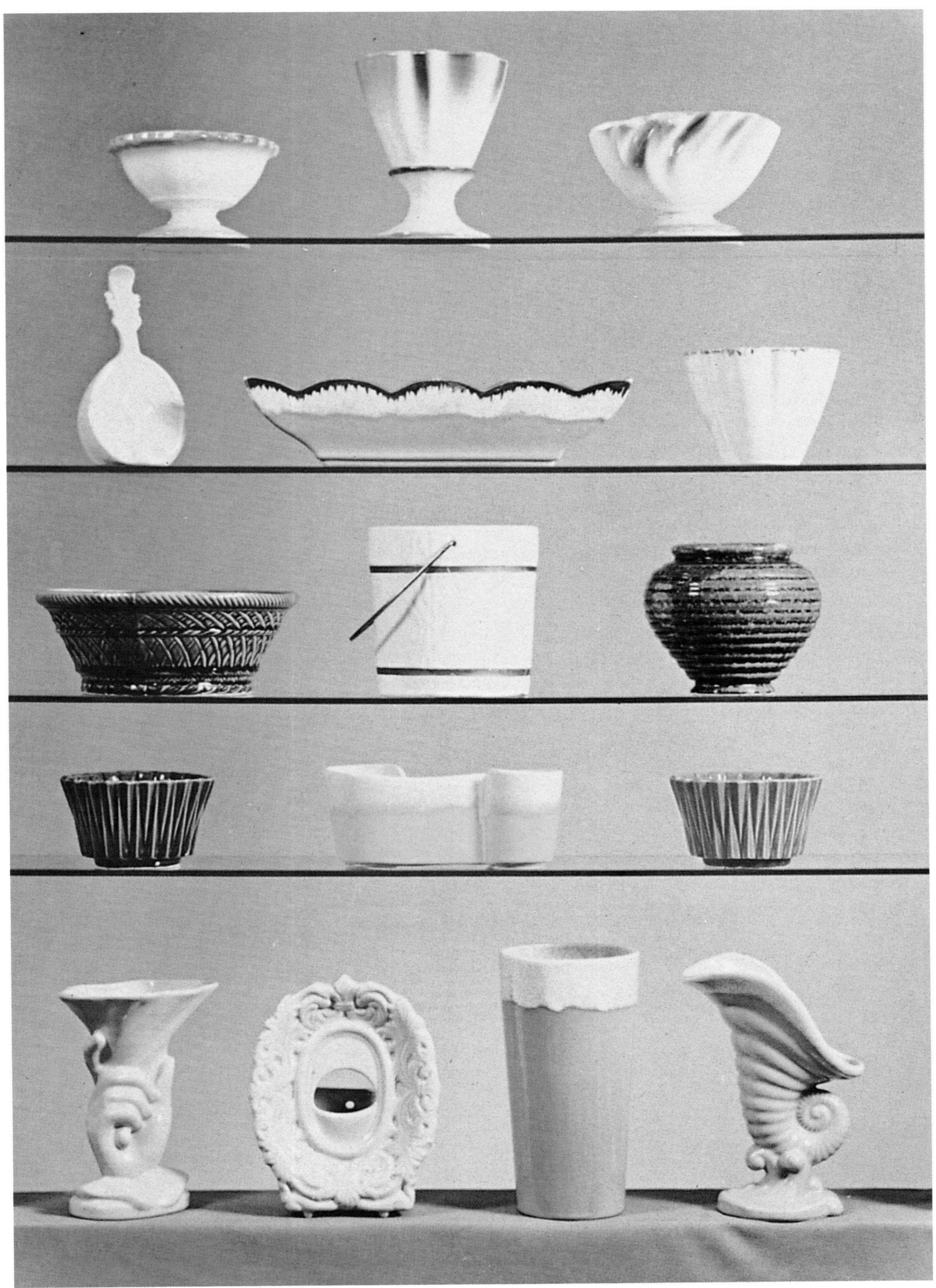

Plate 92

PLATE 93 (1960's-1970's)

Row 1:

1. 10½" Dinner Plate with incised star decoration
2. Mug, incised decor of flowers, tea kettle, bean pot, etc., 3¼"×5"
3. 10" Dinner Plate with incised rooster and weather vane decor

Row 2:

1. 6½" Salad Bowl
2. 5¼" Fruit Bowl
3. 10½" Dinner Plate
4. 6½" Saucer
5. 3¼"×5" Mug

PLATE 94

Handled Skillet Trays, 9¼"×15½", all unmarked with the exception of Row 2., No. 2, which is incised No. 27

These trays were produced in the late 1950's. (Recognize the Persimmon and Evergreen of Continental?) They would appear to have been made for only a short period of time — pretty, but impractical.

Of present-day production is a Mirror Brown Skillet Serving Tray that measures 11¼"×7¾"×2" — surely not as interesting, but nice.

The following House n' Garden Serving-ware items were discontinued in December, 1970.

590 Individual Leaf Dish, 7¼"×4¾"
505 Carafe with Cover, 2 Cup
508 Oval Chicken Salad, 6½"×5¼"
528 Coffee Carafe Set, 2 Cup
577 Double Serving Dish, 14½"×8½"
584 Sauce Bowl, 5½" Diameter
585 Tray, 12"×11"
586 Chip 'n Dip, 2 pc. set

Plate 93

Plate 94

HOUSE 'N GARDEN SERVING-WARE (1960's-1970's)

PLATE 95

Carafe, unmarked, but bears Hull seal 6½". This particular carafe is in Olive Green. Carafes are discontinued items in the House 'n Garden line.

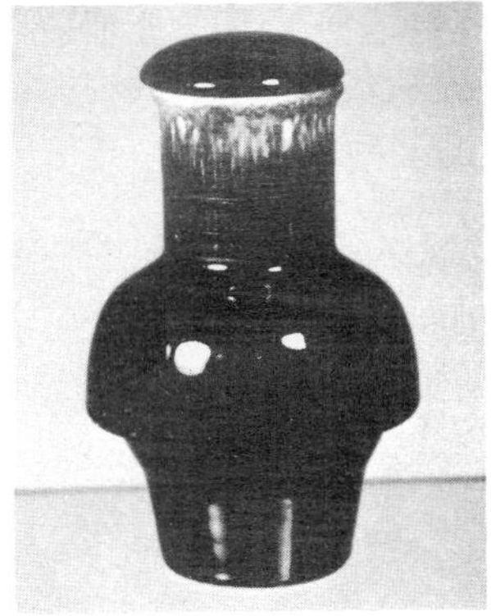

Plate 95

PLATE 96

Row 1:

1. Butter Dish, 7¾", Avocado
2. Teapot, 6¾", of present day production. This mold has been in use since the early 1960's.
3. RAINBOW Green Agate Soup 'n Sandwich, tray 9¾", mug 5"

Row 2:

1. Fish Tray, 11", present-day production
2. Shaker, unmarked, discontinued
3. Spoon Rest, 6¾", present-day production.
4. Shaker, unmarked, discontinued
5. RAINBOW Butterscotch Luncheon Plate, 8½"

Row 3:

1. RAINBOW Green Agate Pitcher, 7½"
2. CRESTONE Coffee, 11"
3. RAINBOW Tangerine Bud Vase, 9", discontinued
4. RAINBOW Tangerine Tid Bit, 10"

Row 4:

Canister Set, 9", 8", 7", & 6", present-day production limited.

Also of present-day production are Mirror Brown vinegar and oil cruets and cheese bottles, all measuring 6¾" high.

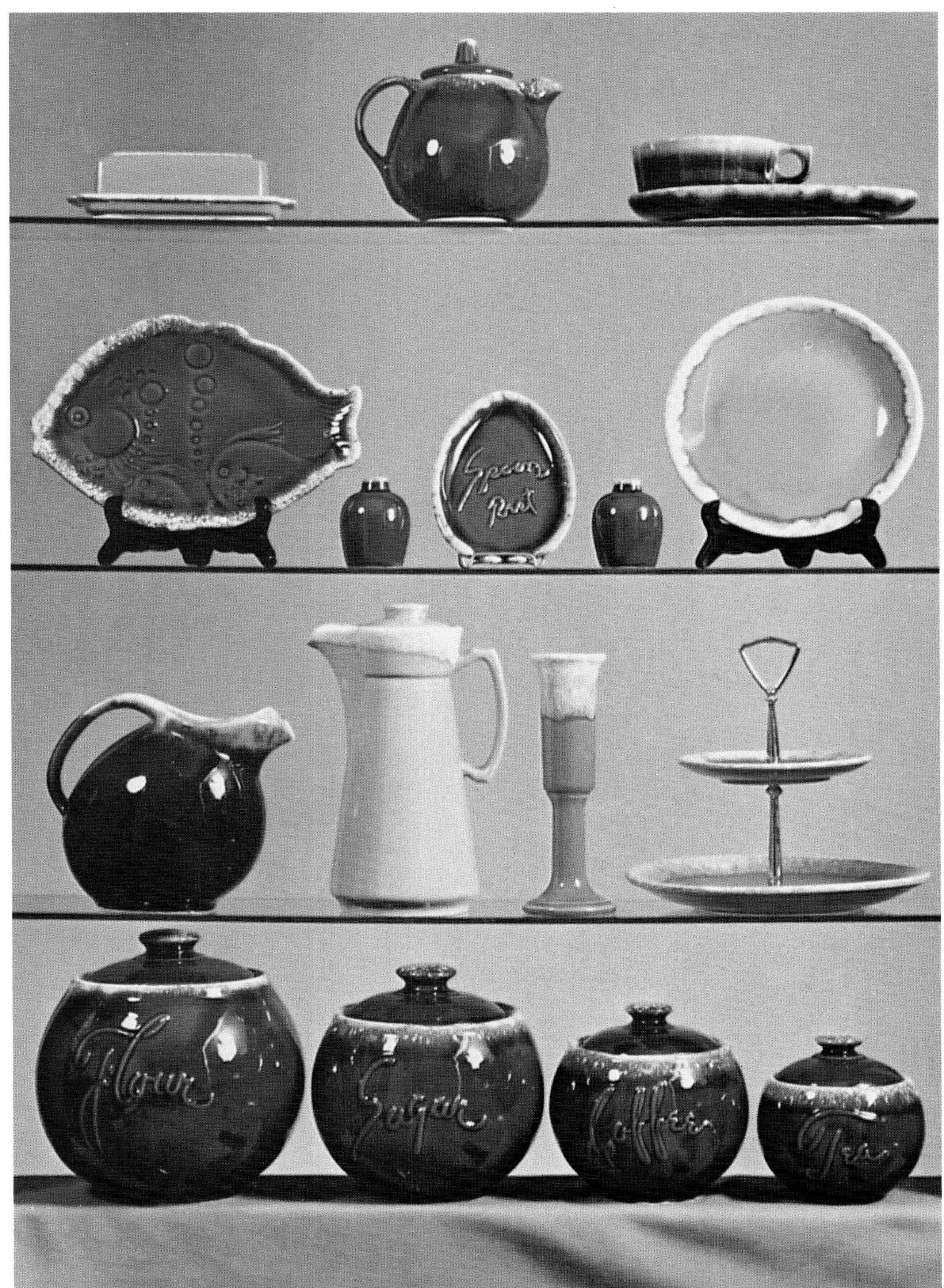

Plate 96

PLATE 97

Square Stand, experimental, for either a picture frame or a wall pocket, 6½″×8″, unmarked, stippled, white gloss finish. (Late 1960's)

PLATE 98 (1960's)

Row 1:

1. RUB OFF, Experimental Imperial blank, F27, 6¾″

Row 2:

1. RUB OFF, Experimental Imperial blank, unmarked, 4¾″
2. RUB OFF, Experimental Imperial blank, unmarked, 4¾″

Row 3:

1. Experimental Imperial blank, unmarked, 4½″
2. Experimental Leaf dish, unmarked, 12″. This lacy item proved to be disastrous to remove from the mold. It was remolded, without the lace-work sides.
3. RUB OFF, Experimental Imperial blank, unmarked, 8″

Row 4: (1970's)

1. 10½″ Dinner Plate, Experimental swirl design
2. 10½″ Dinner Plate, Experimental swirl design

Plate 97

Plate 98

GREENWARE

PLATE 99

Row 1:

1. Parrot Planter, 6″×9½″
2. Pheasant Planter, 6″×8″

Row 2:

1. Planter, embossed bird decor
2. Bank, premium item made in 1972 for Graham Chevrolet, Mansfield, Ohio, "The Little Texan"
3. Planter

Row 3:

1. Shaker, embossed eagle decor
2. "70" Swan mold piece
3. Shaker, embossed eagle decor

PLATE 100

1. Experimental Vase, marked 72, 8½″
2. Experimental Vase with rough texture, 8½″

PLATE 101

Experimental 10½″ Dinner Plates

PLATE 102

Experimental Lids

Plate 99

Plate 100

Plate 101

Plate 102

BROCHURE REPRINTS

In addition to Hull Company brochure pages included in the preceeding text, the following reprints are shown to aid the collector in identification of Hull's early utilitarian lines such as banded kitchenware, yellow ware, square cereal sets, porcelain toliet ware, and Zane Grey kitchenware—all of which were distributed by The American Clay Products Company.

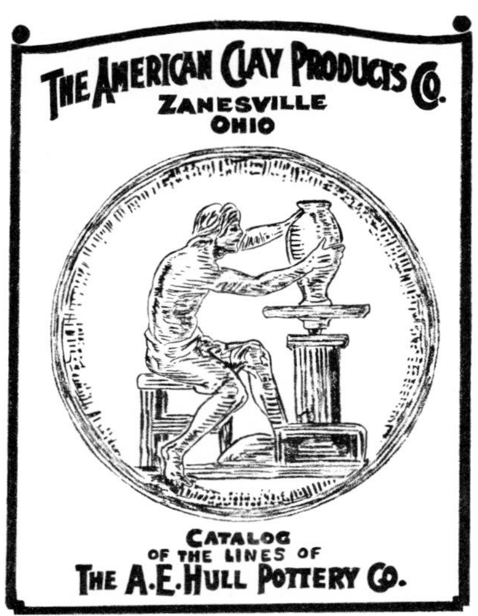

Hull's American Clay Products Company logo, sketched from the original catalog, included the Potter-at-Wheel figure.

This symbol has served as company trademark for over fifty years, appearing in label form, on company brochure pages, and on the pottery firm's official letterhead.

The American Clay Products Company catalog has been reprinted in its entirety.

Also included for your reference are catalogue pages on Hull's casual serving ware lines Rainbow, Crestone and Mirror Brown.

For those who wish to pursue the extensive Imperial lines, these too have been added for your information.

White Blue Band Kitchen Ware

Bowls, Nappies, Butter Jars, Custards and Jugs

THE A. E. Hull Pottery Co. are the first and original producers of American White Body, underglaze, raised blue banded kitchen ware. A careful and constant study of the lines needed in the kitchen, together with excellent modeler to transform ideas to actual plaster models, and ceramic engineers to supervise the manufacturing processes in one of the most modern potteries, insures the buyer of Hull Ware, the most practical shapes possible, made of absolutely white body, with the deep blue raised bands under the glaze. The ware is strong and durable on account of the selection of clays in the body, and the high temperature attained in the kilns. Description of the items will be found on the following pages.

Page Three

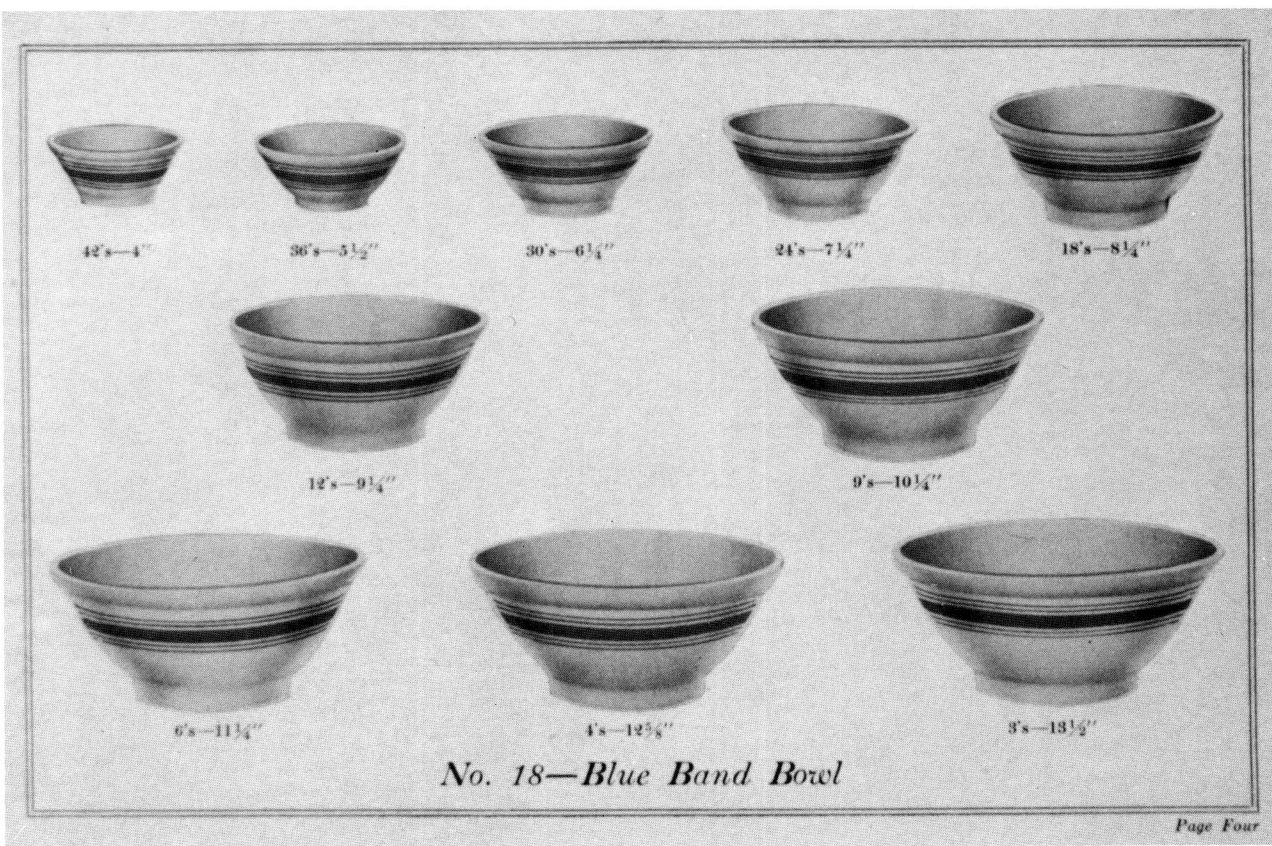

42's—4''
36's—5½''
30's—6¼''
24's—7¼''
18's—8¼''
12's—9¼''
9's—10¼''
6's—11¾''
4's—12⅝''
3's—13½''
No. 18—Blue Band Bowl
Page Four

36's—5⅜''
30's—6¼''
24's—7½''
18's—8½''
12's—9⅝''
9's—10⅝''
No. 19—Blue Band Panelled Bowl
Page Five

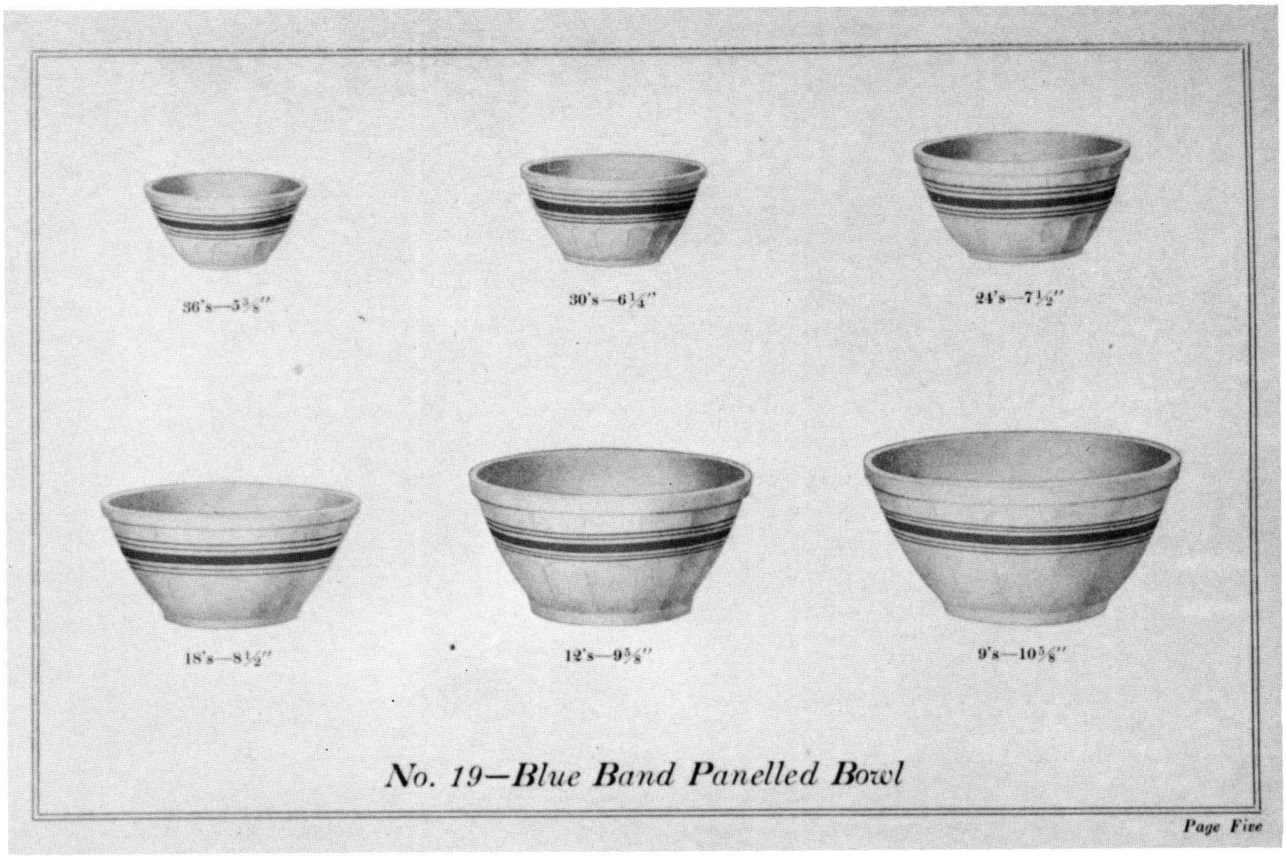

List of Weights of All Items Shown

For the Convenience of the Buyer in Calculating Shipment Weights

No. 18— 4″ Bowl— 6 lbs doz
5″ Bowl— 8 lbs doz
6″ Bowl—12 lbs doz
7″ Bowl—15 lbs doz
8″ Bowl—21 lbs doz
9″ Bowl—30 lbs doz
10″ Bowl—39 lbs doz
11″ Bowl—48 lbs doz
12″ Bowl—54 lbs doz
13″ Bowl—69 lbs doz

No. 19— 5″ Bowl— 9 lbs doz
6″ Bowl—14 lbs doz
7″ Bowl—24 lbs doz
8″ Bowl—30 lbs doz
9″ Bowl—36 lbs doz
10″ Bowl—54 lbs doz

No. 101— 4″ Bowl— 6 lbs doz
5″ Bowl— 8 lbs doz
6″ Bowl—12 lbs doz
7″ Bowl—15 lbs doz
8″ Bowl—21 lbs doz

No. 41— 6 Pc Set— 7½ lbs set

No. 23— 6 Pc Set— 7½ lbs set

No. 5—48's Jug— 7½ lbs doz
42's Jug— 12 lbs doz
36's Jug— 15 lbs doz
30's Jug— 21 lbs doz
24's Jug— 25½ lbs doz
18's Jug— 27 lbs doz

No. 7—2 lb Butter—24 lbs doz
3 lb Butter—30 lbs doz
4 lb Butter—39 lbs doz

No. 4—Size 1 Custard—3 lbs doz
Size 2 Custard—6 lbs doz

No. 1—Combinet—110 lbs doz

No. 5—Covered Chamber—72 lbs doz

No. 5—Open Chamber—48 lbs doz

No. 4—Hall Boy Jug—27 lbs doz

No. 55—Coffee Mug—12 lbs doz

Parlor Cuspidor—24 lbs doz

Hotel Cuspidor—33 lbs doz

Square Cereal Jar—27 lbs doz

Square Spice Jar—7 lbs doz

Square Bottle—12 lbs doz

Square Salt Box—27 lbs

15 Pc Cereal Set—21 lb per set

4″ Yellow Bowl— 5½ lbs per doz
5″ Yellow Bowl— 9 lbs per doz
6″ Yellow Bowl—13 lbs per doz
7″ Yellow Bowl—18 lbs per doz
8″ Yellow Bowl—25 lbs per doz
9″ Yellow Bowl—32 lbs per doz
10″ Yellow Bowl—41 lbs per doz
11″ Yellow Bowl—51 lbs per doz
12″ Yellow Bowl—69 lbs per doz
13″ Yellow Bowl—78 lbs per doz
14″ Yellow Bowl—99 lbs per doz
15″ Yellow Bowl—108 lbs per doz

No. 400— ½ Gal Jar— 39 lbs doz
1 Gal Jar— 60 lbs doz
1½ Gal Jar— 72 lbs doz
2 Gal Jar—102 lbs doz
3 Gal Jar—144 lbs doz
4 Gal Jar—186 lbs doz
5 Gal Jar—225 lbs doz
6 Gal Jar—288 lbs doz

No. 400— ½ Gal Cover—12 lbs doz
1 Gal Cover—18 lbs doz

No. 400— 1½ Gal Cover—24 lbs doz
2 Gal Cover—28½ lbs doz
3 Gal Cover—39 lbs doz
4 Gal Cover—45 lbs doz
5 Gal Cover—57 lbs doz
6 Gal Cover—69 lbs doz

No. 420— 4″ Bowl— 5½ lbs doz
5″ Bowl— 9 lbs doz
6″ Bowl— 13 lbs doz
7″ Bowl— 18 lbs doz
8″ Bowl— 25 lbs doz
9″ Bowl— 32 lbs doz
10″ Bowl— 41 lbs doz
11″ Bowl— 51 lbs doz
12″ Bowl— 69 lbs doz
13″ Bowl— 78 lbs doz
14″ Bowl— 99 lbs doz
15″ Bowl—108 lbs doz

No. 430— 6 Pc Nappy Set—8 lbs set

No. 440—48's Jug— 9 lbs doz
42's Jug—12 lbs doz
36's Jug—18 lbs doz
30's Jug—24 lbs doz
24's Jug—27 lbs doz
18's Jug—33 lbs doz

No. 450—2 lb Butter—24 lbs doz
3 lb Butter—33 lbs doz
4 lb Butter—39 lbs doz

No. 460—Size 1 Custard— 6 lbs doz
Size 2 Custard—12 lbs doz

No. 470—Cuspidor—33 lbs doz

No. 480—Salt Box—25 lbs doz.

Shipping Facilities

THE A. E. Hull Pottery Co. factory is located on both The Pennsylvania and New York Central Lines. Shipments can be made on either road. An expert traffic manager is in charge of all shipments at all times. By this method the best possible service is rendered to our customer. For customers who can purchase in car load lots, we are able to make mixed car shipments of any quantities of Hull Ware. Facilities for making L.C.L. shipments are excellent. Hardwood crates, strongly made, with expert packers to fill the crates, reduce breakage to a minimum.

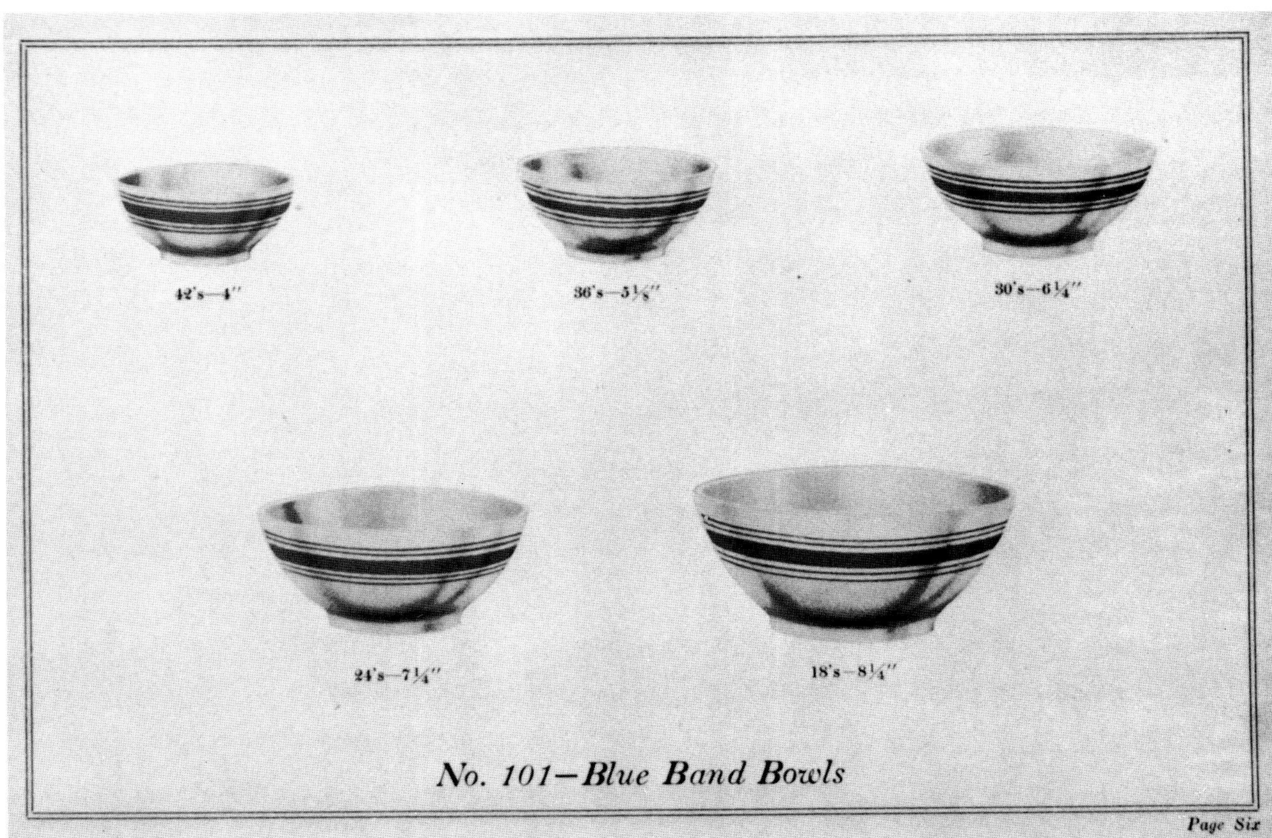
42's—4"
36's—5⅛"
30's—6¼"
24's—7¼"
18's—8¼"
No. 101—Blue Band Bowls
Page Six

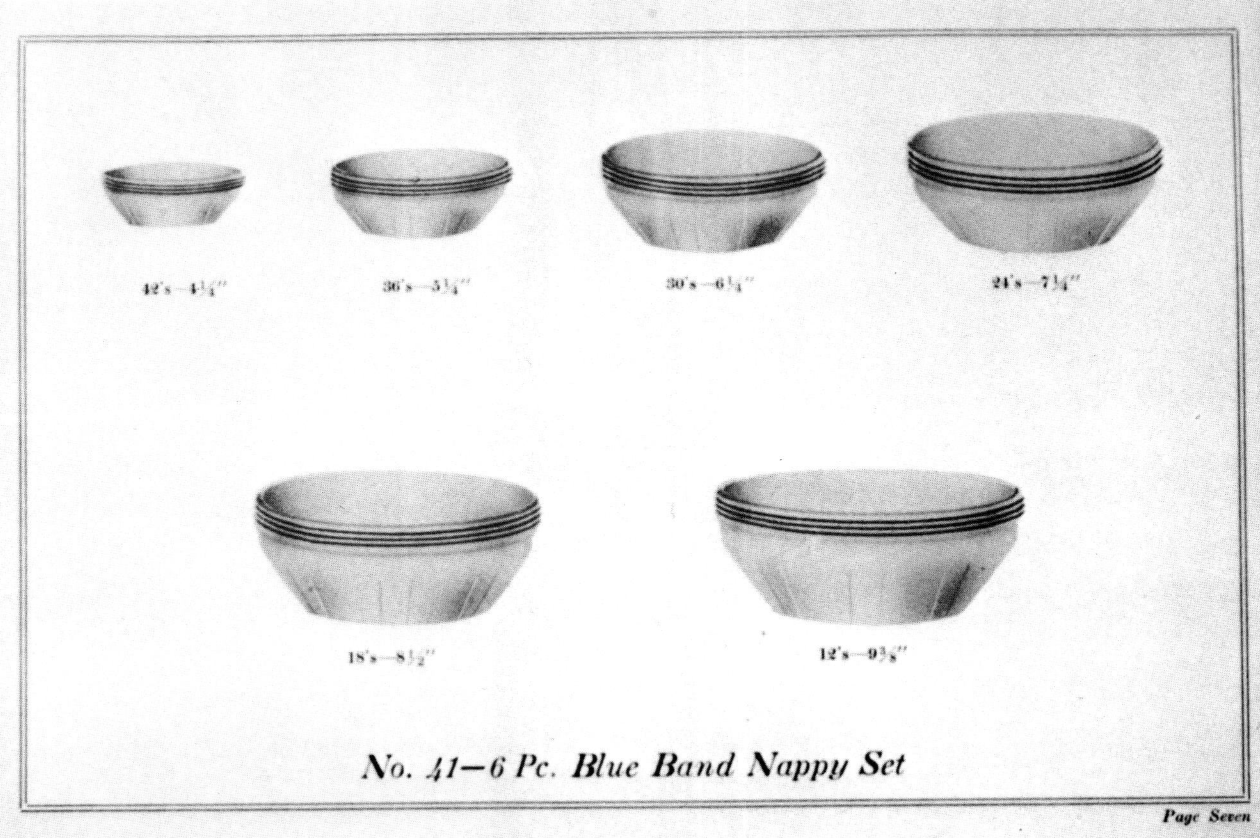
42's—4¼"
36's—5¼"
30's—6¼"
24's—7¼"
18's—8½"
12's—9⅜"
No. 41—6 Pc. Blue Band Nappy Set
Page Seven

The following original wholesale prices once applied to the No. 5 — Blue Band Jugs as shown on the opposite page.

48's	....	per dozen	1.50
42's	....	per dozen	2.00
36's	....	per dozen	2.75
30's	....	per dozen	3.25
24's	....	per dozen	4.50
18's	....	per dozen	5.50

POPULAR KITCHEN SET
COMPOSITION
1—No. 423, 9″ Bowl.
1—No. 423, 7″ Bowl.
1—No. 440, 36s Jug.
1—No. 453, 7″ Casserole.
6—No. 460/1 Custard Cups.
10 piece Kitchen-Set
Price
75c
Per Set

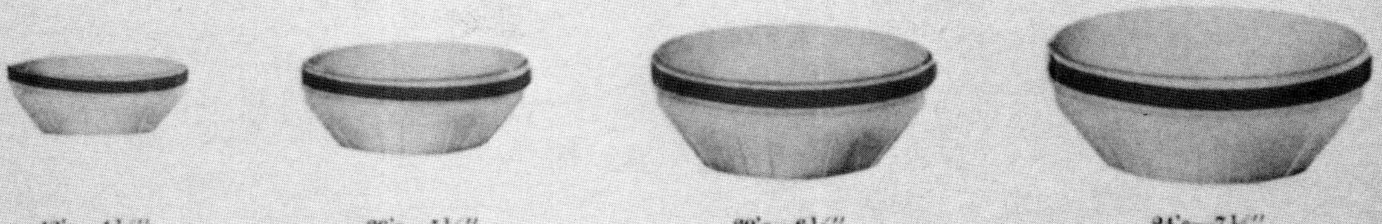

42's—4¼″ 36's—5¼″ 30's—6¼″ 24's—7¼″

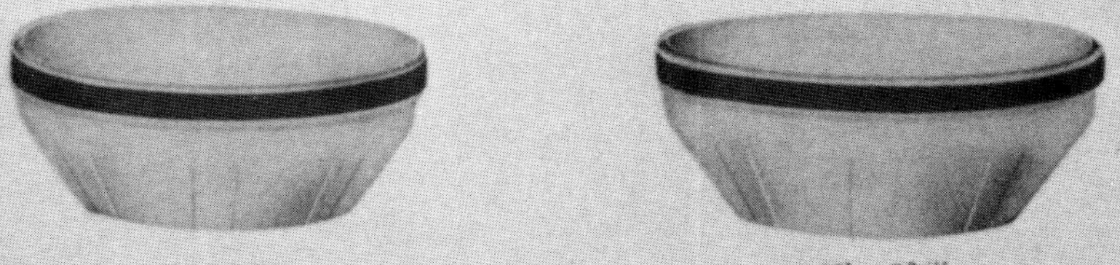

18's—8½″ 12's—9⅝″

No. 23—6 Pc. Blue Band Nappy Set

48's—¾ pt. 42's—1 pt. 36's—1½″ pt.

30's—2½ pt. 24—4 pt. 18's—5 pt.

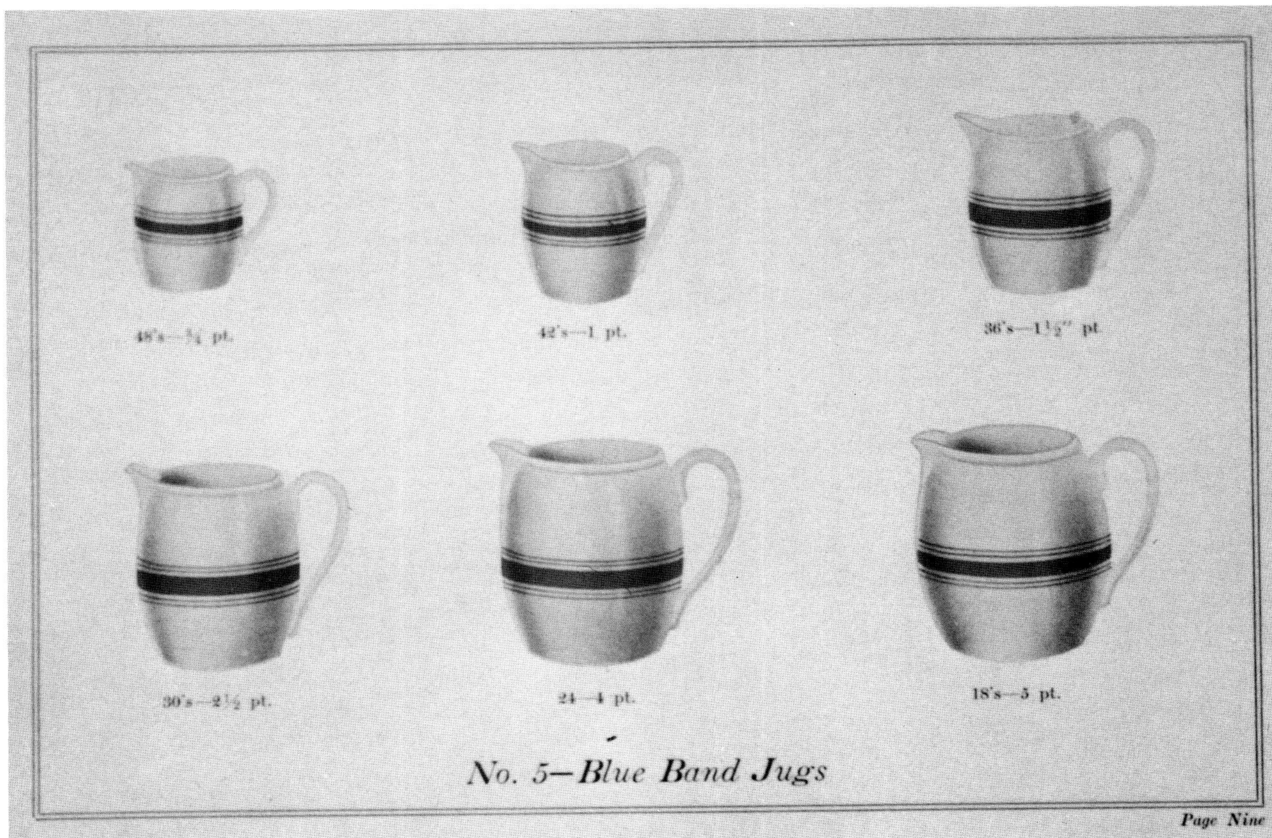

No. 5—Blue Band Jugs

LEADER COOKING ASSORTMENT

COMPOSITION

1—No. 423, 7″ Bowl.
1—No. 423, 9″ Bowl.
1—No. 423, 5″ Bowl.
1—No. 440, 30s Jug.
1—No. 440, 42s Jug.
1—No. 453, 7″ Casserole.
6—No. 460/1 Custard Cups.

Price
95c
Per Set

Yellow Bowls

YELLOW Bowls have come to be almost a household necessity. For the kitchen they find a multitude of uses such as bread mixing, as food containers, and for handy receptacles for anything the house-wife uses in her kitchen. The Yellow-Bowl is first of all a more inexpensive bowl than most any other. The A. E. Hull Pottery Co. are manufacturing Yellow Bowls in large quantity at a remarkably low figure and combined with several other notable features. The Hull Yellow Bowl is made with a Round Spherical Bottom which offers no hindrance to the housewife in stirring or cleaning the bowl. There are no sharp creases in the bottom. This yellow bowl is also made of a body that is fired until practically vitreous, thereby insuring a highly bonded and durable bowl with a bright Glossy Glaze and Brown Bands for decoration.

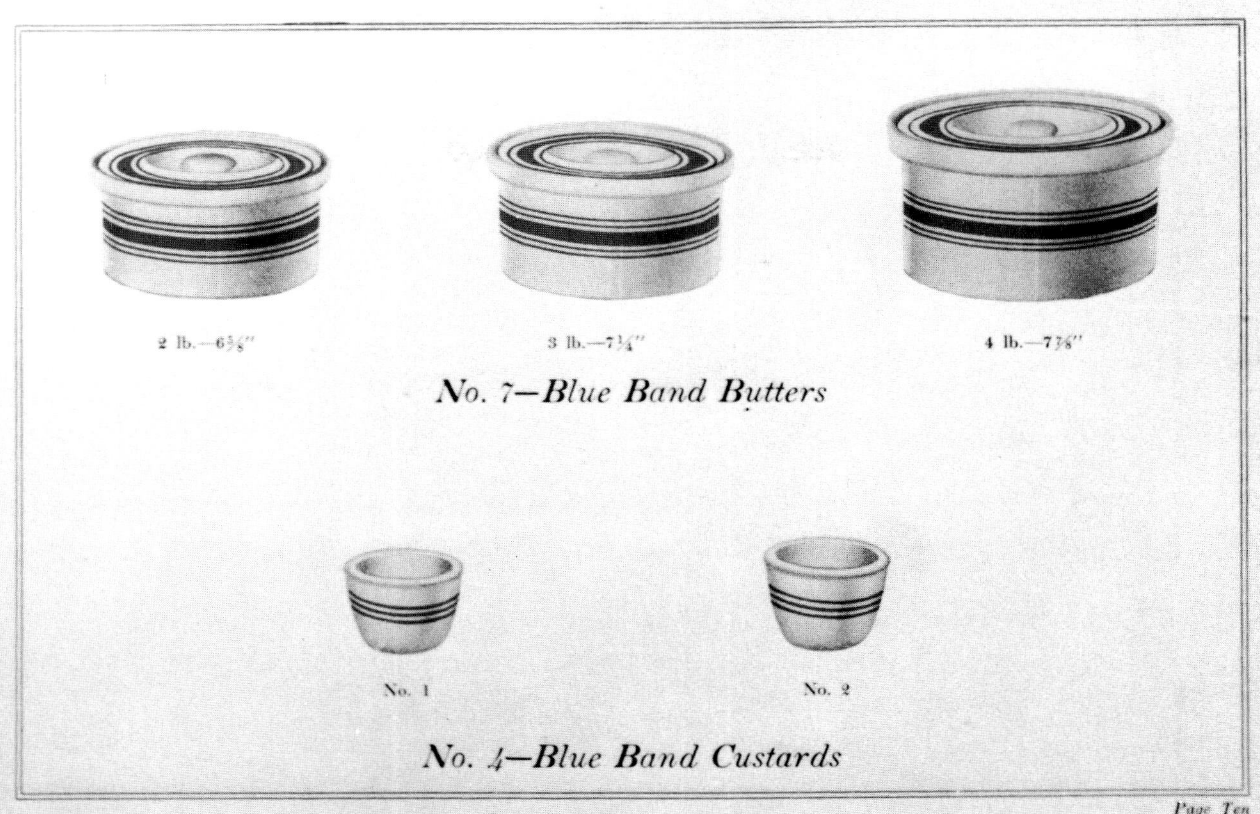
2 lb.—6⅝" 3 lb.—7¼" 4 lb.—7⅞"

No. 7—Blue Band Butters

No. 1 No. 2

No. 4—Blue Band Custards

Page Ten

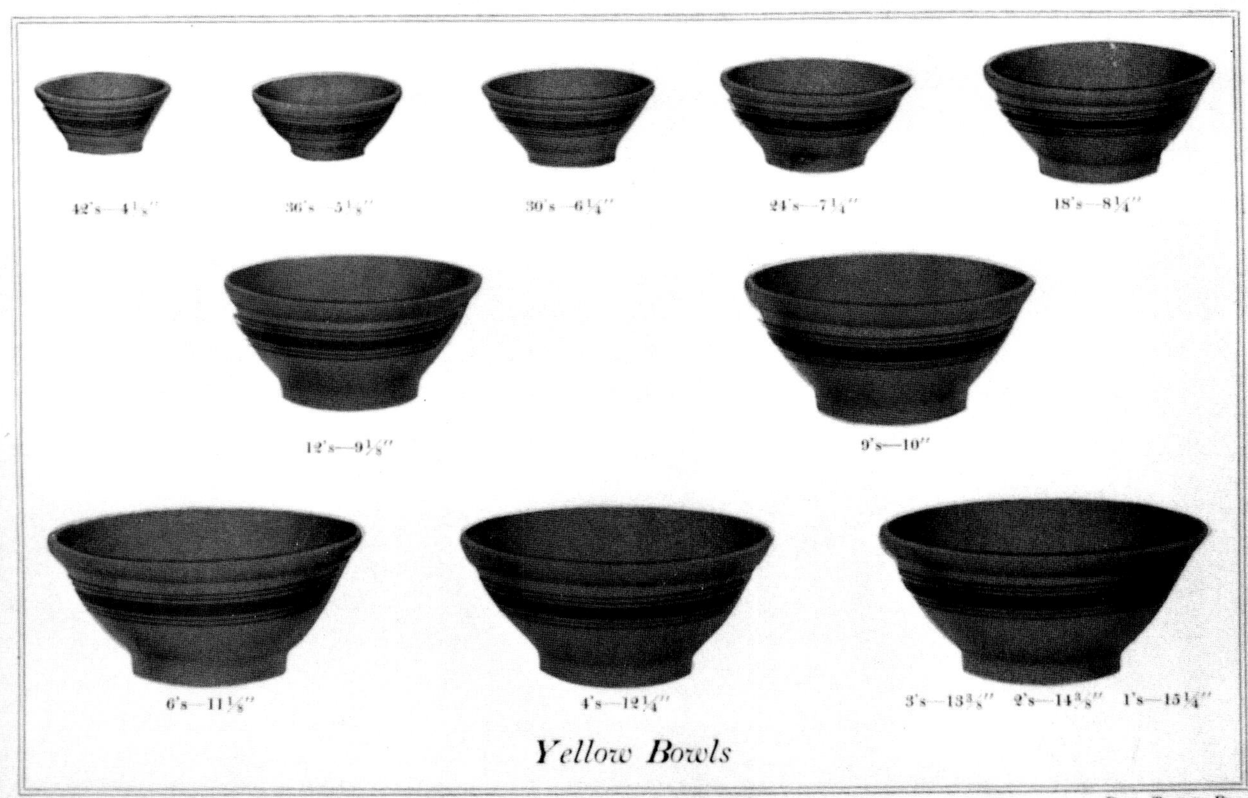
42's—4⅛" 36's—5⅛" 30's—6¼" 24's—7¼" 18's—8¼"

12's—9⅛" 9's—10"

6's—11⅛" 4's—12¼" 3's—13⅜" 2's—14⅜" 1's—15¼"

Yellow Bowls

Page Twenty-Four

Square Cereal Sets

THE Square Cereal Set has been sold heretofore as a general rule in sets of fifteen pieces. We have decided to establish a new method in regard to the marketing of our standard square cereal set. Now, the buyer may make up his own set composition or buy open stock as he pleases. We offer seven decorations from which to choose, which are representative as to designs and colorings. The following names will be furnished in any of our decorations in any quantity. For Cereal Jars we have COFFEE, TEA, RICE, CEREAL, FLOUR, SUGAR. For Spice Jars: CINNAMON, GINGER, PEPPER, ALLSPICE, MUSTARD, NUTMEG. For Bottles either OIL or VINEGAR. Salt Boxes are furnished in every decoration. These sets are made by the casting process from the white body, used in our Blue Band Ware, which insures a close, durable body.

Page Fourteen

Square Cereal Sets No. 119, No. 121, No. 131, No. 132, No. 133, No. 136, and No. 150, were marketed through The American Clay Products Company in the early 1930's. In 1933, this Yellow or Green Cereal Ware was offered by the Hull Pottery Company at these wholesale prices:

			Wt. Per Dozen
No. 880 —	Cereal and Cover	1.80 per dozen	21 lbs.
	Coffee and Cover	1.80 per dozen	21 lbs.
	Tea and Cover	1.80 per dozen	21 lbs.
	Rice and Cover	1.80 per dozen	21 lbs.
	Sugar and Cover	1.80 per dozen	21 lbs.
	Flour and Cover	1.80 per dozen	21 lbs.
No. 880 —	Spice and Cover	0.90 per dozen	8 lbs.
	Nutmeg and Cover	0.90 per dozen	8 lbs.
	Ginger and Cover	0.90 per dozen	8 lbs.
	Cinnamon and Cover	0.90 per dozen	8 lbs.
	Mustard and Cover	0.90 per dozen	8 lbs.
	Pepper and Cover	0.90 per dozen	8 lbs.
No. 880 —	Salt Box and Cover	1.80 per dozen	16 lbs.
No. 880 —	13-pc. Cereal Set	1.50 per set	16 lbs.
	9-pc. Cereal Set	1.05 per set	11 lbs.
	5-pc. Cereal Set	0.75 per set	8½ lbs.

No. 119—Blue Grecian Border Cereal Ware

Page Fifteen

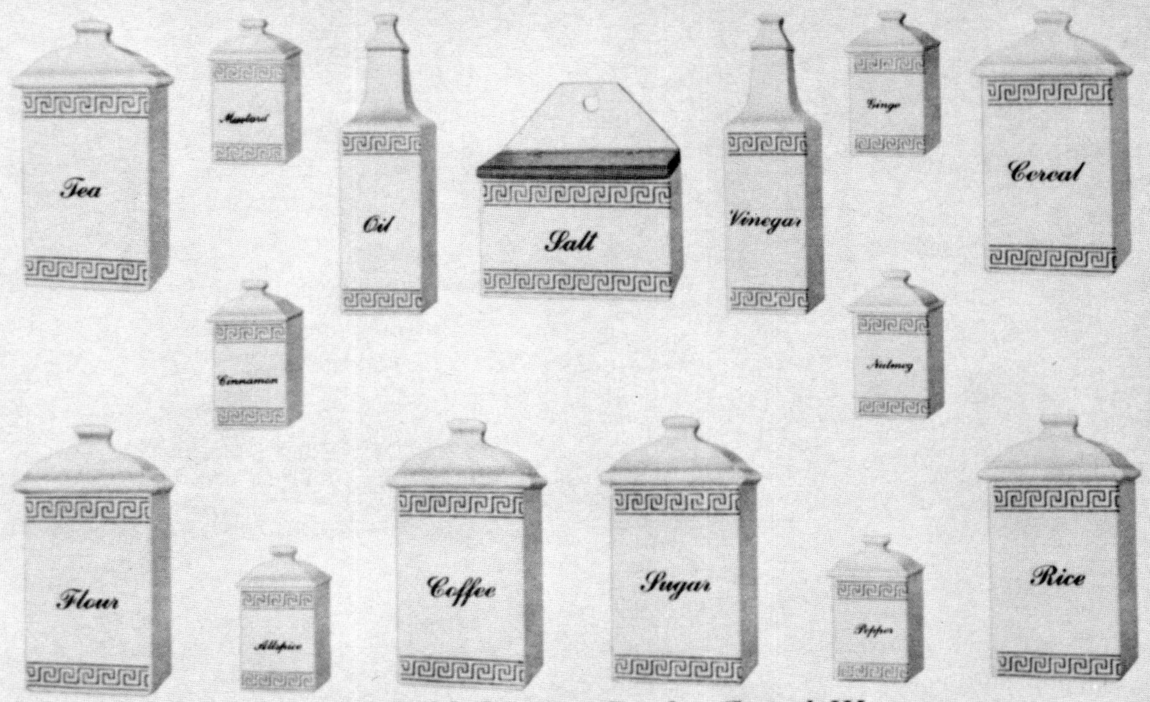

Tea
Mustard
Oil
Salt
Vinegar
Cereal
Cinnamon
Nutmeg
Flour
Allspice
Coffee
Sugar
Pepper
Rice

No. 121—Gold Grecian Border Cereal Ware

Page Sixteen

THE A. E. HULL POTTERY COMPANY, CROOKSVILLE, OHIO

TOP ROW	SECOND ROW	THIRD ROW	BOTTOM ROW
300 4 CUSTARD	300 2 PIE PLATES	300 BOWL SET	300 [illegible] BAKE SET
300 [illegible] JUGS	300 5 FRENCH CASSEROLES	300 [illegible] CASSEROLES	300 [illegible] COVERED BEAN POT
300 [illegible] RAMEKIN	300 [illegible] COVERED BEAN POT	300 6 PLATE	300 4 DEEP BOWLS
	300 7 BAKED APPLE		

OVEN PROOF, REFRIGERATOR PROOF, IVORY WHITE BODY AND GLAZE DECORATED WITH PIMENTO RED OR NUBIAN BLACK STRIPES

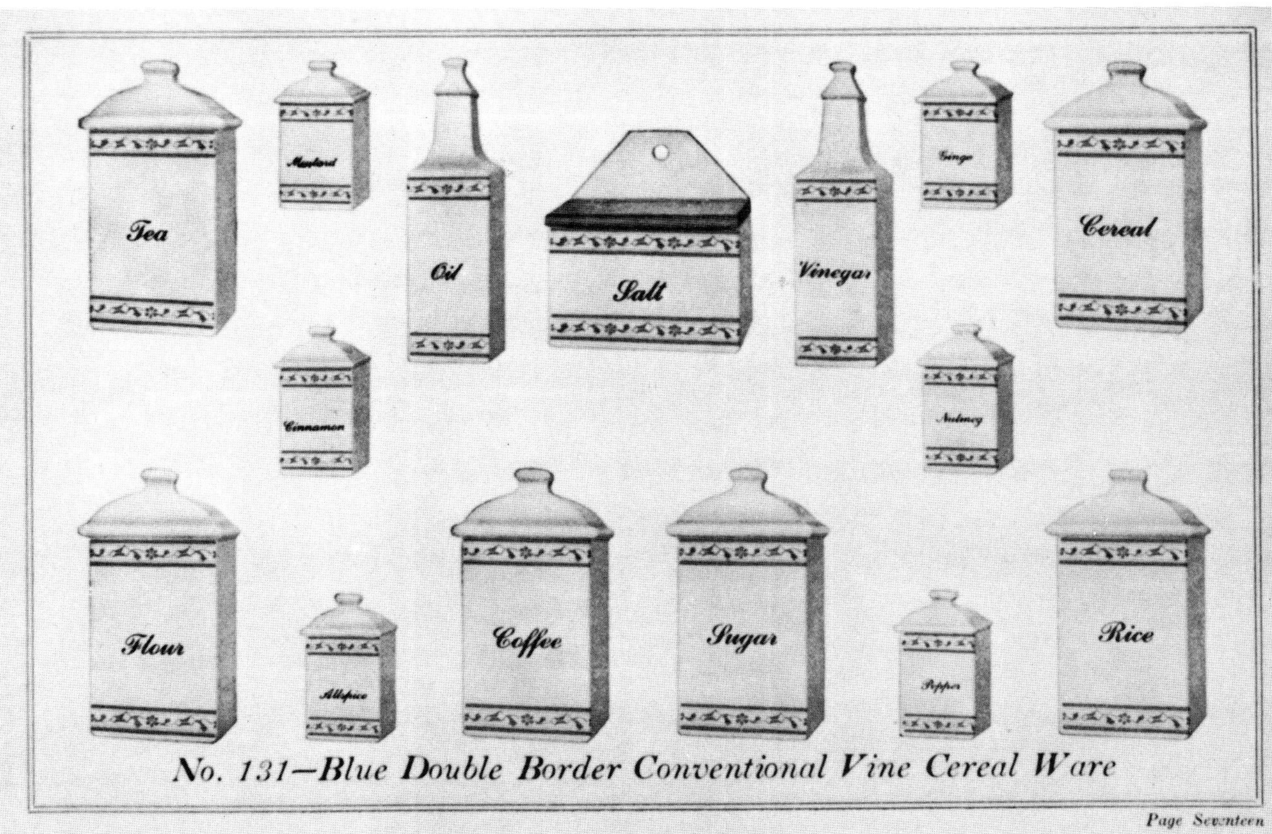

No. 131—Blue Double Border Conventional Vine Cereal Ware

Page Seventeen

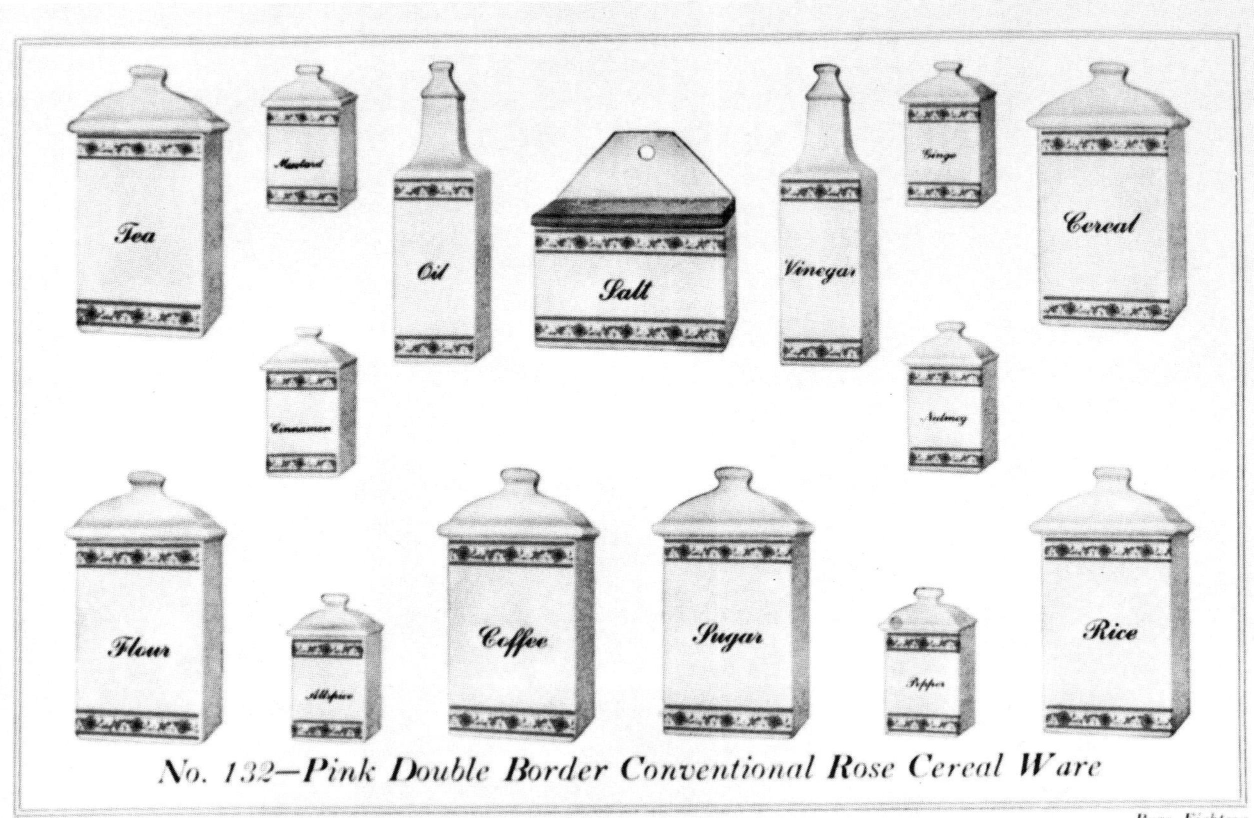

No. 132—Pink Double Border Conventional Rose Cereal Ware

Page Eighteen

THE A. E. HULL POTTERY COMPANY, CROOKSVILLE, OHIO

No. 300/6 BAKE DISH
No. 300/16 FRENCH HANDLED CASSEROLE
HEAT PROOF, COLD PROOF, IVORY WHITE BODY AND GLAZE, DECORATED WITH PIMENTO RED OR NUBIAN BLACK STRIPES.

THE A. E. HULL POTTERY COMPANY, CROOKSVILLE, OHIO

KITCHEN ENSEMBLE
No. 300/1 BOWL
No. 300/14 CUSTARD CUPS

OVEN PROOF
COLD PROOF
IVORY WHITE
BODY AND GLAZE

DECORATION—PIMENTO RED OR NUBIAN BLACK

THE A. E. HULL POTTERY COMPANY, CROOKSVILLE, OHIO

No. 300/4—DEEP BOWLS DESIGNED FOR QUICK, FAST STIRRING EITHER MECHANICALLY OR BY HAND.

THE A. E. HULL POTTERY COMPANY, CROOKSVILLE, OHIO

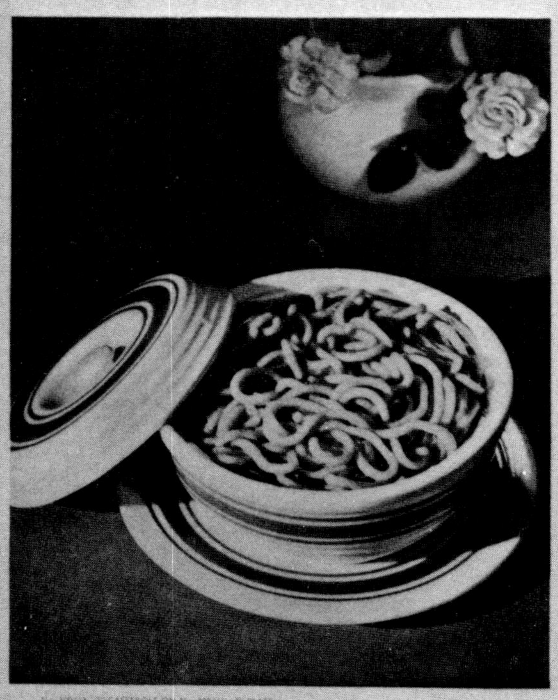

No. 300/13—9" CASSEROLE ON No. 300/16—7" PLATE.
HEAT PROOF—COLD PROOF. BODY AND GLAZE DONE IN IVORY WHITE—DECORATION IN UNDERGLAZE EITHER, SPRING GREEN OR ALICE BLUE STRIPES.

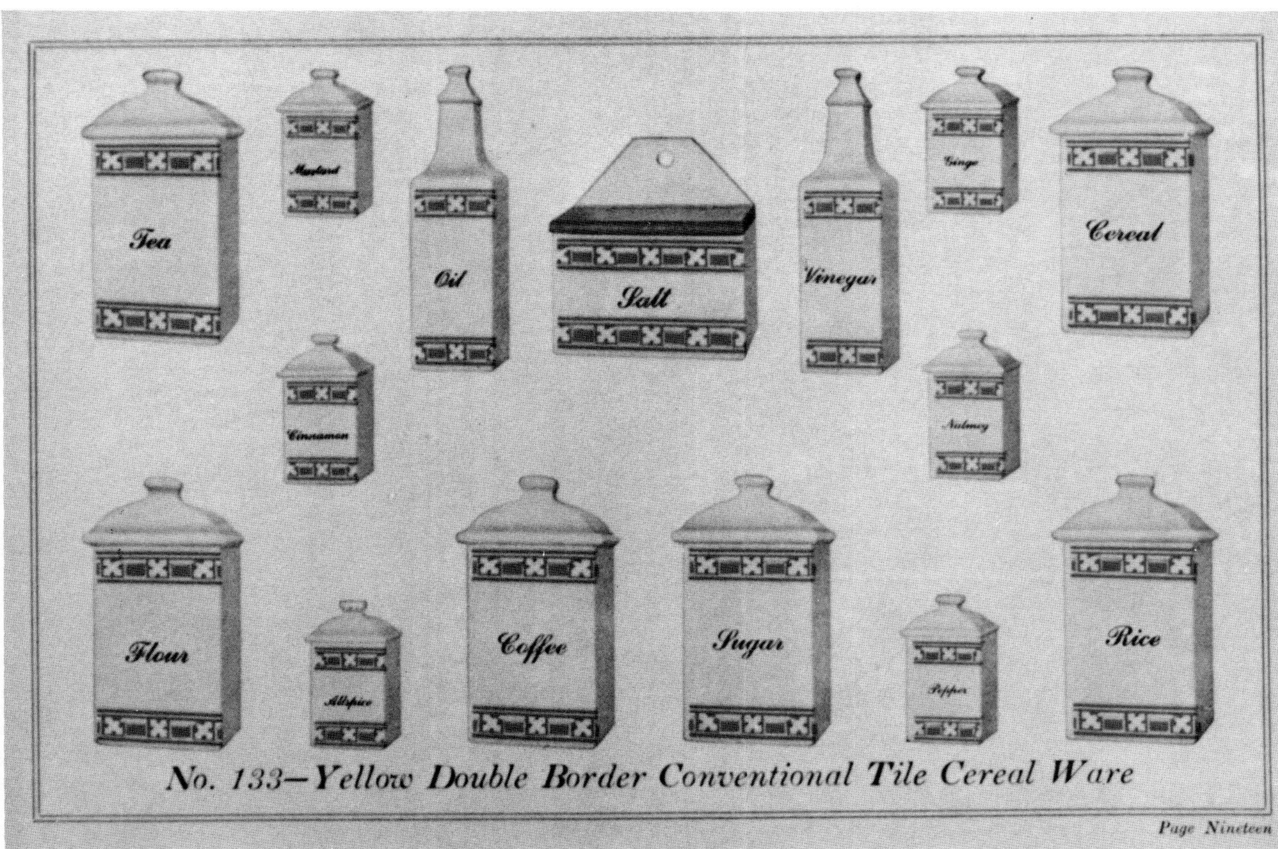

Tea
Mustard
Oil
Salt
Vinegar
Ginger
Cereal
Cinnamon
Nutmeg
Flour
Allspice
Coffee
Sugar
Pepper
Rice
No. 133—Yellow Double Border Conventional Tile Cereal Ware

Page Nineteen

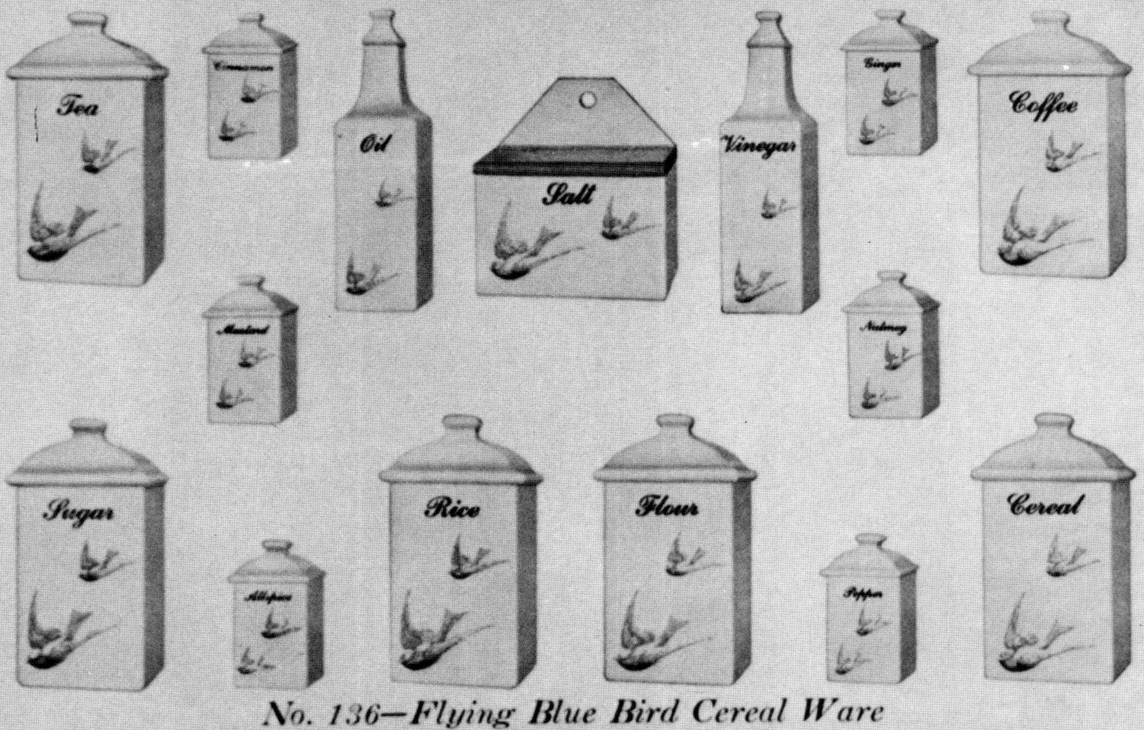

Tea
Cinnamon
Oil
Salt
Vinegar
Ginger
Coffee
Mustard
Nutmeg
Sugar
Allspice
Rice
Flour
Pepper
Cereal
No. 136—Flying Blue Bird Cereal Ware

Page Twenty

THE A. E. HULL POTTERY COMPANY, CROOKSVILLE, OHIO

KITCHEN WORK TABLE ENSEMBLE

No. 300/7—¾ PT. JUG No. 300/7—1 QT. JUG

COLD PROOF IVORY WHITE WITH SPRING GREEN OR ALICE BLUE DECORATION

THE A. E. HULL POTTERY COMPANY, CROOKSVILLE, OHIO

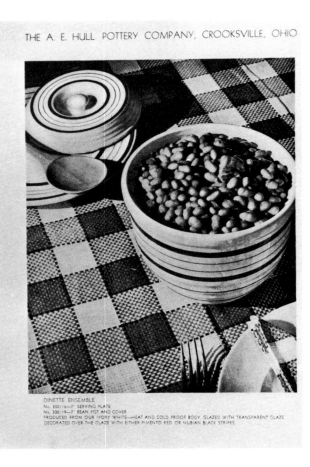

DINETTE ENSEMBLE
No. 300/16—7" SERVING PLATE
No. 300/19—7" BEAN POT AND COVER
PRODUCED FROM OUR IVORY WHITE—HEAT AND COLD PROOF BODY. GLAZED WITH TRANSPARENT GLAZE.
DECORATED OVER THE GLAZE WITH EITHER PIMENTO RED OR NUBIAN BLACK STRIPES.

The following is an October 1, 1935, net price list for Pimento Red or Nubian Black overglaze striped 300 Line Kitchen Ware. Underglaze Spring Green or Alice Blue stripe decoration was only slightly less expensive.

No.	*Size*	*Item*	*Doz.*
300/1	5"	Bowl	1.42
300/1	6"	Bowl	2.08
300/1	7"	Bowl	2.75
300/1	8"	Bowl	3.45
300/1	9"	Bowl	4.15
300/4	4"	Deep Bowl	1.30
300/4	5"	Deep Bowl	1.78
300/4	6"	Deep Bowl	2.46
300/4	7"	Deep Bowl	3.33
300/6	4"	Bake Dish	1.08
300/6	5"	Bake Dish	1.22
300/6	6"	Bake Dish	1.88
300/6	7"	Bake Dish	2.50
300/6	8"	Bake Dish	3.14
300/6	9"	Bake Dish	3.76
300/7	¾ pt.	Jug	2.46
300/7	1 pt.	Jug	3.24
300/7	1 qt.	Jug	4.66

No.	*Size*	*Item*	*Doz.*
300/9	4"	Ramekin	1.08
300/12	9"	Pie Plate	2.85
300/12	10"	Pie Plate	3.50
300/13	6"	Cov. Casserole	3.64
300/13	7"	Cov. Casserole	4.40
300/13	8"	Cov. Casserole	5.18
300/14	3"	Custard Cup	.77
300/15	4"	Fr. Casserole	1.42
300/15	5"	Fr. Casserole	1.80
300/16	7"	Plate	2.42
300/17	5"	Baked Apple	1.42
300/19	3"	Cov. Bean Pot	1.50
300/19	4"	Cov. Bean Pot	2.36
300/19	5"	Cov. Bean Pot	3.12
300/19	6"	Cov. Bean Pot	4.15
300/19	7"	Cov. Bean Pot	5.18

Tea
Cinnamon
Oil
Salt
Vinegar
Ginger
Coffee
Mustard
Nutmeg
Sugar
Allspice
Rice
Flour
Pepper
Cereal

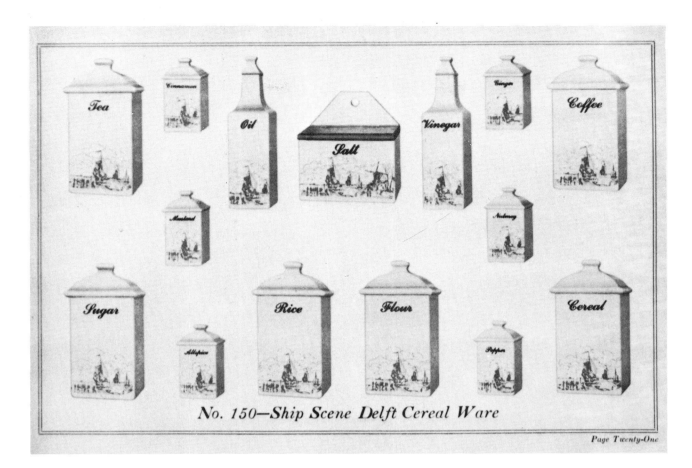

No. 150—Ship Scene Delft Cereal Ware

Page Twenty-One

No. 11—Blue | No. 12—Gold | No. 203—Blue Bird | No. 206—Delft

Round Salt Box

No. 15—Blue | No. 14—Gold | No. 16—Blue Bird | No. 13—Delft

Panelled Salt Box

Semi-Porcelain Hotel and Toilet Ware

Combinets, Chambers, Cuspidors, Mugs and Jugs

THE A. E. Hull Pottery Co. have become large manufacturers of Toilet and Kitchen ware. These lines are made in such quantities that the price can be made extremely reasonable at all times. The quality of the ware is the same as the Blue Band Ware since the same body and glaze is used. The Cuspidors in the line are decorated in the numerous decorations shown on following pages. These decorations are made over the glaze with decalcomania and color bands both selected for their pleasing colors and the fact that they fit nicely into the average color scheme of the ordinary room, be it hotel or residence.

No. 1 Combinet | No. 55 Coffee Mug | No. 4 Hall Boy Jug | No. 5 Chamber and Cover

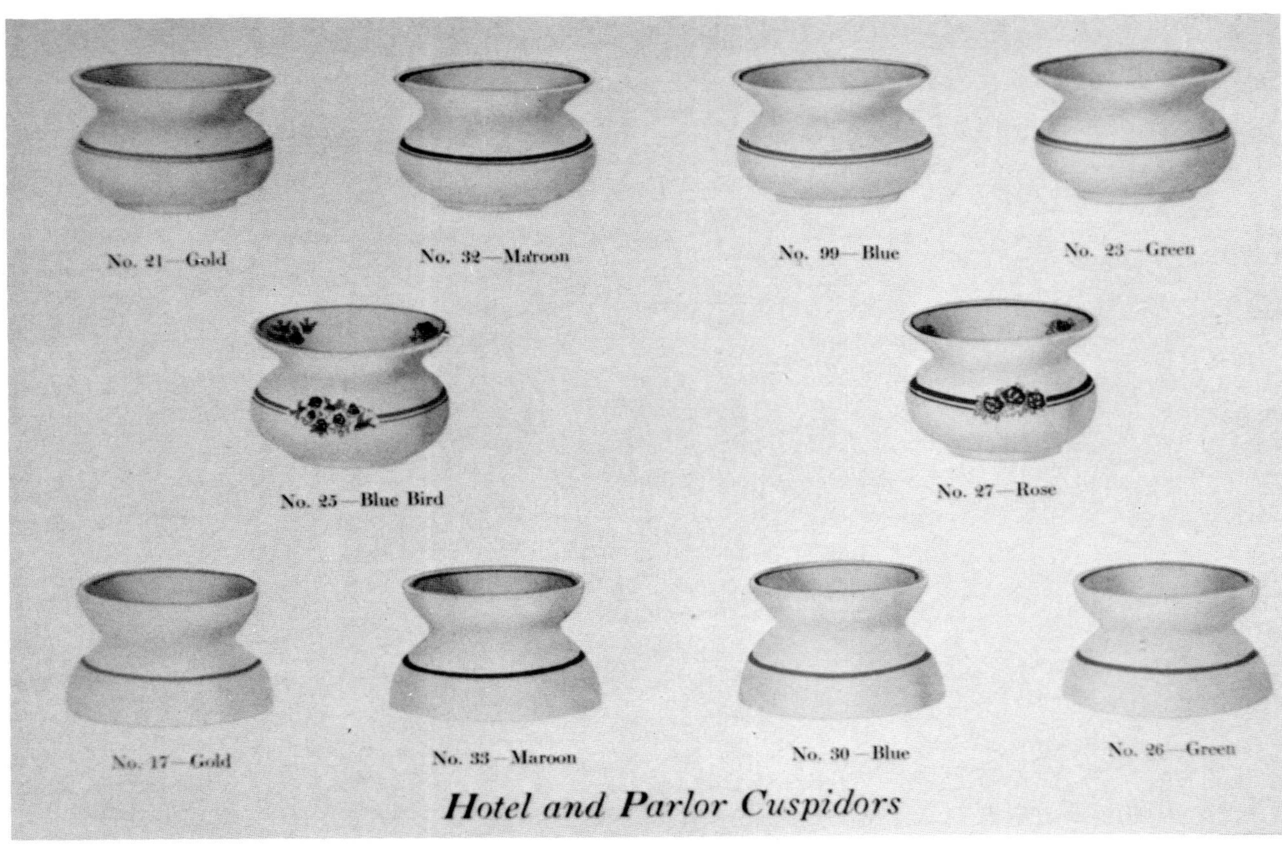

Hotel and Parlor Cuspidors

½ Gal. 1 Gal. 1½ Gal. 2 Gal. 3 Gal.

No. 400—Zane Grey Jars

Page Twenty-Six

Zane Grey Ware

Jars, Bowls, Nappies, Jugs, Butters, Custards

THE Zane Grey Line is being introduced to the trade to meet the growing demand for a lower priced kitchen ware. The A. E. Hull Pottery Co. ceramists, after a year of research and experiments, have devised a body made of refined clays and a glaze of extra soft, glossy texture free from excessive pinholes and crazing, to suit this body. The shapes of the bowls, nappies, jugs and butters are the same as the white and blue band ware with the above body practically vitreous and the blue band decoration under the glaze. Besides these kitchen specialties a line of Food Containers from one-half gallon capacity, including all sizes, to six gallons capacity are made, using the Zane Grey Body, Decoration and Glazes. The quality of the whole line is on a par with the white ware and the price is substantially lower. With these qualifications we are recommending this line to the trade where Cheapness, Quality, Design and Texture, together with usual Hull service is desired.

4 Gal. 5 Gal. 6 Gal.

No. 400—Zane Grey Jars

42's—4 1/8" 36's—5 1/8" 30's—6 1/4" 24's—7 1/4" 18's—8 1/4"

12's—9 [illegible]" 9's—10"

6's—11 1/8" 4's—12 1/4" 3's—13 3/8" 2's—14 3/8 1's—15 1/4

No. 420—Zane Grey Bowls

Page Twenty-Eight

48's—3/4 pt. 42's—1 pt. 36's—1 1/2 pt.

30's—2 1/2 pt. 24's—4 pt. 18's—5 pt.

No. 440—Zane Grey Jugs

Page Twenty-Nine

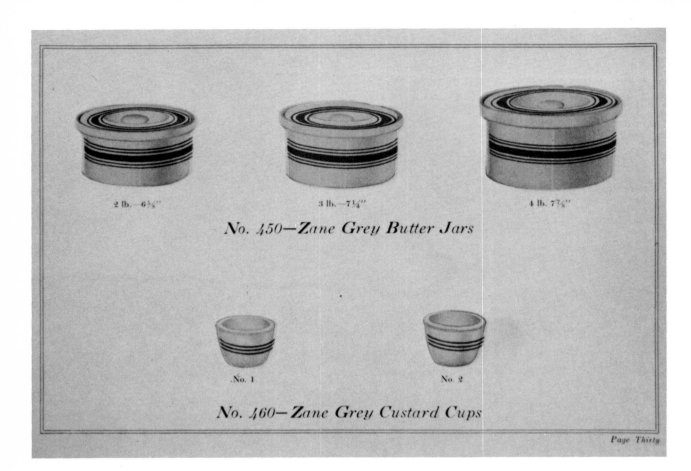

2 lb.—6⅝″ 3 lb.—7¼″ 4 lb. 7⅞″

No. 450—Zane Grey Butter Jars

No. 1 No. 2

No. 460—Zane Grey Custard Cups

Page Thirty

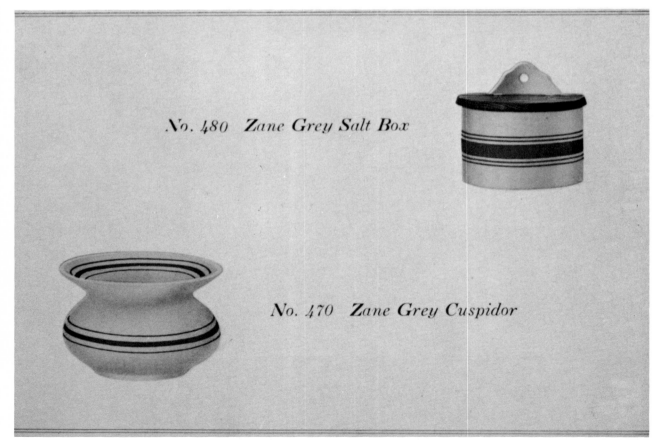

No. 480 Zane Grey Salt Box

No. 470 Zane Grey Cuspidor

RAINBOW
BY HULL
#260—12 Piece Rainbow Dinnerware Set
consisting of:
4 only 10½ Plates
4 only 9 oz. Mugs
4 only Soup & Salad Bowls—6½
Hull Pottery Company - - Crooksville, Ohio

#232—12 pc.
Plate 8½
Cup 6 oz.
Saucer 5½
RAINBOW
LUNCHEON SET
Illustrated
by Hull
Mixing Bowls and Serv-all Trays sold only
in Mirror Brown and Tangerine.
The complete line of House 'n Garden is available in Mirror Brown or Tangerine, each trimmed in Ivory Foam . . . See list for other items also offered in "Rainbow" assorted colors.
Hull Pottery Company - - Crooksville, Ohio

hull u.s.a.
Crestone
©
OVEN-PROOF
an
ovenproof
creation
hull pottery company —
crooksville, ohio u.s.a.

for
casual living ---

Mirror Brown trimmed in Ivory Foam

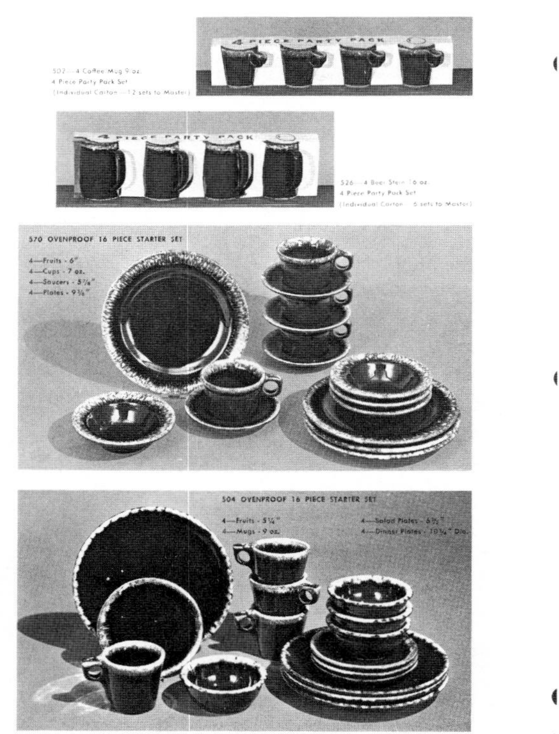

hull pottery company–crooksville, ohio *u.s.a.*

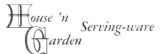

New Addition to Hull's Famous Ovenproof House 'n Garden Serving-ware

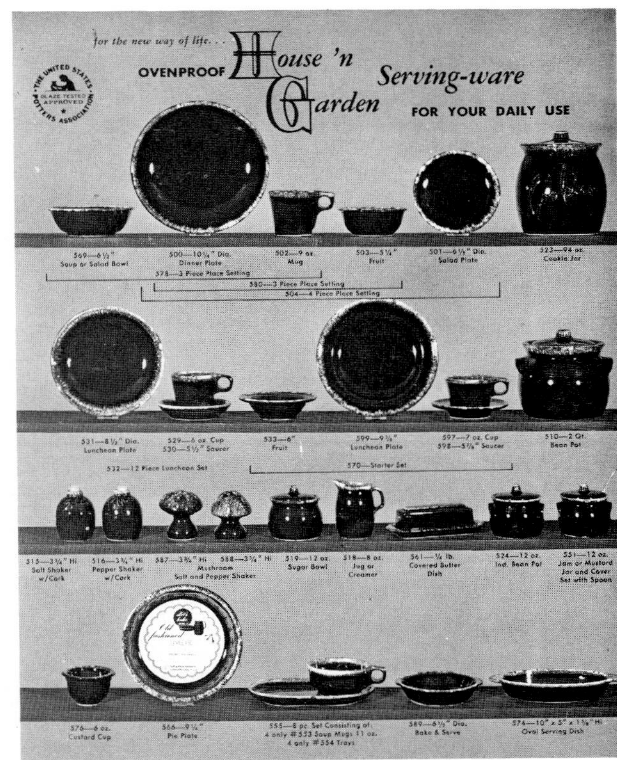

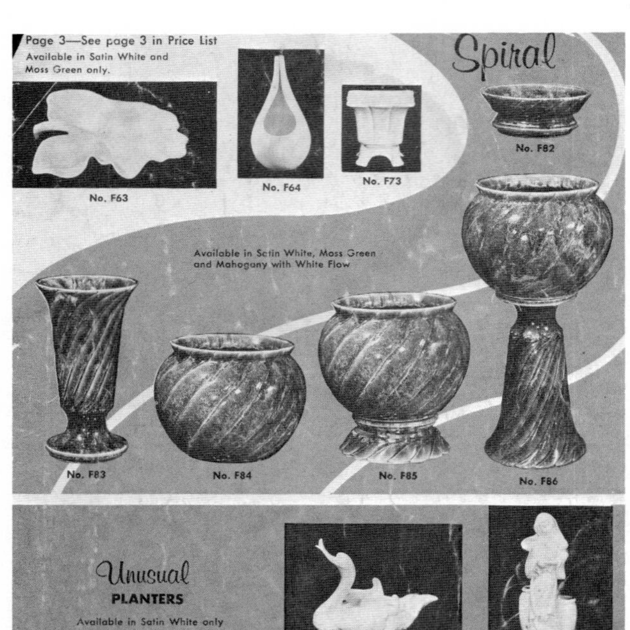
Page 3—See page 3 in Price List
Available in Satin White and Moss Green only.
Spiral
No. F63
No. F64
No. F73
No. F82
Available in Satin White, Moss Green and Mahogany with White Flow
No. F83
No. F84
No. F85
No. F86
Unusual
PLANTERS
Available in Satin White only
No. F21, F22, F23
No. F23 Shown
No. F40

SW—Satin White
SP—Satin Pink
SG—Satin Green
JG—Jade Green
Imperial Ware By HULL
Urn Planters Flower Bowls
Urn Vases Baskets
F43 Urn Jardiniere 5¾" x 5½"
F401 Low Round Flower Bowl 6" dia. x 3"
F411 Square Footed Planter 5½" x 4¾" Hi.
F422 Oriental Planter 6¾" x 4½" x 2¼"
F425 Footed Octagonal Compote 7½" x 4¼"
F434 Urn Vase 7"
*F454 Urn Vase 5¼" dia. x 4¾"
*F455 Hand Turned Urn Planter 4½" dia. x 4¾"
*F456 Pedestaled Pagoda Planter 5¼" x 5¼" x 5"
*F457 Basket w/Handle 7" x 7"
*F458 Pedestaled Octagonal Planter 5½" x 7" Hi.
*F463 Urn Planter w/Handles 5½" dia. x 4¾"
*F464 Flower Bowl w/Leaf Embossing 5½" dia. x 4½"
*F465 Modern Flower Bowl 5⅝" dia. x 3⅞"
*F466 Grecian Urn Planter Bowl 8¼" dia. x 5½"
NOTE: Items marked with an * are new for 1964. Colors will be assorted to the carton as requested.
Hull Pottery Company - - Crooksville, Ohio

SW—Satin White
SP—Satin Pink
SG—Satin Green
JG—Jade Green
Imperial Ware By HULL
Flower Dishes
F71 Flower Dish 11¾" x 5" x 3"
F72 Flower Dish 14" x 5" x 3½"
F75 Flower Dish 6½" x 3⅞" x 2¼"
F76 Flower Dish 7" x 4" x 3⅛"
F77 Flower Dish 8¼" x 4½" x 3¼"
F402 Free Form Flower Dish 7" x 3½" x 3"
F404 Footed Flower Dish 7" x 4" x 3"
F405 Footed Flower Dish 8¼" x 4½"
F406 Scroll Flower Dish 12" x 6½" x 4"
F423 Modern Low Flower Bowl 8¼" x 6" x 2"
F437 Candle Holder 4½" x 4½" x 1¾"
F438 Flower Dish 8¾" x 4¾" x 3½"
*F446 Round Fluted Flower Bowl 5" x 2¾"
*F447 Panelled Flower Dish 6¼" x 4" x 2⅝"
*F448 Oval Flower Dish 6½" x 3½" x 2⅞"
*F450 Cart Flower Dish 6½" x 3¾" x 2¾"
*F451 Rectangular Flower Dish 8¼" x 4½" x 3¼"
*F452 Footed Oval Flower Dish 10" x 4¼" x 3¼"
*F467 Oriental Planter 7½" x 4¾" x 1½"
NOTE: Item marked with an * are new for 1964. Colors will be assorted to the carton as requested.
Hull Pottery Company - - Crooksville, Ohio

SW—Satin White
SP—Satin Pink
SG—Satin Green
JG—Jade Green
Imperial Ware By HULL
Novelty Planter
Jardinieres Vases
F21 Baby Swan Planter/Ash Tray 4" Hi. 3" x 2¼" opening (Satin White Only)
F23 Large Swan Planter 8½" Hi. 7" x 6" opening (Satin White Only)
F63 Caladium Leaf Planter 14" x 10½"
F81 Twin Swan Planter 10½" x 8¼" x 5" (Satin White Only)
F416 Bell Vase 10"
F417 Madonna 9½" (Satin White Only)
NOTE: Items marked with an * are new for 1964. Colors will be assorted to the carton as requested.
F432 Chalice Vase 8¾"
F433 Pedestaled Ivy Bowl 10"
*F435 Dutch Shoe Planter 8" x 4" x 3¾"
*FG8 Jardiniere w/Brass Plated Stand 22½" Over-all
*F427 Free Form Jardiniere only 10½"
*F459 Cylindrical Vase 4⅜" dia. x 10¾"
*F460 Embossed Chalice Vase 5⅜" dia. x 9"
*F461 Pitcher Vase 11¾" Hi.
*F462 Pedestaled Rose Vase 5" dia. x 10⅞"
Hull Pottery Company - - Crooksville, Ohio

FLOWER CLUB CERAMICS
IN SATIN WHITE - JADE GREEN - WILD HONEY
821 Grecian Urn 5" x 5½"
822 Flower Basket 7"
823 Pedestaled Planter 4¾" x 5¾"
Hull Pottery Company, Crooksville, Ohio
824 Leaf Shaped Flower Bowl 9¾" x 7" x 2½"
825 Low Bowl with Scallops 9¾" x 6" x 2"
826 Square Pagoda Planter 6" sq.
827 Pagoda Flower Bowl 7½" x 5¼" x 4"
828 Usubata Jardiniere 7¼" x 4½"
829 Dish Garden 6" x 3½" x 2⅛"
830 Dish Garden 6½" x 3¾" x 2¾"
831 Compote 6½" dia. x 7" hi.
MILK WHITE W/GREEN TRIM (only)
SATIN WHITE (only)
815 Baby Swan Planter 4½" x 4"
812 Swan Planter 9" x 7½"
213 Swan Centerpiece or Planter 7½" x 9½" x 10"
813 Madonna Planter 9" x 7½"

SL—SATIN LIME
JG—JADE GREEN
SW—SATIN WHITE
Imperial
LARGE PEDESTAL PLANTERS
FLOWER VASES
MADONNAS
F456 Pedestaled Pagoda Planter 5¼" x 5¼" x 5"
F454 Urn Vase 5¼" Dia. x 4¾"
F411 Square Footed Planter 5½" x 4¾" Hi.
F43 Urn Jardiniere 5¾" x 5½"
F434 Urn Vase 7"
F466 Grecian Urn Planter Bowl 8¼" x 5½"
F425 Footed Oriental Compote 7½" x 4¼"
F460 Embossed Chalice Vase 5⅜" Dia. x 9"
F416 Bell Vase 10"
F462 Pedestaled Rose Vase 5" Dia. x 10⅞" Hi.
*F24 Long Stem Flower Vase 11¾" x 6¼" Opening
*F20 6¼" Madonna (Satin White Only)
*F7 Small Madonna 7¼" High (Satin White Only)
F417 Madonna 9½" (Satin White Only)
NOTE: All items marked with an * are new for 1965. Colors will be assorted to cartons as requested.
hull pottery company — crooksville, ohio u.s.a

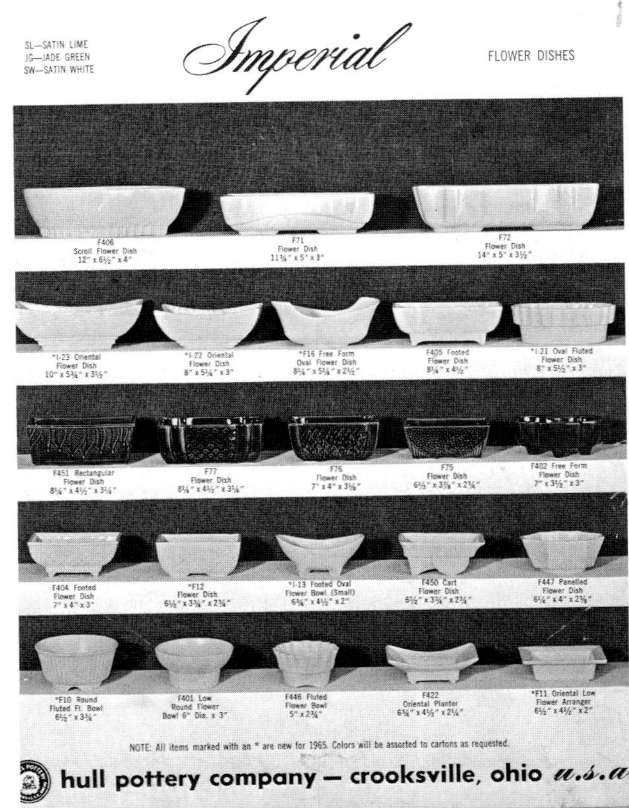
SL—SATIN LIME
JG—JADE GREEN
SW—SATIN WHITE
Imperial
FLOWER DISHES
F406 Scroll Flower Dish 12" x 6½" x 4"
F71 Flower Dish 11¾" x 5" x 3"
F72 Flower Dish 14" x 5" x 3½"
*I-23 Oriental Flower Dish 10" x 5¾" x 3½"
*I-22 Oriental Flower Dish 8" x 5¼" x 3"
*F16 Free Form Oval Flower Dish 8¼" x 5¼" x 2½"
F405 Footed Flower Dish 8¼" x 4½"
*I-21 Oval Fluted Flower Dish 8" x 5½" x 3"
F451 Rectangular Flower Dish 8¼" x 4½" x 3¼"
F77 Flower Dish 8¼" x 4½" x 3¼"
F76 Flower Dish 7" x 4" x 3⅛"
F75 Flower Dish 6½" x 3⅞" x 2⅛"
F402 Free Form Flower Dish 7" x 3½" x 3"
F404 Footed Flower Dish 7" x 4" x 3"
*F12 Flower Dish 6½" x 3¾" x 2¾"
*I-13 Footed Oval Flower Bowl (Small) 6¾" x 4½" x 2"
F450 Cart Flower Dish 6½" x 3¾" x 2¾"
F447 Panelled Flower Dish 6¼" x 4" x 2⅜"
*F10 Round Fluted Fl. Bowl 6½" x 3¾"
F401 Low Round Flower Bowl 6" Dia. x 3"
F446 Fluted Flower Bowl 5" x 2¾"
F422 Oriental Planter 6¾" x 4½" x 2¼"
*F11 Oriental Low Flower Arranger 6½" x 4½" x 2"
NOTE: All items marked with an * are new for 1965. Colors will be assorted to cartons as requested.
hull pottery company — crooksville, ohio u.s.a.

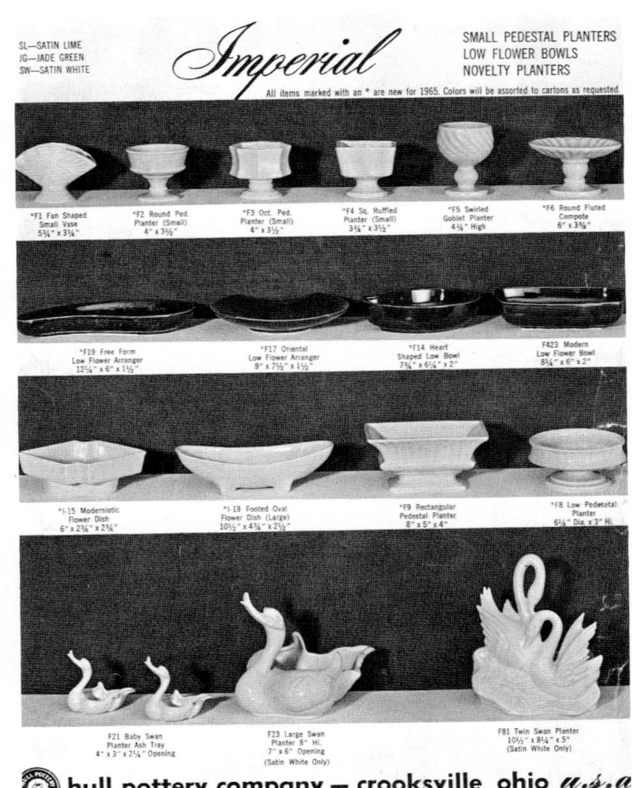
SL—SATIN LIME
JG—JADE GREEN
SW—SATIN WHITE
Imperial
SMALL PEDESTAL PLANTERS
LOW FLOWER BOWLS
NOVELTY PLANTERS
All items marked with an * are new for 1965. Colors will be assorted to cartons as requested
*F1 Fan Shaped Small Vase 5¾" x 3¾"
*F2 Round Ped. Planter (Small) 4" x 3½"
*F3 Oct. Ped. Planter (Small) 4" x 3½"
*F4 Sq. Ruffled Planter (Small) 3¾" x 3½"
*F5 Swirled Goblet Planter 4¼" High
*F6 Round Fluted Compote 6" x 3⅝"
*F19 Free Form Low Flower Arranger 12¼" x 6" x 1½"
*F17 Oriental Low Flower Arranger 9" x 7½" x 1½"
*F14 Heart Shaped Low Bowl 7¾" x 6¼" x 2"
F423 Modern Low Flower Bowl 8¼" x 6" x 2"
*I-15 Modernistic Flower Dish 6" x 2¾" x 2¾"
*I-18 Footed Oval Flower Dish (Large) 10½" x 4¾" x 2½"
*F9 Rectangular Pedestal Planter 8" x 5" x 4"
*F8 Low Pedesetal Planter 6¼" Dia. x 3" Hi.
F21 Baby Swan Planter Ash Tray 4" x 3" x 2¼" Opening
F23 Large Swan Planter 8" Hi. 7" x 6" Opening (Satin White Only)
F81 Twin Swan Planter 10½" x 8¼" x 5" (Satin White Only)
hull pottery company — crooksville, ohio u.s.a

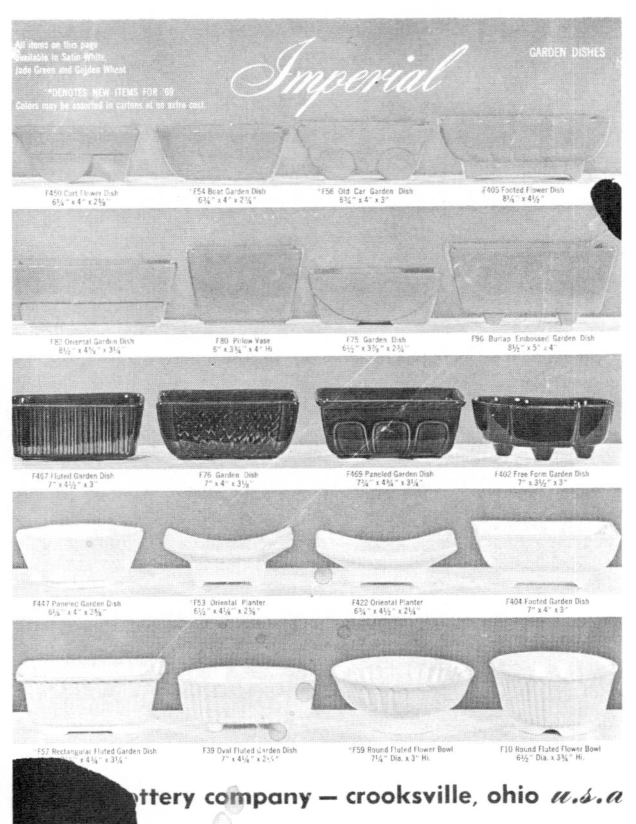
All items on this page
available in Satin White,
Jade Green and Golden Wheat
*DENOTES NEW ITEMS FOR '69
Colors may be assorted in cartons at no extra cost.
Imperial
GARDEN DISHES
F450 Cart Flower Dish 6¼" x 4" x 2⅝"
*F54 Boat Garden Dish 6¾" x 4" x 2¾"
*F56 Old Car Garden Dish 6¾" x 4" x 3"
F405 Footed Flower Dish 8¼" x 4½"
F82 Oriental Garden Dish 8½" x 4⅝" x 3¼"
F80 Pillow Vase 5" x 3¾" x 4" Hi
F75 Garden Dish 6½" x 3⅜" x 2¾"
F96 Burlap Embossed Garden Dish 8½" x 5" x 4"
F467 Fluted Garden Dish 7" x 4½" x 3"
F76 Garden Dish 7" x 4" x 3⅛"
F469 Paneled Garden Dish 7¾" x 4¾" x 3¼"
F402 Free Form Garden Dish 7" x 3½" x 3"
F447 Paneled Garden Dish 6¼" x 4" x 2⅝"
*F53 Oriental Planter 6½" x 4¼" x 2⅜"
F422 Oriental Planter 6¾" x 4½" x 2¼"
F404 Footed Garden Dish 7" x 4" x 3"
*F57 Rectangular Fluted Garden Dish x 4¾" x 3¼"
F39 Oval Fluted Garden Dish 7" x 4¼"
*F59 Round Fluted Flower Bowl 7¼" Dia. x 3" Hi.
F10 Round Fluted Flower Bowl 6½" Dia. x 3¾" Hi.
ttery company — crooksville, ohio u.s.a

The following twelve items available in:
Satin White, Jade Green and Satin Avocado
*DENOTES NEW ITEMS FOR '69
Colors may be assorted in carton at no extra cost
Imperial
PEDESTALED PLANTERS
NOVELTY PLANTERS
GARDEN DISHES
63 Leaf Design Pedestaled Planter 4¾" Dia. x 6¼" Hi.
*F66 Lg. Square Beaded Ped. Planter
*F68 Lg. Fluted Pedestaled Planter 7½" Dia. x 7⅝" Hi
*F67 Lg. Swirl Pedestaled Planter
*F64 Massive Pedestaled Planter 5" Dia. Top x 6¾" Hi.
*F65 Lg. Ruffled Top Pedestaled Planter 7⅜" Dia. x 5¼" Hi.
F83 Pressed Pedestaled Planter 6" x 3½" Hi.
*F62 Pedestaled Compote 6" Dia. x 3½" Hi.
*F52 Owl Planter 6⅛" Hi. x 5" Wide
*F51 Baby Planter 5" Hi. x 4½" Wide
F85 Fluted Pedestaled Planter 4¾" Dia. x 4½" Hi.
*F60 Embossed Jardiniere 6¾" Dia. x 5½" Hi.
The following six items available in: Satin White, Jade Green and Golden Wheat.
F21 Oval Fluted Flower Dish 8" x 5½" x 3"
F45 Shell Embossed Garden Dish 10" x 6" x 3¾"
F42 Rec't Fluted Garden Dish 8½" x 5" x 3¼"
F47 Rec't Garden Dish 11¾" x 4¾" x 4"
F406 Scroll Flower Dish 12" x 6½" x 4"
F72 Garden Dish 14" x 5" x 3½"
hull pottery company — crooksville, ohio u.s.a.

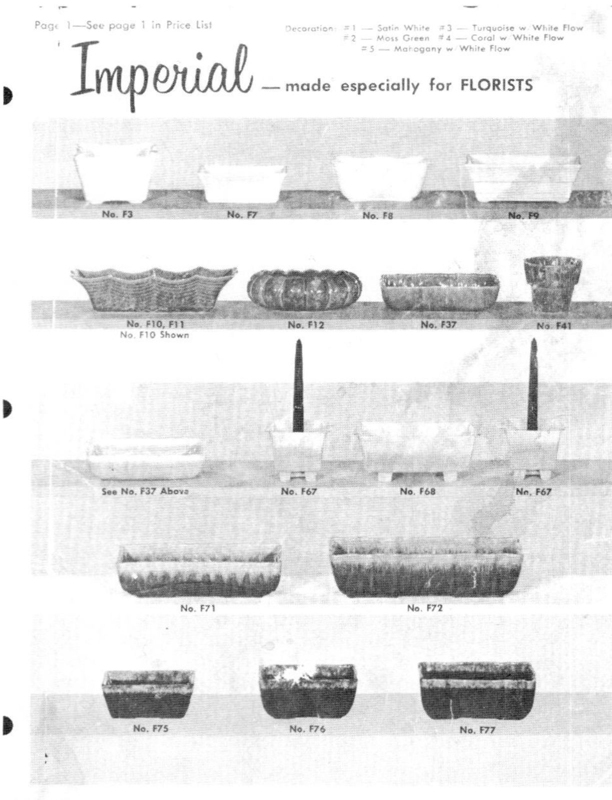
Page 1—See page 1 in Price List
Decoration: #1 — Satin White #3 — Turquoise w/White Flow
#2 — Moss Green #4 — Coral w/White Flow
#5 — Mahogany w/White Flow
Imperial — made especially for FLORISTS
No. F3
No. F7
No. F8
No. F9
No. F10, F11
No. F10 Shown
No. F12
No. F37
No. F41
See No. F37 Above
No. F67
No. F68
No. F67
No. F71
No. F72
No. F75
No. F76
No. F77

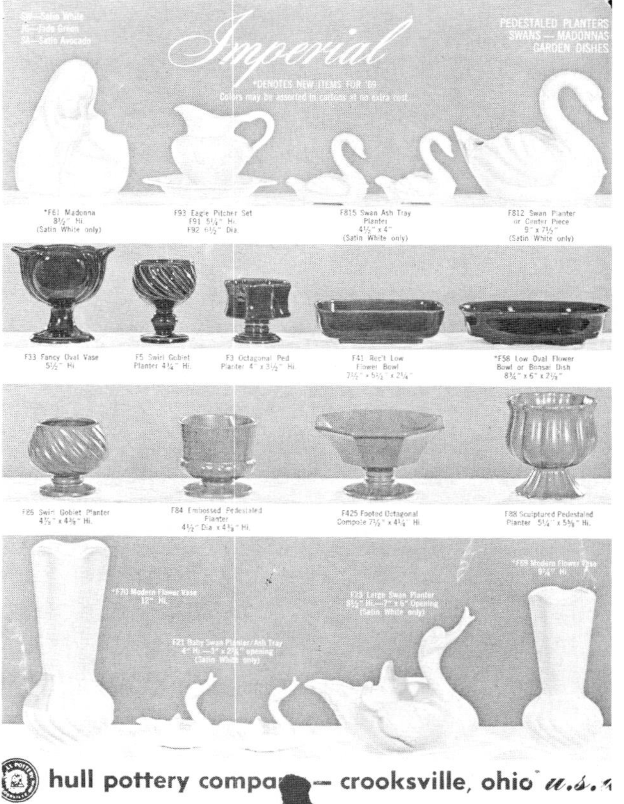
SW—Satin White
JG—Jade Green
SA—Satin Avocado
Imperial
PEDESTALED PLANTERS
SWANS — MADONNAS
GARDEN DISHES
*DENOTES NEW ITEMS FOR '69
Colors may be assorted in cartons at no extra cost.
*F61 Madonna 8½" Hi. (Satin White only)
F93 Eagle Pitcher Set F91 5¼" Hi. F92 6½" Dia.
F815 Swan Ash Tray Planter 4½" x 4" (Satin White only)
F812 Swan Planter or Center Piece 9" x 7½" (Satin White only)
F33 Fancy Oval Vase 5½" Hi
F5 Swirl Goblet Planter 4¾" Hi.
F3 Octagonal Ped Planter 4" x 3½" Hi.
F41 Rec't Low Flower Bowl 7½" x 5½" x 2¼"
*F58 Low Oval Flower Bowl or Bonsai Dish 8¾" x 6" x 2⅛"
F86 Swirl Goblet Planter 4½" x 4⅜" Hi.
F84 Embossed Pedestaled Planter 4½" Dia. x 4⅜" Hi.
F425 Footed Octagonal Compote 7½" x 4¼" Hi.
F88 Sculptured Pedestaled Planter 5¼" x 5⅝" Hi.
*F70 Modern Flower Vase 12" Hi.
F23 Large Swan Planter (Satin White only)
F21 Baby Swan Planter/Ash Tray (Satin White only)
*F69 Modern Flower Vase 9¾" Hi.
hull pottery company — crooksville, ohio u.s.a.

GO—GOLDEN OLIVE
JG—JADE GREEN
SW—SATIN WHITE
Imperial
FLOWER DISHES
Items prefaced by an asterisk (*) are new for 1966
Colors will be assorted to cartons as requested.
F446 Rd. Fluted Flower Bowl
F441 Paneled Flower Dish
F422 Oriental Planter
F11 Oriental Low Flower Arranger
F402 Free Form Flower
F42 Rect. Fluted Dish Garden
F21 Oval Fluted Flower Dish
F404 Footed Flower Dish
F75 Flower Dish
F450 Cart Flower Dish
F76 Flower Dish
F405 Footed Flower Dish
F22 Oriental Flower Dish
*F47 Rectangular Dish Garden
*F45 Shell Embossed Dish Garden
F406 Scroll Dish Garden
*F37 Paneled Dish Garden
F72 Flower Dish
hull pottery company — crooksville, ohio u.s.a

—GOLDEN OLIVE
—JADE GREEN
—SATIN WHITE
Imperial
SMALL PEDESTAL PLANTERS
LOW FLOWER BOWLS
NOVELTY PLANTERS
F25 Low Shell Flower Bowl
F2 Round Ped. Planter (Small)
*F38 Ped. Planter
F3 Oct. Ped. Planter (Small)
F4 Sq. Ruffled Ped. Planter (Small)
*F26 Low Ped. Flower Arranger
F22 Rect. Ped. Flower Arranger
F27 High Ped. Flower Arranger
F5 Swirled Goblet Planter
F31 Chalice Vase
F32 Free Form Oval Vase
F6 Round Fluted Compote
*F39 Oval Fluted Dish Garden
*F41 Rect. Low Flower Bowl
F14 Heart Shape Low Bowl
*F46 Rd. Swirl Bulb Bowl
F48 Free Form Low Bowl
F401 Low Rd. Flower Bowl
F10 Rd. Fluted Flower Bowl
F21 Baby Swan Planter Ash Tray
F23 Large Swan Planter
F8 Low Ped. Planter
hull pottery company — crooksville, ohio u.s.a.

GM—GOLDEN MIST
JG—JADE GREEN
SW—SATIN WHITE
Imperial
GARDEN DISHES
*DENOTES NEW ITEMS FOR '67
Colors may be assorted in cartons at no extra cost
F468 Round Flower Bowl
F402 Free Form Flower Dish
F467 Fluted Dish Garden
*F469 Paneled Dish Garden
F441 Paneled Flower Dish
F450 Cart Flower Dish
F39 Oval Fluted Dish Garden
F404 Footed Flower Dish
F10 Rd. Fluted Flower Bowl
F21 Oval Fluted Flower Dish
F76 Flower Dish
F405 Footed Flower Dish
F42 Rect. Fluted Dish Garden
F45 Shell Embossed Dish Garden
F47 Rect. Dish Garden
F37 Paneled Dish Garden
F406 Scroll Flower Dish
F72 Flower Dish
hull pottery company — crooksville, ohio

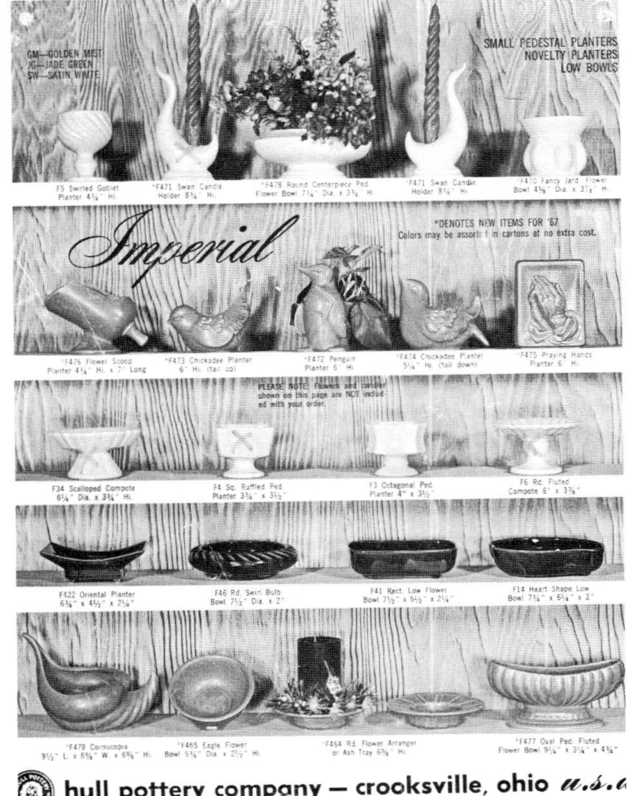
GM—GOLDEN MIST
JG—JADE GREEN
SW—SATIN WHITE
SMALL PEDESTAL PLANTERS
NOVELTY PLANTERS
LOW BOWLS
F5 Swirled Goblet Planter
*F471 Swan Candle Holder
*F478 Round Centerpiece Ped. Flower Bowl
*F471 Swan Candle Holder
*F470 Fancy Jard. Flower Bowl
Imperial
*DENOTES NEW ITEMS FOR '67
Colors may be assorted in cartons at no extra cost.
*F476 Flower Scoop Planter
*F473 Chickadee Planter
*F472 Penguin Planter
*F474 Chickadee Planter
*F475 Praying Hands Planter
PLEASE NOTE: Flowers and candles shown on this page are NOT included with your order.
F34 Scalloped Compote
F4 Sq. Ruffled Ped. Planter
F3 Octagonal Ped. Planter
F6 Rd. Fluted Compote
F422 Oriental Planter
F46 Rd. Swirl Bulb Bowl
F41 Rect. Low Flower Bowl
F14 Heart Shape Low Bowl
*F479 Cornucopia
*F465 Eagle Flower Bowl
*F454 Rd. Flower Arranger or Ash Tray
*F477 Oval Ped. Fluted Flower Bowl
hull pottery company — crooksville, ohio u.s.a

GARDEN DISHES
Imperial
*DENOTES NEW ITEMS FOR '70
COLORS MAY BE ASSORTED IN CARTONS AT NO EXTRA COST

hull pottery company — crooksville, ohio u.s.a

Imperial
COLORS MAY BE ASSORTED IN CARTONS AT NO EXTRA COST
*DENOTES NEW ITEMS FOR '70
hull pottery company — crooksville, ohio

Designed Especially for Florists
by Hull

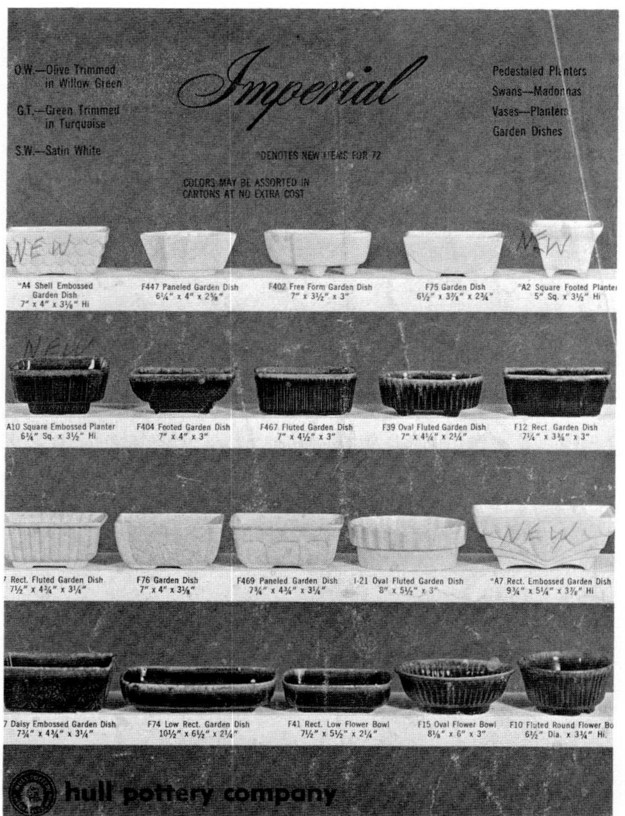
O.W.—Olive Trimmed in Willow Green
G.T.—Green Trimmed in Turquoise
S.W.—Satin White
Imperial
*DENOTES NEW ITEMS FOR '72
COLORS MAY BE ASSORTED IN CARTONS AT NO EXTRA COST
hull pottery company

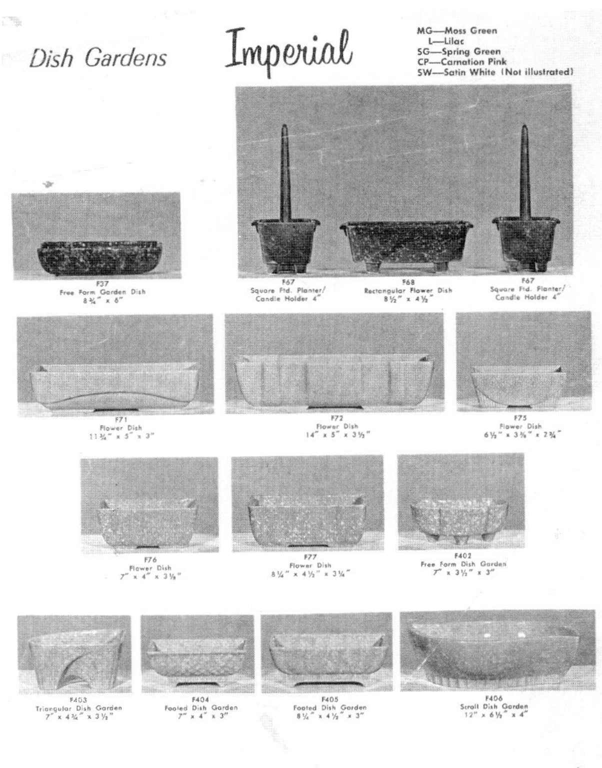
Dish Gardens
Imperial
MG—Moss Green
L—Lilac
SG—Spring Green
CP—Carnation Pink
SW—Satin White (Not illustrated)
F37
Free Form Garden Dish
8¾" x 6"
F67
Square Ftd. Planter/
Candle Holder 4"
F68
Rectangular Flower Dish
8½" x 4½"
F67
Square Ftd. Planter/
Candle Holder 4"
F71
Flower Dish
11¾" x 5" x 3"
F72
Flower Dish
14" x 5" x 3½"
F75
Flower Dish
6½" x 3⅞" x 2¾"
F76
Flower Dish
7" x 4" x 3⅛"
F77
Flower Dish
8¼" x 4½" x 3¼"
F402
Free Form Dish Garden
7" x 3½" x 3"
F403
Triangular Dish Garden
7" x 4¾" x 3½"
F404
Footed Dish Garden
7" x 4" x 3"
F405
Footed Dish Garden
8¼" x 4½" x 3"
F406
Scroll Dish Garden
12" x 6½" x 4"

Hull Pottery Company - - Crooksville, Ohio

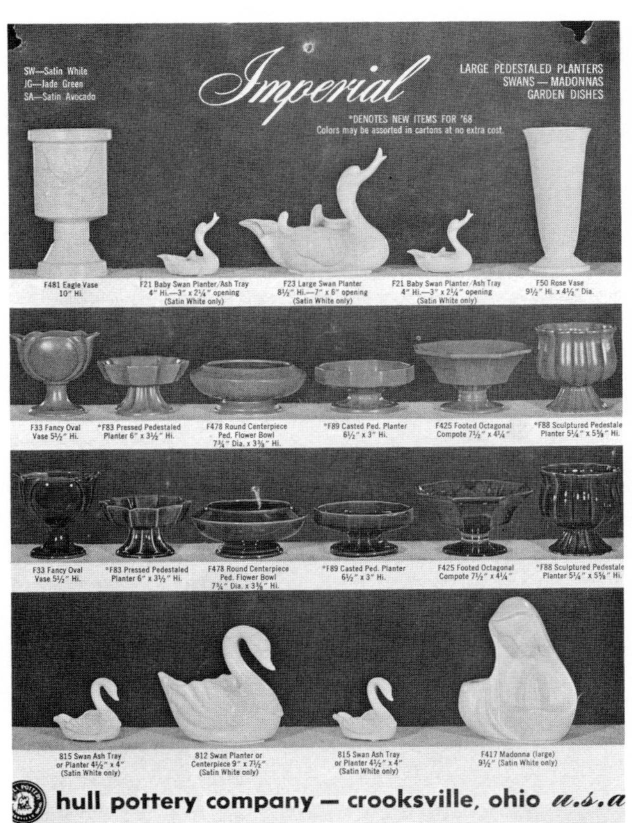
SW—Satin White
JG—Jade Green
SA—Satin Avocado
Imperial
LARGE PEDESTALED PLANTERS
SWANS — MADONNAS
GARDEN DISHES
*DENOTES NEW ITEMS FOR '68
Colors may be assorted in cartons at no extra cost.
F481 Eagle Vase
10" Hi.
F21 Baby Swan Planter/Ash Tray
4" Hi.—3" x 2¼" opening
(Satin White only)
F23 Large Swan Planter
8½" Hi.—7" x 6" opening
(Satin White only)
F21 Baby Swan Planter/Ash Tray
4" Hi.—3" x 2¼" opening
(Satin White only)
F50 Rose Vase
9½" Hi. x 4½" Dia.
F33 Fancy Oval
Vase 5½" Hi.
*F83 Pressed Pedestaled
Planter 6" x 3½" Hi.
F478 Round Centerpiece
Ped. Flower Bowl
7¾" Dia. x 3⅜" Hi.
*F89 Casted Ped. Planter
6½" x 3" Hi.
F425 Footed Octagonal
Compote 7½" x 4¼"
*F88 Sculptured Pedestale
Planter 5¼" x 5⅝" Hi.
F33 Fancy Oval
Vase 5½" Hi.
*F83 Pressed Pedestaled
Planter 6" x 3½" Hi.
F478 Round Centerpiece
Ped. Flower Bowl
7¾" Dia. x 3⅜" Hi.
*F89 Casted Ped. Planter
6½" x 3" Hi.
F425 Footed Octagonal
Compote 7½" x 4¼"
*F88 Sculptured Pedestale
Planter 5¼" x 5⅝" Hi.
815 Swan Ash Tray
or Planter 4½" x 4"
(Satin White only)
812 Swan Planter or
Centerpiece 9" x 7½"
(Satin White only)
815 Swan Ash Tray
or Planter 4½" x 4"
(Satin White only)
F417 Madonna (large)
9½" (Satin White only)
hull pottery company — crooksville, ohio u.s.a

All items on this page
available in Satin White,
Jade Green and Golden Wheat
*DENOTES NEW ITEMS FOR '68
Colors may be assorted in cartons at no extra cost.
Imperial
GARDEN DISHES
*F82 Oriental Dish Garden
8½" x 4⅝" x 3¼"
*F80 Pillow Vase
6" x 3¾" x 4" Hi
F75 Dish Garden
6½" x 3⅞" x 2¾"
*F96 Burlap Embossed Dish Garden
8½" x 5" x 4"
F467 Fluted Dish Garden
7" x 4½" x 3"
F468 Round Flower Bowl
(Ten Panels) 5¾" Dia. x 2¾" Hi
F402 Free Form Flower Dish
7" x 3½" x 3"
F469 Paneled Dish Garden
7¾" x 4¾" x 3¼"
F450 Cart Flower Dish
6½" x 3¾" x 2¾"
F447 Paneled Flower Dish
6¼" x 4" x 2⅝"
F422 Oriental Planter
6¾" x 4½" x 2¼"
F404 Footed Flower Dish
7" x 4" x 3"
I-21 Oval Fluted Flower Dish
8" x 5½" x 3"
F39 Oval Fluted Dish Garden
7" x 4¼" x 2¼"
F10 Rd. Fluted Flower Bowl
6½" x 3¾"
F405 Footed Flower Dish
8¼" x 4½"
F45 Shell Embossed Dish Garden
10" x 6" x 3¾"
F76 Flower Dish
7" x 4" x 3⅛"
F42 Rect. Fluted Dish Garden
8½" x 5" x 3¼"
F47 Rect. Dish Garden
11¾" x 4¾" x 4"
F37 Paneled Dish Garden
12¼" x 6½" x 4"
F406 Scroll Flower Dish
12" x 6½" x 4"
F72 Flower Dish
14" x 5" x 3½"
hull pottery company — crooksville, ohio u.s.a.

All items on this page
available in Satin White,
Jade Green and Satin Avocado
Imperial
SMALL PEDESTAL PLANTERS
NOVELTY PLANTERS
LOW BOWLS
F473 Chickadee Planter
6" Hi. (tail up)
*F86 Swirl Goblet Planter
4⅞" x 4⅜" Hi.
F5 Swirled Goblet
Planter 4¾" Hi.
F474 Chickadee Planter
5¼" Hi. (tail down)
F3 Octagonal Ped.
Planter 4" x 3½"
*F87 Embossed Flower
Bowl 5½" Dia. x 3" Hi.
F470 Fancy Jard./Flower
Bowl 4⅝" Dia. x 3⅞" Hi.
*F97 Tub Planter
5" Dia. x 3¼" Hi.
*DENOTES NEW ITEMS FOR '68
Colors may be assorted in cartons at no extra cost.
*F95 Bowl Planter
6⅜" x 3½" Hi.
*F78 Square Fluted Planter
3⅞" x 3½" Hi.
F41 Rect. Low Flower
Bowl 7½" x 5½" x 2¼"
*F79 Fancy Jardiniere
4¾" x 3⅞" Hi.
hull pottery company —
*F93 Eagle Pitcher Set
*F91—5¼" Hi.
*F92—6½" Dia.
*F81 Tall Square Jardiniere
4⅝" x 4½" Hi.
F476 Flower Scoop Planter
4¾" Hi. x 7" Long
*F94 Novelty Boy Planter
8" Hi.
crooksville, ohio u.s.a.
F479 Cornucopia
9½" L. x 6⅝" W. x 6⅝" Hi.
*F85 Fluted Pedestaled
Planter 4¾" x 4½" Hi.
*F84 Embossed Pedestaled Planter
4½" Dia. x 4⅜" Hi.
*F90 Flower Arranger Vase
6¾" x 3⅜" x 6½" Hi.

Pressed Ped. Planter
F22 Oval Ped. Planter 6⅛" x 4½" x 4½"
F3 Octagonal Ped. Planter 4" x 3½" Hi.
F5 Swirl Goblet Planter 4¾" Hi.
*A55 Oval Ped. Planter 6¼" x 3¾" x 5¾"
*A3 Sq. Emb. Planter 4½" Sq. x 4½" Hi.
*A5 Rect. Fluted Garden Dish 9¼" x 5¼" x 3½" Hi.
*A6 Scroll Flower Dish 9" x 5½" x 3½"
F42 Rect. Fluted Garden Dish 8½" x 5" x 3¼"
F405 Footed Flower Dish 8¼" x 4½" x 3¼"
Imperial
Shell Embossed Garden Dish 10" x 6" x 3¾"
Floristware
*A9 Rect. Paneled Garden Dish 15" x 5½" x 3¾" Hi.
F406 Scroll Flower Dish 12" x 6½" x 4"
F78 Rect. Leaf Design Grdn. Dish 10½" x 5¼" x 3⅝"
F77 Fancy Oval Grdn. Dish 11½" x 5¼" x 3"
F34 Urn Shaped Planter 4¾" Dia. x 5" Hi.

F42 Rect. Fluted Garden Dish 8½" x 5" x 3¼"
F82 Oriental Garden Dish
F405 Footed Flower Dish 8¼" x 4½" x 3¼"
F45 Shell Embossed Garden Dish 10" x 6" x 3¾"
F47 Rectangular Garden Dish 11¾" x 4¾" x 4"
*F79 Rect. Flower Dish 10½" x 5¼" x 3¾"
F72 Rect. Garden Dish 11" x 5" x 3½"
F406 Scroll Flower Dish 12" x 6½" x 4"
*F78 Rect. Leaf Design Grdn. Dish 10½" x 5¼" x 3⅝"
*F77 Fancy Oval Grdn. Dish 11½" x 5¼" x 3"
F34 Urn Shaped Planter 4¾" Dia. x 5" Hi.
F3 Octagonal Ped. Planter 4" x 3½" Hi.
F5 Swirl Goblet Planter 4¾" Hi.
F22 Oval Ped. Planter
F33 Fancy Oval Vase 5½" Hi.
*F87 Embossed Box Planter

D.W.—Olive Trimmed in Willow Green
G.T.—Green Trimmed in Turquoise
S.W.—Satin White
Imperial by Hull
Pedestaled Planters
Vases
Planters
Garden Dishes
COLORS MAY BE ASSORTED IN CARTONS AT NO EXTRA COST
F68 Sculptured Ped. Planter
F24 Flower Basket 7" x 6¾" x 6"
A55 Oval Ped. Planter
F447 Paneled Garden Dish
F404 Footed Garden Dish
hull pottery company
crooksville, ohio

Designed Especially for Florists
F12 Rect. Garden Dish
F39 Oval Fluted Garden Dish
F52 Rect. Fluted Garden Dish
F76 Garden Dish
F469 Paneled Garden Dish
F42 Rect. Fluted Garden Dish
F18 Fruit Emb. Garden Dish 8¾" x 4¾" x 3¼"
A6 Scroll Flower Dish 9" x 5½" x 3½"
F77 Fancy Oval Grdn. Dish 11½" x 5¼" x 3"
F10 Fluted Round Flower Bowl
F15 Oval Flower Bowl
A2 Square Footed Planter
A3 Sq. Emb. Planter 4½" Sq. x 4½" Hi.
B14 Cart Planter
A12 Rnd. Flower Bowl
B6 Fancy Ruffled Bowl
A10 Square Embossed Planter
B5 Diamond Shaped Dish
F41 Rect. Low Flower
F406 Scroll Flower Dish 12" x 6½" x 4"
F72 Rect. Garden Dish 14" x 5" x 3½"
F47 Rectangular Garden Dish

Designed Especially for Florists

BIBLIOGRAPHY

Antiques Research Publications, ST. LOUIS: BLACKWELL WIELANDY COMPANY, 1940, reprinted edition, Menton, Alabama, 1968.

BETTER HOMES AND GARDENS, Hull advertisements, February, 1946; May, 1946; October, 1946; November, 1946; December, 1946; February; 1947, April, 1947; May, 1947; August, 1947; October, 1947; November, 1947; April, 1948; June, 1948; November, 1948; December, 1948; April, 1949; June, 1949; August, 1949; October, 1949; April, 1950.

Coleman, Duke, HULL, American Art Pottery, Number 4, September, 1976.

COLUMBUS SUNDAY DISPATCH, Columbus, Ohio, June 18, 1950.

Crooks, Guy E., BRIEF HISTORY OF THE POTTERY INDUSTRY OF CROOKSVILLE, 1868-1932, printed in booklet form after publication in *The Crooksville Messenger,* courtesy The Ohio Historical Society.

Crooksville Advance, The. THE STONEWARE STORY, Crooksville, Ohio, circa 1902.

Crooksville-Roseville Messenger, The. A BRIEF HISTORY OF THE HULL POTTERY COMPANY, reprinted edition, Vol. 23, Number 35, Crooksville, Ohio, 1974.

ECHOES, A PUBLICATION OF THE OHIO HISTORICAL SOCIETY, Vol. I, Number 11, November, 1962.

Hammer, Michael L., HISTORY OF THE HULL POTTERY COMPANY, Pottery Festival Souvenir, 1967.

HOUSE AND GARDEN, Hull advertisement, May, 1950.

Holmquist, Betsy, HULL'S LITTLE RED RIDING HOOD, private correspondence.

Hull, Addis Emmet, Jr., letter to Norris Schneider dated August 10, 1960. During this period Mr. Hull was serving as President of Western Stoneware Company of Monmouth, Illinois.

Hull, Byron E., private correspondence, 1979.

Hull, James Brannon, private correspondence, 1974.

Hull Pottery Company Personnel, personal interviews with current and retired personnel of the Hull plant: Helen Aichele, Isabella Dusenberry, Lois and Russell Lee, Esta Marshall, Daine Neff, Elsie Robinson, Harold Showers, Hattie Sturgill, Bernice Walpole, Douglas Young.

Hull, Robert W., private correspondence, 1979.

Huxford, Sharon and Bob, THE COLLECTOR'S ENCYCLOPEDIA OF McCOY POTTERY, Collector Books, Paducah, Kentucky, 1978.

Lewis, Thomas William, A HISTORY OF SOUTHEASTERN OHIO AND THE MUSKINGUM VALLEY, Vol. III, S.J. Clarke Publishers, Chicago, 1928.

McCALL'S, Shulton-Hull advertisement, December, 1942.

McCoy, Mrs. Nelson, company brochure pages and price guides, pre-1950.

Modern Packaging Magazine, SHULTON'S OLD SPICE, September, 1953, Modern Packaging Corp., New York.

Ohio Historical Society Archives Library, company brochure pages, post-1950.

Patent and Trademark Office, patent information, HULL'S LITTLE RED RIDING HOOD, Washington, D.C.

PROSPECTUS OF SHAWNEE POTTERY COMPANY, May 6, 1937.

Roberts, Brenda, private collection of company brochure pages, price guides, and company photographs, pre and post-1950.

Robinson, Elsie, private correspondence, 1977, 1978.

Schaefer, Granville, private correspondence, personal interview, 1978, 1979.

Schneider, Norris, HULL POTTERY, Zanesville Times Recorder, April 25, 1965, Zanesville, Ohio.

Shulton Company, EARLY AMERICAN TOILETRIES, OLD SPICE, 1938, 1939, 1940, 1942 catalogues, Shulton, New Jersey.

Sulens, Henry, private correspondence, 1979.

Whitlatch, Gene, personal interviews.

ZANESVILLE NEWS, THE. June 17, 1950, Zanesville, Ohio.

Zanesville Times-Recorder, PERRY COUNTY TOWNS FLOODED, June 17, 1950; STRICKEN VILLAGES CLEAN UP FLOOD DEBRIS, June 19, 1950; MORALE MOUNTING IN FLOODED AREAS, June 20, 1950; SHIP POTTERY FROM CROOKSVILLE, June 23, 1950, Zanesville, Ohio.

Price Guide

Page 33

Plate 1, Lusterware/Acme
1. Candleholder, 3" .....$ 30.00- 40.00
2. Plate, 11" ....$ 25.00- 35.00
3. Pitcher, 4" ....$ 30.00- 40.00

Plate 2, Lusterware
1. Vase, 3½" ....$ 30.00- 42.00
2. Bud Vase, 8" ....$ 35.00- 48.00

Plate 3, Novelty
Row 1:
1. Bear, 1½" ....$ 15.00- 20.00
2. Owl Bank, 3¾" ......$ 25.00- 35.00
3. Rabbit, 5½" ....$ 12.00- 18.00
4. Frog Bank, 3¾" ......$ 50.00- 65.00
5. Kitten, 1½" ....$ 15.00- 20.00

Row 2:
1. Rabbit, 2¾" ....$ 15.00- 20.00
2. Rabbit, 2¾" ....$ 15.00- 20.00
3. Musician, 5¾" ....$ 25.00- 40.00
4. Kitten, 1½" ....$ 15.00- 20.00
5. Musician, 6" ....$ 25.00- 40.00
6. Rabbit, 2¾" ....$ 15.00- 20.00
7. Rabbit, 2¾" ....$ 15.00- 20.00

Page 34

Brochure Page, Early Art
1. Flower Pot/Saucer, 6½" ....$ 30.00- 45.00
2. Flower Pot/Saucer, 6½" ....$ 30.00- 45.00
3. Jardinier, 6½" ....$ 30.00- 40.00
4. Jardinier, 6½" ....$ 30.00- 40.00

Page 35

Plate 4, Early Art
Row 1:
1. Vase, 5½" ....$ 22.00- 32.00
2. Vase, 8" ....$ 25.00- 35.00
3. Jardinier, 4" ....$ 18.00- 25.00

Row 2:
1. Vase, 7" ....$ 25.00- 35.00
2. Vase, 8" ....$ 20.00- 22.00
3. Vase, 7" ....$ 25.00- 35.00

Row 3:
1. Vase, 4½" ....$ 22.00- 32.00
2. Vase, 8" ....$ 25.00- 40.00
3. Vase, 8" ....$ 25.00- 40.00
4. Pitcher, 6½" ....$ 90.00-140.00

Row 4:
1. Jardinier, 7" ....$ 40.00- 60.00
2. Vase, 8" ....$ 25.00- 35.00
3. Vase, 8" ....$ 25.00- 40.00
4. Jardinier, 6½" ....$ 35.00- 50.00

Page 36

Brochure Page, Top, Early Art
1. Top, Jardinier, 3½" ...$ 15.00- 20.00
2. Top Right, Jardinier, 3½" ....$ 15.00- 20.00
3. Left, Jardinier, 3½" ...$ 15.00- 20.00
4. Center, Jardinier, 3½" $ 15.00- 20.00
5. Bottom Left, Jardinier, 3½" ....$ 12.00-15.00
6. Bottom Right, Jardinier, 2½" ....$ 15.00- 20.00

Brochure Page, Bottom
1. Vase, 7" ....$ 22.00- 32.00
2. Vase, 5½" ....$ 22.00- 32.00
3. Vase, 5" ....$ 22.00- 32.00

Page 37

Plate 5, Tile
1. Plain Tile, 4¼"x4¼" ..$ 14.00- 20.00
2. Decorated Border Tiles, 2⅞"x6" ....$ 30.00- 40.00

Plate 6, Early Art
1. Vase, 5" ....$ 22.00- 32.00
2. Vase, 5" ....$ 22.00- 32.00

Plate 7, Early Utility
Row 1:
1. Pitcher, 4¾" ....$ 20.00- 30.00
2. Bowl, 6" ....$ 15.00- 20.00
3. Pitcher, 4¼" ....$ 20.00- 30.00

Row 2:
1. Bowl, 5" ....$ 12.00- 15.00
2. Salt Box, 6" ....$ 48.00- 70.00
3. Pitcher, 3¾" ....$ 20.00- 30.00
4. Custard, 2½" ....$ 8.00- 12.00

Row 3:
1. Flower Pot/Saucer, 4" .$ 20.00- 28.00
2. Canister, 6½" ....$ 35.00- 50.00
3. Cruet, 6½" ....$ 35.00- 50.00
4. Spice Jar, 3½" ......$ 25.00- 35.00
5. Spice Jar, 3½" ......$ 25.00- 35.00

Page 39

Plate 8, Early Utility
Row 1:
1. Mug, 4½" ....$ 15.00- 20.00
2. Stein, 6½" ....$ 25.00- 40.00
3. Tankard, 9½" ....$ 95.00-140.00
4. Stein, 6½" ....$ 15.00- 20.00
5. Mug, 4¼" ....$ 22.00- 28.00

Row 2:
1. Mug, 4½" ....$ 18.00- 20.00
2. Pretzel Jar, 9½" .....$ 110.00-165.00
3. Pretzel Jar, 9½",sp.dec. ....$ 225.00-300.00
4. Mug, 5" ....$ 18.00- 20.00
5. Mug, 3¾" ....$ 18.00- 24.00

Row 3:
1. Covered Casserole, 7½" ....$ 25.00- 40.00
2. Bowl, 7" ....$ 12.00- 18.00
3. Bowl, 7" ....$ 18.00- 25.00
4. Bowl, 8" ....$ 15.00- 22.00

Row 4:
1. Bowl, 10" ....$ 30.00- 40.00
2. Nested Bowls, 5",6",7",8", and 9" ...$ 45.00- 70.00
3. Bowl, 7" ....$ 15.00- 18.00

Page 40

Plate 9, Utility
Row 1:
1. Bowl, 8" ....$ 18.00- 25.00

Row 2:
1. Jug, 6" ....$ 30.00- 40.00
2. Jardinier, 3" ....$ 16.00- 22.00
3. Bean Pot, 6" ....$ 25.00- 38.00

Row 3:
1. Flower Pot, 4" ....$ 18.00- 24.00
2. Bean Pot, 5" ....$ 18.00- 25.00

Brochure Page, Mardi Gras
Spanish Pots:
1. 3¼" ....$ 3.00- 5.00
2. 4¾" ....$ 5.00- 7.00
3. 6" ....$ 6.00- 10.00
4. 7" ....$ 12.00- 15.00
5. 8¼" ....$ 15.00- 20.00
6. 9½" ....$ 18.00- 25.00

Italian Pots:
1. 6¾" ....$ 6.00- 10.00
2. 7½" ....$ 12.00- 15.00
3. 8½" ....$ 15.00- 20.00

Flower Vases:
1. 6" ....$ 8.00- 12.00
2. 8" ....$ 12.00- 16.00
3. 10" ....$ 15.00- 22.00

Jardiniers:
1. 6" ....$ 10.00- 15.00
2. 7" ....$ 15.00-18.00
3. 8" ....$ 16.00- 22.00

Mixing Bowls:
1. 5¼" ....$ 4.00- 5.00
2. 6¼" ....$ 5.00- 8.00
3. 7¼" ....$ 6.00- 10.00
4. 8¼" ....$ 10.00- 15.00
5. 9¼" ....$ 15.00- 18.00
6. 10¼" ....$ 16.00- 22.00

Page 41

Plate 10, Utility
Row 1:
1. Bowl, 7" ....$ 16.00- 22.00
2. Bowl, 10" ....$ 25.00- 40.00
3. Bowl, 7" ....$ 15.00- 18.00

Nuline Bak-Serve
Row 2:
1. Pitcher, 7" ....$ 25.00- 35.00
2. Pitcher, 8½" ....$ 45.00- 75.00
3. Pitcher, 6" ....$ 28.00- 38.00

Row 3:
1. Custard, 2¾" ....$ 5.00- 8.00
2. Covered Casserole, 7½" ....$ 25.00- 35.00
3. Cookie Jar, 8" ....$ 35.00- 45.00
4. Bean Pot, 5½" ....$ 25.00- 40.00
5. Mug, 3½" ....$ 12.00- 18.00

Row 4:
1. Bowl, 10¼" ....$ 16.00- 22.00
2. Vase, 6" ....$ 8.00- 12.00
3. Vase, 6" ....$ 8.00- 12.00
4. Nested Bowls, 5",6",7",8", and 9" ...$ 45.00- 80.00

Page 42

Plate 11, Calla Lily
Row 1:
1. Bowl, 10" ....$ 55.00- 85.00

Row 2:
1. Vase, 6½" ....$ 35.00- 45.00
2. Console Bowl, 13" ....$ 50.00- 75.00

Page 43

Plate 12, Calla Lilly
Row 1:
1. Vase, 6" ....$ 35.00- 45.00
2. Cornucopia, 8" ....$ 35.00- 50.00
3. Vase, 5" ....$ 35.00- 45.00

Row 2:
1. Candleholder, 2¼" ...$ 30.00- 40.00
2. Vase, 8" ....$ 50.00- 75.00
3. Vase, 7" ....$ 50.00- 75.00
4. Candleholder, 2¼" ...$ 30.00- 40.00

Row 3:
1. Vase, 8" ....$ 50.00- 75.00
2. Vase, 13" ....$ 100.00-150.00
3. Ewer, 10" ....$ 100.00-150.00
4. Vase, 7½" ....$ 45.00- 65.00

Page 44

Plate 13, Sueno Tulip
1. Vase, 8" ....$ 45.00- 65.00
2. Vase, 10" ....$ 75.00-120.00

Brochure Page, Sueno
Row 1:
1. Vase, 9" ....$ 45.00- 65.00
2. Vase, 6½" ....$ 35.00- 45.00
3. Vase, 8½" ....$ 45.00- 65.00
4. Vase, 10½" ....$ 75.00-120.00
5. Vase, 6" ....$ 35.00- 45.00
6. Vase, 8" ....$ 45.00- 65.00

Row 2:
1. Basket, 6" ....$ 60.00-110.00
2. Vase, 6½" ....$ 60.00- 90.00
3. Bud Vase, 6" ....$ 35.00- 50.00
4. Vase, 8" ....$ 45.00- 65.00

Row 3:
1. Vase, 6½" ....$ 35.00- 45.00
2. Vase, 6½" ....$ 35.00- 45.00
3. Vase, 6½" ....$ 35.00- 45.00
4. Vase, 7" ....$ 38.00- 48.00
5. Ewer, 8" ....$ 65.00- 95.00
6. Ewer, 13" ....$ 135.00-180.00

Row 4:
1. Jardinier, 7" ....$ 90.00-140.00
2. Flower Pot/Saucer, 6" .$ 45.00- 75.00
3. Jardinier, 5" ....$ 35.00- 45.00
4. Cornucopia, 8" ....$ 35.00- 50.00

Row 5:
1. Vase, 6½" ....$ 25.00- 32.00
2. Vase, 6½" ....$ 25.00- 32.00
3. Vase, 6½" ....$ 25.00- 32.00
4. Vase, 6½" ....$ 25.00- 32.00
5. Vase, 6½" ....$ 35.00- 45.00

Page 45

Plate 14, Sueno Tulip

Row 1:
1. Vase, 6″ . . . . $ 35.00- 45.00
2. Vase, 6″ . . . . $ 35.00- 45.00
3. Vase, 6″ . . . . $ 35.00- 45.00

Row 2:
1. Bud Vase, 6″ . . . . $ 35.00- 50.00
2. Vase, 6½″ . . . . $ 35.00- 45.00
3. Basket, 6″ . . . . $ 60.00-110.00
4. Vase, 6″ . . . . $ 38.00- 48.00

Row 3:
1. Vase, 6″ . . . . $ 35.00- 45.00
2. Jardinier, 7″ . . . . $ 90.00-140.00
3. Flower Pot/Saucer, 6″ . $ 45.00- 75.00
4. Flower Pot/Saucer, 4¼″ . . . . $ 35.00- 45.00

Row 4:
1. Vase, 9″ . . . . $ 70.00- 95.00
2. Ewer, 13″ . . . . $ 135.00-180.00
3. Ewer, 8″ . . . . $ 65.00- 95.00
4. Vase, 6″ . . . . $ 60.00- 90.00

Page 46

Plate 15, Orchid
1. Bookends, 7″,(Pair) . . . $ 210.00-285.00
2. Basket, 7″ . . . . $ 110.00-175.00

Plate 16, Orchid
1. Jardinier, 6″ . . . . $ 65.00- 95.00
2. Console Bowl, 13″ . . . . $ 120.00-185.00

Page 47

Plate 17, Orchid

Row 1:
1. Vase, 4¼″ . . . . $ 30.00- 45.00
2. Vase, 6″ . . . . $ 35.00- 50.00
3. Vase, 6″ . . . . $ 30.00- 50.00
4. Vase, 4¾″ . . . . $ 30.00- 45.00

Row 2:
1. Jardinier, 4¾″ . . . . $ 35.00- 50.00
2. Vase, 4¾″ . . . . $ 30.00- 45.00
3. Bud Vase, 6¾″ . . . . . . $ 40.00- 65.00
4. Low Bowl, 7″ . . . . $ 40.00- 65.00

Row 3:
1. Vase, 6″ . . . . $ 35.00- 50.00
2. Candleholder, 4″ . . . . . $ 30.00- 50.00
3. Lamp Base, 10″ . . . . . . $ 160.00-230.00
4. Candleholder, 4″ . . . . . $ 30.00- 50.00
5. Vase, 6½″ . . . . $ 40.00- 60.00

Row 4:
1. Vase, 10″ . . . . $ 110.00-185.00
2. Vase, 10¾″ . . . . $ 110.00-185.00
3. Ewer, 13″ . . . . $ 170.00-250.00

Page 49

Plate 18, Iris

Row 1:
1. Vase, 7″ . . . . $ 45.00- 65.00
2. Vase, 8½″ . . . . $ 55.00- 85.00
3. Bud Vase, 7½″ . . . . . . $ 40.00- 65.00
4. Vase, 7″ . . . . $ 45.00- 65.00

Row 2:
1. Rose Bowl, 7″ . . . . $ 55.00- 80.00
2. Vase, 8½″ . . . . $ 50.00- 85.00
3. Vase, 8½″ . . . . $ 50.00- 85.00
4. Basket, 7″ . . . . $ 75.00-125.00

Row 3:
1. Vase, 8½″ . . . . $ 50.00- 85.00
2. Vase, 10½″ . . . . $ 95.00-165.00
3. Ewer, 13½″ . . . . $ 155.00-210.00
4. Vase, 10½″ . . . . $ 95.00-165.00

Page 50

Brochure Page

Row 1:
1. Vase, 5″ . . . . $ 18.00- 25.00
2. Vase, 5″ . . . . $ 18.00- 25.00
3. Vase, 5″ . . . . $ 18.00- 25.00
4. Advertising Plaque, 5″x11″ . . . . $ 600.00-850.00
5. Vase, 5″ . . . . $ 18.00- 25.00
6. Vase, 5″ . . . . $ 18.00- 25.00
7. Vase, 5″ . . . . $ 18.00- 25.00

Row 2:
1. Vase, 5″ . . . . $ 18.00- 25.00
2. Jardinier, 5″ . . . . $ 35.00- 45.00
3. Vase, 6½″ . . . . $ 25.00- 32.00
4. Vase, 6½″ . . . . $ 25.00- 32.00
5. Vase, 6½″ . . . . $ 25.00- 32.00
6. Vase, 6½″ . . . . $ 25.00- 32.00
7. Vase, 6½″ . . . . $ 35.00- 45.00
8. Bud Vase, 6″ . . . . $ 35.00- 50.00

Row 3:
1. Vase, 6½″ . . . . $ 35.00- 45.00
2. Cornucopia, 8″ . . . . $ 35.00- 50.00
3. Vase, 8″ . . . . $ 50.00- 75.00
4. Basket, 6″ . . . . $ 60.00-110.00
5. Flower Pot/Saucer, 6″ . $ 45.00- 75.00

Page 51

Plate 19, Iris

Row 1:
1. Vase, 4¾″ . . . . $ 30.00- 40.00
2. Vase, 4¾″ . . . . $ 30.00- 40.00
3. Advertising Plaque, 5″x11″ . . . . $ 600.00-850.00
4. Vase, 4¾″ . . . . $ 30.00- 40.00
5. Vase, 4¾″ . . . . $ 30.00- 40.00

Row 2:
1. Jardinier, 5½″ . . . . $ 38.00- 55.00
2. Ewer, 8″ . . . . $ 75.00-115.00
3. Ewer, 5″ . . . . $ 35.00- 48.00
4. Rose Bowl, 4″ . . . . $ 32.00- 45.00

Row 3:
1. Candleholder, 5″ . . . . . $ 30.00- 45.00
2. Console Bowl, 12″ . . . . $ 90.00-150.00
3. Candleholder, 5″ . . . . . $ 30.00- 45.00
4. Jardinier, 9″ . . . . $ 125.00-185.00

Row 4: **Thistle and Pinecone**
1. Vase, 6½″ . . . . $ 25.00- 32.00
2. Vase, 6½″ . . . . $ 25.00- 32.00
3. Vase, 6½″ . . . . $ 25.00- 32.00
4. Vase, 6½″ . . . . $ 25.00- 32.00
5. Vase, 6½″ . . . . $ 35.00- 45.00

Page 52

Brochure Page

Vases:
1. 6″ . . . . $ 8.00- 12.00
2. 8″ . . . . $ 12.00- 16.00
3. 10″ . . . . $ 15.00- 20.00
4. 12″ . . . . $ 18.00- 25.00

Jardiniers:
1. 3⅜″ . . . . $ 4.00- 5.00
2. 4¾″ . . . . $ 5.00- 6.00
3. 5½″ . . . . $ 6.00- 8.00
4. 6½″ . . . . $ 10.00- 15.00
5. 7¾″ . . . . $ 15.00- 18.00
6. 8¾″ . . . . $ 16.00- 22.00

Flower Pots/Saucers:
1. 3¾″ . . . . $ 4.00- 7.00
2. 4¾″ . . . . $ 5.00- 8.00
3. 5½″ . . . . $ 10.00- 12.00
4. 6½″ . . . . $ 12.00- 15.00
5. 7¾″ . . . . $ 15.00- 20.00
6. 8¾″ . . . . $ 18.00- 22.00

Round Jardiniers:
1. 6″ . . . . $ 10.00- 15.00
2. 7″ . . . . $ 15.00- 18.00
3. 8″ . . . . $ 16.00- 22.00

Hanging Baskets:
1. 4¾″ . . . . $ 10.00- 15.00
2. 6½″ . . . . $ 15.00- 22.00

Bottom:
1. Planter, 5½″ . . . . $ 20.00- 25.00
2. Planter, 5″ . . . . $ 20.00- 25.00
3. Planter, 5½″ . . . . $ 20.00- 25.00
4. Planter, 5½″ . . . . $ 20.00- 25.00

Page 53

Plate 20, Dogwood

Row 1:
1. Cornucopia, 3¾″ . . . . . $ 30.00- 42.00
2. Low Bowl, 7″ . . . . $ 40.00- 65.00
3. Window Box, 10½″ . . . $ 60.00- 95.00
4. Jardinier, 4″ . . . . $ 32.00- 40.00

Row 2:
1. Basket, 7½″ . . . . $ 80.00-140.00
2. Candleholder, 3¾″ . . . $ 30.00- 45.00
3. Console Bowl, 11½″ . . $ 90.00-125.00
4. Candleholder, 3¾″ . . . $ 30.00- 45.00

Row 3:
1. Ewer, 4¾″ . . . . $ 35.00- 48.00
2. Vase, 4¾″ . . . . $ 30.00- 40.00
3. Vase, 6½″ . . . . $ 35.00- 45.00
4. Ewer, 8½″ . . . . $ 70.00-110.00
5. Vase, 6½″ . . . . $ 60.00- 95.00
6. Vase, 4¾″ . . . . $ 30.00- 40.00

Row 4:
1. Vase, 10½″ . . . . $ 90.00-130.00
2. Ewer, 13½″ . . . . $ 225.00-300.00
3. Ewer, 11½″ . . . . $ 110.00-165.00
4. Vase, 6½″ . . . . $ 40.00- 60.00

Page 54

Plate 21, Poppy
1. Planter, 6½″ . . . . $ 50.00- 80.00
2. Basket, 12″ . . . . $ 210.00-300.00

Page 55

Plate 22, Poppy

Row 1:
1. Vase, 6½″ . . . . $ 40.00- 55.00
2. Basket, 9″ . . . . $ 125.00-200.00
3. Vase, 6½″ . . . . $ 40.00- 50.00

Row 2:
1. Lamp Base, 9″ . . . . $ 100.00-165.00
2. Ewer, 4¾″ . . . . $ 40.00- 50.00
3. Vase, 8½″ . . . . $ 65.00- 95.00

Row 3:
1. Vase, 10½″ . . . . $ 125.00-175.00
2. Ewer, 13½″ . . . . $ 225.00-325.00
3. Wall Pocket, 9″ . . . . . . $ 85.00-125.00

Page 56

Plate 23

Row 1:
1. Vase, 8½″ . . . . $ 65.00- 95.00
2. Teapot, 6½″ . . . . $ 90.00-155.00
3. Wall Pocket, 8½″ . . . . $ 110.00-160.00

Row 2:
1. Jardinier, 5″ . . . . $ 35.00- 45.00
2. Vase, 4″ . . . . $ 8.00- 10.00

Page 57

Plate 24, Open Rose (Camellia)

Row 1:
1. Vase, 6½″ . . . . $ 35.00- 48.00
2. Planter, 10½″ . . . . $ 175.00-250.00
3. Hanging Basket, 8″ . . . $ 70.00-100.00

Row 2:
1. Vase, 6½″ . . . . $ 35.00- 48.00
2. Vase, 6¼″ . . . . $ 35.00- 40.00
3. Ewer, 8½″ . . . . $ 70.00-115.00
4. Vase, 6¼″ . . . . $ 35.00- 42.00
5. Vase, 6¼″ . . . . $ 35.00- 42.00

Row 3:
1. Cornucopia, 8½″ . . . . . $ 45.00- 65.00
2. Vase, 4¾″ . . . . $ 20.00- 30.00
3. Vase, 8½″ . . . . $ 50.00- 75.00
4. Ewer, 4¾″ . . . . $ 30.00- 40.00
5. Vase, 8½″ . . . . $ 45.00- 65.00

Row 4:
1. Vase, 6¼″ . . . . $ 35.00- 40.00
2. Basket, 8″ . . . . $ 80.00-140.00
3. Ewer, 13¼″ . . . . $ 175.00-260.00
4. Ewer, 7″ . . . . $ 70.00- 95.00
5. Vase, 4¾″ . . . . $ 28.00- 32.00

Page 58

Plate 25, Open Rose (Camellia)
1. Bud Vase, 7″ . . . . $ 40.00- 60.00
2. Vase, 10½″ . . . . $ 95.00-160.00
3. Vase, 8½″ . . . . $ 45.00- 65.00

Page 59

Plate 26, Open Rose (Camellia)

Row 1:
1. Creamer, 5″ . . . . $ 24.00- 32.00
2. Teapot, 8½″ . . . . $ 90.00-140.00
3. Sugar, 5″ . . . . $ 24.00- 32.00
4. Basket, 6¼″ . . . . $ 60.00- 95.00

Row 2:
1. Candleholder, 6½" ...$ 40.00- 50.00
2. Console Bowl, 12" ....$ 95.00-155.00
3. Candleholder, 6½" ...$ 40.00- 50.00

Row 3:
1. Low Bowl, 7" ....$ 50.00- 65.00
2. Vase, 8½" ....$ 85.00-135.00
3. Vase, 8½" ....$ 50.00- 70.00
4. Vase, 6¼" ....$ 35.00- 45.00

Row 4:
1. Basket, 10½" ....$ 195.00-240.00
2. Jardinier, 8¼" ....$ 95.00-150.00
3. Vase, 8½" ....$ 50.00- 70.00

Page 61

Plate 27, Novelty

Row 1:
1. Flower Pot, 4½" .....$ 8.00- 10.00
2. Planter, 5" ....$ 20.00-25.00
3. Planter, 5½" ....$ 20.00- 25.00
4. Mug, 3" ....$ 12.00- 15.00

Row 2:
1. Basket Girl, gloss finish, 8" ....$ 20.00- 28.00
2. Dancing Girl, 7" ......$ 24.00- 30.00
3. Basket Girl, matte finish, 8" ....$ 24.00- 30.00

Row 3:
1. Pig Planter, 5" ....$ 20.00- 24.00
2. Rooster 7" ....$ 25.00- 35.00
3. Baby Planter, 6¼" ....$ 18.00- 24.00
4. Lamb Planter, 8" .....$ 18.00- 24.00

Row 4:
1. Kitten Planter, 7½" ...$ 20.00- 28.00
2. Cat Bank, 11" ....$ 55.00- 85.00
3. Cat Figural, 7" ....$ 50.00- 80.00

Page 63

Plate 28, Mardi Gras/Granada

Row 1:
1. Vase, 9" ....$ 20.00- 25.00
2. Vase, 9" ....$ 20.00- 25.00
3. Vase, 9" ....$ 20.00- 25.00
4. Planter, 6" ....$ 20.00- 25.00

Row 2:
1. Ewer, 10" ....$ 45.00- 65.00
2. Basket, 8" ....$ 45.00- 65.00
3. Basket, 8" ....$ 45.00- 65.00
4. Ewer, 10" ....$ 45.00- 65.00

Row 3:
1. Vase, 9" ....$ 20.00- 25.00
2. Ewer, 10", sp.dec. ....$ 65.00- 90.00
3. Ewer, 10½" ....$ 55.00- 80.00
4. Vase, 9" ....$ 20.00- 25.00

Page 64

Plate 29, Little Red Riding Hood
1. Teapot, 8" ....$ 100.00-160.00
2. Pitcher, 8" ....$ 100.00-160.00

Plate 30, Little Red Riding Hood
1. Shaker, Set, 5½" .....$ 45.00- 75.00

Page 65

Plate 31, Little Red Riding Hood

Row 1:
1. Shaker, 3¼" ....$ 12.00- 15.00
2. Shaker, 3¼" ....$ 12.00- 15.00
3. Shaker, 5¼" ....$ 20.00- 30.00
4. Mustard with Spoon, 5¼" ....$ 110.00-160.00
5. Shaker, 3¼" ....$ 12.00- 15.00
6. Shaker, 3¼" ....$ 12.00- 15.00

Row 2:
1. Casserole, 11¾" .....$ 150.00-250.00
2. Wall Pocket, 4¾" ....$ 20.00- 25.00

Row 3:
1. Pitcher, 7" ....$ 110.00-160.00
2. Covered Jar, 8½" ....$ 160.00-225.00
3. Covered Jar, 9" ......$ 160.00-225.00
4. Bank, 7" ....$ 225.00-275.00

Row 4:
1. Cookie Jar, 13" ......$ 80.00-120.00
2. Cookie Jar, 13" ......$ 80.00-120.00
3. Cookie Jar, 13" ......$ 80.00-120.00

Page 66

Plate 32, Novelty-Banks
1. Bank, 7" ....$ 35.00- 50.00

Page 67

Plate 33, Novelty-Banks

Row 1:
1. Piggy Bank, 3½" .....$ 20.00- 28.00
2. Pig Bottle, 7¾" ......$ 15.00- 22.00
3. Piggy Bank, 3½" .....$ 20.00- 28.00

Row 2:
1. Corky Piggy Bank, 5" .$ 25.00- 35.00
2. Elephant Bottle, 7¾" ..$ 15.00- 22.00
3. Corky Piggy Bank, 5" .$ 25.00-35.00

Row 3:
1. Corky Piggy Bank, 5" .$ 12.00- 15.00
2. Piggy Bank, 6" ....$ 12.00- 15.00
3. Piggy Lamp Base, 6" .$ 30.00- 40.00
4. Jumbo Corky Piggy Bank, 8" ....$ 15.00- 20.00

Row 4:
1. Piggy Bank, 14" ......$ 40.00- 60.00
2. Piggy Bank, 14" ......$ 40.00- 60.00

Page 68

Plate 34, Rosella
1. Vase, 5" ....$ 22.00- 30.00
2. Vase, 5" ....$ 22.00- 30.00

Page 69

Plate 35, Rosella

Row 1:
1. Sugar, Open, 5½" ....$ 22.00- 30.00
2. Vase, 6½" ....$ 30.00- 45.00
3. Ewer, 6½" ....$ 30.00- 45.00
4. Wall Pocket, 6½" ....$ 35.00- 50.00
5. Creamer, 5½" ....$ 22.00- 30.00

Row 2:
1. Vase, 6½" ....$ 24.00- 32.00
2. Vase, 6½" ....$ 24.00- 32.00
3. Basket, 7" ....$ 90.00-115.00
4. Vase, 6½" ....$ 24.00- 32.00

Row 3:
1. Cornucopia, 8½" .....$ 35.00- 50.00
2. Ewer, 7" ....$ 40.00- 60.00
3. Ewer, 7" ....$ 40.00- 60.00
4. Cornucopia, 8½" .....$ 35.00- 50.00

Row 4:
1. Vase, 8½" ....$ 35.00- 50.00
2. Ewer, 9½" ....$ 90.00-140.00
3. Vase, 8½" ....$ 35.00- 50.00

Page 71

Plate 36, Lamps

Row 1:
1. Lamp Base, 6" ....$ 25.00- 35.00

Row 2:
1. Lamp Base, 11" ......$ 165.00-210.00
2. Lamp Base, 13" ......$ 75.00-110.00
3. Lamp Base, 10¾" ....$ 175.00-240.00

Row 3:
1. Lamp Base, 6¾" .....$ 80.00-135.00
2. *Lamp Base, 14¾" sp.dec. ....$ 175.00-300.00
3. Lamp Base, 7¾" .....$ 50.00- 75.00
   *Decorated in usual colors, without castor's signature ....$ 145.00-210.00

Page 73

Plate 37, Magnolia Matte

Row 1:
1. Basket, 10½", sp. dec. ....$ 100.00-150.00
2. Vase, 10½" ....$ 55.00- 80.00
3. Basket, 10½" ....$ 90.00-140.00

Row 2:
1. Vase, 8½" ....$ 45.00- 60.00
2. Vase, 12¼" ....$ 80.00-125.00
3. Vase, 10½" ....$ 55.00- 80.00

Row 3:
1. Vase, 15" ....$ 160.00-220.00
2. Lamp Base, 12½" ....$ 150.00-210.00
3. Vase, 15" ....$ 160.00-220.00

Page 75

Plate 38, Magnolia Matte

Row 1:
1. Vase, 4¾" ....$ 22.00- 28.00
2. Double Cornucopia, 12" ....$ 60.00- 90.00
3. Ewer, 4¾" ....$ 25.00- 35.00

Row 2:
1. Vase, 6¼" ....$ 26.00- 38.00
2. Sugar, 3¾" ....$ 22.00- 28.00
3. Teapot, 6½" ....$ 65.00-100.00
4. Creamer, 3¾" ....$ 22.00- 28.00

Row 3:
1. Vase, 6¼" ....$ 26.00- 38.00
2. Vase, 6¼" ....$ 26.00- 38.00
3. Vase, 6¼" ....$ 26.00- 38.00
4. Ewer, 7" ....$ 45.00- 65.00

Row 4:
1. Vase, 12½" ....$ 90.00-130.00
2. Vase, 10½", sp.dec...$ 75.00-110.00
3. Vase, 12½" ....$ 90.00-130.00

Page 77

Plate 39, Magnolia Matte

Row 1:
1. Candleholder, 4" .....$ 20.00- 28.00
2. Console Bowl, 12" ....$ 60.00- 85.00
3. Candleholder, 4" .....$ 20.00- 28.00

Row 2:
1. Vase, 8½" ....$ 40.00- 60.00
2. Vase, 12½" ....$ 90.00-130.00
3. Vase, 8½" ....$ 40.00- 60.00

Row 3:
1. Vase, 8½" ....$ 45.00- 65.00
2. Ewer, 13½" ....$ 125.00-165.00
3. Cornucopia, 8½" .....$ 40.00- 60.00

Page 79

Plate 40, Magnolia Glass

Row 1:
1. Sugar, 3¾" ....$ 20.00- 24.00
2. Teapot, 6½" ....$ 60.00- 85.00
3. Creamer, 3¾" ....$ 20.00- 24.00

Row 2:
1. Ewer, 8½" ....$ 35.00- 45.00
2. Vase, 5½" ....$ 20.00- 24.00
3. Cornucopia, 8½" .....$ 30.00- 42.00

Row 3:
1. Candleholder, 4" .....$ 18.00- 22.00
2. Console Bowl, 13" ....$ 45.00- 65.00
3. Candleholder, 4" .....$ 18.00- 22.00

Row 4:
1. Vase, 8½" ....$ 26.00- 40.00
2. Ewer, 13½" ....$ 135.00-165.00
3. Vase, 12½" ....$ 60.00-90.00

Page 81

Plate 41, Magnolia Gloss

Row 1:
1. Vase, 6½" ....$ 25.00- 30.00
2. Basket, 10½" ....$ 85.00-130.00
3. Vase, 6½" ....$ 25.00- 30.00

Row 2:
1. Vase, 5½" ....$ 20.00- 28.00
2. Double Cornucopia, 12" ....$ 45.00- 65.00
3. Ewer, 5½" ....$ 25.00- 35.00

Row 3:
1. Vase, 8½" ....$ 40.00- 48.00
2. Vase, 12½" ....$ 60.00- 90.00
3. Vase, 10½" ....$ 40.00- 55.00

Page 82

Plate 42, Wildflower (Number Series)
1. Vase, 8½" ....$ 60.00- 95.00
2. Sugar, 4¾" ....$ 30.00- 45.00
3. Teapot, 8" ....$ 140.00-210.00
4. Creamer, 4¾" ....$ 35.00- 45.00

Page 83

Plate 43, Wildflower (Number Series)

Row 1:
1. Double Candleholder,4" ....$ 35.00- 45.00

2. Console Bowl, 12″ . . . . $ 95.00-160.00
3. Double Candleholder, 4″ . . . . $ 35.00- 45.00

Row 2:
1. Cornucopia, 6¼″ . . . . . $ 35.00- 50.00
2. Jardinier, 4″ . . . . $ 30.00- 42.00
3. Vase, 5¼″ . . . . $ 35.00- 45.00

Row 3:
1. Vase, 8½″ . . . . $ 95.00-150.00
2. Vase, 8½″ . . . . $ 50.00- 75.00
3. Vase, 5¼″ . . . . $ 35.00- 50.00

Row 4:
1. Vase, 10½″ . . . . $ 60.00- 85.00
2. Vase, 12″ sp.dec. . . . . $ 125.00-200.00
3. Ewer, 13½″ . . . . $ 175.00-210.00

Page 85

Plate 44, Wildflower

Row 1:
1. Vase, 5½″ . . . . $ 22.00- 28.00
2. Vase, 7½″ . . . . $ 35.00- 45.00
3. Cornucopia, 8½″ . . . . . $ 45.00- 65.00
4. Vase, 7½″ . . . . $ 35.00- 45.00
5. Ewer, 5½″ . . . . $ 30.00- 50.00

Row 2:
1. Vase, 6½″ . . . . $ 35.00- 45.00
2. Vase, 9½″ . . . . $ 50.00- 75.00
3. Vase, 9½″ . . . . $ 45.00- 65.00
4. Vase, 8½″ . . . . $ 45.00- 65.00

Row 3:
1. Vase, 12½″ . . . . $ 90.00-130.00
2. Lamp Base, 12½″ . . . . $ 95.00-145.00
3. Vase, 12½″ . . . . $ 90.00-130.00
4. Ewer, 13½″ . . . . $ 140.00-175.00

Page 86

Plate 45, Wildflower
1. Vase, 15½″ . . . . $ 130.00-200.00

Page 87

Plate 46, Wildflower

Row 1:
1. Vase, 5½″ . . . . $ 20.00- 30.00
2. Candleholder . . . . $ 20.00- 25.00
3. Console Bowl, 12″ . . . . $ 60.00- 90.00
4. Candleholder . . . . $ 20.00- 28.00

Row 2:
1. Cornucopia, 7½″ . . . . . $ 40.00- 45.00
2. Vase, 10½″ . . . . $ 60.00- 95.00
3. Vase, 6½″ . . . . $ 30.00- 45.00

Row 3:
1. Basket, 10½″ . . . . $ 90.00-140.00
2. Base, 10½″ . . . . $ 60.00- 85.00
3. Ewer, 8½″ . . . . $ 50.00- 80.00

Page 88

Brochure, Water Lily
1. Vase, L-1, 5½″ . . . . . . $ 22.00- 32.00
2. Vase, L-2, 5½″ . . . . . . $ 22.00- 32.00
3. Ewer, L-3, 5½″ . . . . . . $ 28.00- 40.00
4. Vase, L-4, 6½″ . . . . . . $ 30.00- 40.00
5. Vase, L-5, 6½″ . . . . . . $ 22.00- 32.00
6. Vase, L-6, 6½″ . . . . . . $ 22.00- 32.00
7. Cornucopia, L-7, 6½″ . $ 40.00- 45.00
8. Vase, L-8, 8½″ . . . . . . $ 45.00- 65.00
9. Vase, L-9, 8½″ . . . . . . $ 45.00- 65.00
10. Vase, L-10, 9½″ . . . . $ 55.00- 80.00
11. Vase, L-11, 9½″ . . . . $ 55.00- 80.00
12. Vase, L-12, 10½″ . . . $ 60.00- 95.00
13. Vase, L-13, 10½″ . . . $ 60.00- 95.00
14. Basket, L-14, 10½″ . . $ 95.00-145.00
15. Vase, L-15, 12½″ . . . $ 95.00-150.00
16. Vase, L-16, 12½″ . . . $ 90.00-135.00
17. Ewer, L-17, 13½″ . . . $ 155.00-190.00
18. Teapot, L-18, 6″ . . . . . $ 75.00-110.00
19. Creamer, L-19, 5″ . . . $ 20.00- 30.00
20. Sugar, L-20, 5″ . . . . . $ 20.00- 30.00
21. Console Bowl, L-21, 13½″ . . . . $ 80.00-125.00
22. Candleholder, L-22, 4½″ . . . . $ 22.00- 32.00
23. Jardinier, L-23, 5½″ . $ 40.00- 60.00
24. Jardinier, L-24, 8½″ . $ 90.00-140.00
25. Pot/Saucer, 5½″ . . . . $ 45.00- 65.00
26. Vase, L-A, 8½″ . . . . . $ 60.00-110.00
27. Double Cornucopia, L-27, 12″ . . . . $ 60.00- 95.00

Page 89

Plate 47, Water Lily

Row 1:
1. Cornucopia, 6½″ . . . . . $ 40.00- 45.00
2. Vase, 8½″ . . . . $ 45.00- 65.00
3. Vase, 6½″ . . . . $ 22.00- 32.00
4. Jardiniere, 5½″ . . . . . . $ 40.00- 60.00

Row 2:
1. Vase, 10½″ . . . . $ 60.00- 95.00
2. Jardinier, 8½″ . . . . $ 90.00-140.00
3. Vase, 10½″ . . . . $ 60.00- 95.00

Row 3:
1. Vase, 12½″ . . . . $ 95.00-150.00
2. Vase, 5½″ . . . . $ 22.00- 32.00
3. Ewer, 13½″ . . . . $ 155.00-190.00
4. Ewer, 5½″ . . . . $ 28.00- 40.00
5. Vase, 12½″ . . . . $ 90.00-135.00

Page 91

Plate 48, Water Lily

Row 1:
1. Creamer, 5″ . . . . $ 20.00- 30.00
2. Teapot, 6″ . . . . $ 75.00-110.00
3. Sugar, 5″ . . . . $ 20.00- 30.00
4. Vase, 5½″ . . . . $ 22.00- 32.00

Row 2:
1. Candleholder, 4½″ . . . $ 22.00- 32.00
2. Console Bowl, 13½″ . . $ 80.00-125.00
3. Candleholder, 4½″ . . . $ 22.00- 32.00
4. Vase, 6½″ . . . . $ 22.00- 32.00

Row 3:
1. Lamp Base, 7½″ . . . . . $ 60.00- 95.00
2. Vase, 9½″ . . . . $ 55.00- 80.00
3. Vase, 9½″ . . . . $ 55.00- 80.00
4. Vase, 6½″ . . . . $ 30.00- 40.00

Row 4:
1. Basket, 10½″ . . . . $ 95.00-145.00
2. Double Cornucopia, 12″ . . . . $ 60.00- 95.00
3. Vase, 8½″ . . . . $ 60.00-110.00

Page 92

Plate 49, Bow-Knot
1. Basket, 12″ . . . . $ 260.00-340.00

Page 93

Plate 50, Bow-Knot

Row 1:
1. Candleholder, 4″ . . . . . $ 30.00- 40.00
2. Console Bowl, 13½″ . . $ 90.00-160.00
3. Candleholder, 4″ . . . . . $ 30.00- 40.00

Row 2:
1. Cornucopia, 7½″ . . . . . $ 40.00- 60.00
2. Vase, 8½″ . . . . $ 50.00- 90.00
3. Vase, 8½″ . . . . $ 50.00- 90.00
4. Bell, 6½″ . . . . $ 50.00- 85.00
5. Bell, 6″ . . . . $ 50.00- 85.00

Row 3:
1. Jardinier, 5¾″ . . . . $ 50.00- 85.00
2. Flower Pot/Saucer, 6½″ . . . . $ 50.00- 85.00
3. Vase, 8½″ . . . . $ 50.00- 90.00
4. Vase, 6½″ . . . . $ 45.00- 75.00
5. Basket, 6½″ . . . . $ 80.00-110.00

Row 4:
1. Vase, 10½″ . . . . $ 110.00-175.00
2. Vase, 5″ . . . . $ 35.00- 45.00
3. Lamp Base, 12¾″ . . . . $ 110.00-175.00
4. Ewer, 5½″ . . . . $ 45.00- 60.00
5. Vase, 10½″ . . . . $ 110.00-175.00

Page 95

Plate 51, Bow-Knot

Row 1:
1. Cup/Saucer Wall Pocket, 6″ . . . . $ 50.00- 75.00
2. Wall Plaque, 10″ . . . . . $ 265.00-365.00
3. Pitcher Wall Pocket, 6″ $ 50.00- 75.00

Row 2:
1. Iron Wall Pocket, 6¼″ . $ 55.00- 90.00
2. Teapot, 6″ . . . . $ 140.00-190.00
3. Sugar, 4″ . . . . $ 35.00- 50.00
4. Creamer, 4″ . . . . $ 35.00- 50.00

Row 3:
1. Whisk Broom Wall Pocket, 8″ . . . . $ 50.00- 75.00
2. Double Cornucopia, 13″ . . . . $ 75.00-125.00
3. Vase, 6½″ . . . . $ 35.00- 50.00

Row 4:
1. Basket, 10½″ . . . . $ 180.00-275.00
2. Vase, 12½″ . . . . $ 175.00-230.00
3. Jardinier, 9⅜″ . . . . $ 265.00-325.00

Page 97

Plate 52, Cinderella

Row 1:
1. Casserole Dish, 7½″ . . $ 16.00- 22.00
Covered Casserole, 7½″ . . . . $ 22.00- 32.00
2. Pitcher, 16 oz. . . . . $ 25.00- 30.00

Row 2:
1. Creamer, 4½″ . . . . $ 16.00- 22.00
2. Teapot, 42 oz. . . . . $ 55.00- 85.00
3. Sugar, 4½″ . . . . $ 16.00- 22.00

Row 3:
1. Bowl, 7½″ . . . . $ 20.00- 28.00
2. Shaker, 3½″ . . . . $ 10.00- 15.00
3. Grease Jar, 32 oz. . . . . $ 25.00- 35.00
4. Shaker, 3½″ . . . . $ 10.00- 15.00

Row 4:
1. Pitcher, 32 oz. . . . . $ 28.00- 35.00
2. Bowl, 9½″ . . . . $ 25.00- 35.00
3. Teapot, 42 oz. . . . . $ 55.00- 85.00

Row 5:
1. Pitcher, 64 oz. . . . . . . $ 60.00- 80.00
2. Bowl, 9¾″ . . . . $ 40.00- 60.00
3. Pitcher, 64 oz . . . . $ 60.00- 80.00

Page 99

Plate 53, Woodland

Row 1:
1. Cornucopia, 5½″ . . . . . $ 28.00- 38.00
2. Cornucopia, 11″ . . . . . . $ 35.00- 50.00
3. Cornucopia, 6½″ . . . . . $ 30.00- 45.00

Row 2:
1. Ewer, 6½″ . . . . $ 40.00- 55.00
2. Vase, 7½″ . . . . $ 35.00- 45.00
3. Double Bud Vase, 8½″ $ 45.00- 70.00
4. Vase, 6½″ . . . . $ 30.00- 45.00

Row 3:
1. Vase, 7½″ . . . . $ 70.00-115.00
2. Vase, 5½″ . . . . $ 26.00- 36.00
3. Vase, 12½″ . . . . $ 185.00-225.00
4. Ewer, 5½″ . . . . $ 30.00- 45.00
5. Vase, 8½″ . . . . $ 55.00- 80.00

Page 100

The following prices apply only to pre-1950 matt Woodland shapes, open floral, front sides.

Brochure Page, Top Right, Woodland

Row 1:
1. Hanging Basket, 5½″ . $ 60.00-100.00
2. Vase, 12½″ . . . . $ 185.00-225.00

Row 2:
1. Candleholder, 3½″ . . . $ 35.00- 45.00
2. Console Bowl, 14″ . . . . $ 85.00-135.00
3. Candleholder, 3½″ . . . $ 35.00- 45.00

Brochure Page, Bottom Left

Row 1:
1. Vase, 5½″ . . . . $ 26.00- 36.00
2. Cornucopia, 5½″ . . . . . $ 28.00- 38.00
3. Ewer, 5½″ . . . . $ 30.00- 45.00
4. Vase, 6½″ . . . . $ 30.00- 45.00
5. Cornucopia, 6½″ . . . . . $ 30.00- 45.00

Row 2:
1. Cornucopia, 11″ . . . . . . $ 35.00- 50.00
2. Flower Pot/Saucer, 5¾″ . . . . $ 50.00- 80.00
3. Hanging Basket, 7½″ . $ 175.00-250.00

Row 3:
1. Vase, 10½" . . . .$ 95.00-130.00
2. Basket, 10½" . . . .$ 225.00-300.00
3. Planter, 10½" . . . .$ 45.00- 60.00
4. Jardinier, 9½" . . . .$ 225.00-300.00

Brochure Page, Bottom Right

Row 1:
1. Ewer, 6½" . . . .$ 40.00- 55.00
2. Jardinier, 5½" . . . .$ 45.00- 70.00
3. Vase, 7½" . . . .$ 35.00- 45.00
4. Basket, 8¾" . . . .$ 65.00- 95.00

Row 2:
1. Wall Pocket, 7½" . . . .$ 45.00- 70.00
2. Window Box, 10" . . . . .$ 40.00- 60.00
3. Double Bud Vase, 8½" $ 45.00- 70.00
4. Vase, 8½" . . . .$ 55.00- 80.00
5. Vase, 7½" . . . .$ 70.00-115.00

Row 3:
1. Dbl. Cornucopia, 14" . .$ 150.00-225.00
2. Sugar . . . .$ 35.00- 45.00
3. Creamer . . . .$ 35.00- 45.00
4. Teapot . . . .$ 160.00-210.00
5. Ewer, 13½" . . . .$ 185.00-285.00

Page 101

Plate 54, Woodland

Row 1:
1. Candleholder, 3½" . . .$ 35.00- 45.00
2. Console Bowl, 14" . . . .$ 85.00-135.00
3. Candleholder, 3½" . . .$ 35.00- 45.00

Row 2:
1. Window Box, 10" . . . . .$ 40.00- 60.00
2. Wall Pocket, 7½" . . . .$ 45.00- 70.00
3. Planter, 10½" . . . .$ 45.00- 60.00

Row 3:
1. Jardinier, 5½" . . . .$ 45.00- 70.00
2. Hanging Basket, 5½" .$ 60.00-100.00
3. Hanging Basket, 7½" .$ 175.00-250.00
4. Flower Pot/Saucer,
   5¾" . . . .$ 50.00- 80.00

Row 4:
1. Double Cornucopia, 14"
   . . . .$ 150.00-225.00
2. Basket, 8¾" . . . .$ 65.00-95.00
3. Basket, 10½" . . . .$ 225.00-300.00

Page 102

Brochure Page, Left, Woodland, Gloss

Row 1:
1. Cornucopia, 5½" . . . . .$ 18.00- 22.00
2. Ewer, 5½" . . . .$ 20.00- 30.00
3. Vase, 6½" . . . .$ 20.00- 30.00
4. Ewer, 6½" . . . .$ 25.00- 35.00

Row 2:
1. Cornucopia, 11" . . . . . .$ 25.00- 35.00
2. Flower Pot/Saucer,
   5¾" . . . .$ 28.00- 40.00

Row 3:
1. Wall Pocket, 7½" . . . .$ 28.00- 40.00
2. Window Box, 10" . . . . .$ 25.00- 35.00
3. Basket, 10½" . . . .$ 65.00-100.00
4. Ewer, 13½" . . . .$ 95.00-130.00

Brochure Page, Right

Row 1:
1. Jardinier, 5½" . . . .$ 28.00- 38.00
2. Vase, 6½" . . . .$ 24.00- 34.00
3. Basket, 8¾" . . . .$ 40.00- 55.00

Row 2:
1. Double Bud Vase, 8½" $ 30.00- 45.00
2. Vase, 8½" . . . .$ 35.00- 46.00
3. Vase, 10½" . . . .$ 35.00- 50.00

Row 3:
1. Teapot . . . .$ 40.00- 65.00
2. Sugar . . . .$ 14.00- 18.00
3. Creamer . . . .$ 14.00- 18.00
4. Console Bowl, 14" . . . .$ 40.00- 65.00
5. Candleholder, 3½" . . .$ 15.00- 20.00
6. Candleholder, 3½" . . .$ 15.00- 20.00

Page 103

Plate 55, Woodland

Row 1:
1. Vase, 8½" . . . .$ 40.00- 50.00
2. Candleholder, 3½" . . .$ 20.00- 30.00
3. Console Bowl, 14" . . . .$ 60.00- 80.00
4. Candleholder, 3½" . . .$ 20.00- 30.00

Row 2:
1. Cornucopia, 11" . . . . . .$ 25.00- 35.00
2. Window Box, 10" . . . . .$ 25.00- 35.00
3. Cornucopia, 5½" . . . . .$ 18.00- 22.00
4. Basket, 8¾" . . . .$ 35.00- 50.00

Row 3:
1. Flower Pot/Saucer,
   5¾" . . . .$ 28.00- 40.00
2. Sugar, 3½" . . . .$ 14.00- 18.00
3. Teapot, 6½" . . . .$ 40.00- 65.00
4. Creamer, 3½" . . . .$ 14.00- 18.00

Row 4:
1. Double Bud Vase, 8½" $ 30.00- 45.00
2. Vase, 6½" . . . .$ 24.00- 34.00
3. Ewer, 13½" . . . .$ 95.00-130.00
4. Ewer, 5½" . . . .$ 20.00- 30.00
5. Basket, 10½" . . . .$ 65.00-100.00

Page 104

Brochure Page, Parchment and Pine

Row 1:
1. Basket, S-3 . . . .$ 35.00- 45.00
2. Cornucopia, S-2 . . . . . .$ 20.00- 28.00
3. Planter, S-5 . . . .$ 25.00- 35.00
4. Vase, S-1 . . . .$ 18.00- 25.00

Row 2:
1. Creamer, S-12 . . . .$ 15.00- 20.00
2. Teapot, S-11 . . . .$ 40.00- 65.00
3. Sugar, S-13 . . . .$ 15.00- 20.00

Row 3:
1. Cornucopia, S-6 . . . . . .$ 40.00-60.00
2. Candleholder, S-10 . . .$ 15.00- 20.00
3. Console Bowl, S-9 . . . .$ 40.00- 60.00
4. Candleholder, S-6 . . . .$ 15.00- 20.00

Row 4:
1. Vase, S-4 . . . .$ 40.00- 60.00
2. Basket, S-8 . . . .$ 65.00- 95.00
3. Ewer, S-7 . . . .$ 70.00-100.00

Page 105

Plate 56, Parchment and Pine

Row 1:
1. Candleholder, 5" . . . . .$ 15.00- 20.00
2. Console Bowl, 16" . . . .$ 40.00- 60.00
3. Candleholder, 5" . . . . .$ 15.00- 20.00

Plate 57

1. Teapot, 6" sp.dec. . . . .$ 65.00- 85.00

Plate 58

Row 1:
1. Cornucopia, 7¾" . . . . .$ 20.00- 28.00
2. Basket, 16½" . . . .$ 65.00- 95.00
3. Teapot, 6" . . . .$ 40.00- 65.00

Row 2:
1. Ashtray, 14" . . . .$ 55.00- 80.00
2. Ewer, 14¼" . . . .$ 70.00-100.00
3. Teapot, 8" . . . .$ 45.00- 75.00

Page 106

Plate 59

Row 1:
1. Vase, 6½" . . . .$ 20.00- 25.00
2. Planter, 12½" . . . .$ 8.00- 12.00
3. Vase, 8¾" . . . .$ 22.00- 32.00

Row 2:
1. Vase, 8¾" . . . .$ 5.00- 7.00
2. Planter, 11¾" . . . .$ 12.00- 16.00
3. Vase, 9½" . . . .$ 4.00- 6.00

Page 107

Plate 60, Sunglow

Row 1:
1. Flower Pot, 5½" . . . . .$ 12.00- 16.00
2. Basket, 6½" . . . .$ 22.00- 32.00
3. Pitcher, 24 oz. . . . .$ 16.00- 24.00

Row 2:
1. Iron Wall Pocket, 6½" .$ 25.00- 35.00
2. Cup/Saucer Wall Pocket
   6¼" . . . .$ 22.00- 28.00
3. Ewer, 5½" . . . .$ 16.00- 20.00
4. Pitcher Wall Pocket,
   5½" . . . .$ 22.00- 28.00

Row 3:
1. Covered Casserole,
   7½" . . . .$ 25.00- 32.00
2. Shaker, 2¾" . . . .$ 5.00- 7.00
3. Grease Jar, 5½" . . . . .$ 16.00- 22.00
4. Shaker, 2¾" . . . .$ 5.00- 7.00

Row 4:
1. Vase, 5½" . . . .$ 15.00- 20.00
2. Vase, 6½" . . . .$ 20.00- 25.00
3. Vase, 8½" . . . .$ 22.00- 32.00
4. Vase, 8" . . . .$ 22.00- 32.00
5. Whisk Broom Wall
   Pocket, 8¼" . . . .$ 22.00- 28.00

Row 5:
1. Flower Pot, 7½" . . . . .$ 20.00- 28.00
2. Bowl, 9½" . . . .$ 20.00- 30.00
3. Pitcher, 7½" . . . .$ 40.00- 60.00

Page 108

Brochure Page, Just Right Kitchenware

Row 1:
1. Shaker Set, 3½" . . . . .$ 20.00- 30.00
2. Grease Jar, 5¾" . . . . .$ 25.00- 35.00
3. Nested Bowl,
   5",6",7",8",and 9" . . . . . .$ 50.00- 80.00

Row 2:
1. Lipped Mixing Bowl, 9" $ 40.00- 60.00
2. Cookie Jar, 8¾" . . . . .$ 50.00- 80.00

Row 3:
1. Salad Bowl, 10½" . . . .$ 30.00- 40.00
2. Cereal Bowl, 6" . . . . . .$ 8.00- 10.00
3. Nested Bowls,
   5",6",7",8", and 9" . . .$ 50.00- 80.00

Row 4:
1. Pitcher, 1 Quart . . . . . .$ 35.00- 45.00
2. Covered French
   Casserole . . . .$ 15.00- 22.00
3. Covered Casserole,
   7½" . . . .$ 35.00- 50.00

Page 109

Plate 61, Floral

Row 1:
1. Shaker, 3½" . . . .$ 5.00- 7.00
2. Grease Jar, 5¾" . . . . .$ 16.00- 24.00
3. Shaker, 3½" . . . .$ 5.00- 7.00

Row 2:
1. Salad Bowl, 10" . . . . . .$ 20.00- 25.00
2. Bowl, 5" . . . .$ 6.00- 8.00

Row 3:
1. Pitcher, 6" . . . .$ 20.00- 30.00
2. Cookie Jar, 8¾" . . . . .$ 30.00- 45.00
3. Bowl, 9" . . . .$ 20.00- 30.00

Utility

Row 4:
1. Cookie Jar, 8¾" . . . . .$ 30.00- 45.00
2. Cookie Jar, 8¾" . . . . .$ 22.00- 32.00
3. Cookie Jar, 8¾" . . . . .$ 50.00- 80.00

Row 5:
1. Bowl, 7½" . . . .$ 15.00- 20.00
2. Bowl, 7½" . . . .$ 20.00- 25.00
3. Bowl, 7½" . . . .$ 15.00- 20.00

Page 111

Plate 62, Crescent

Row 1:
1. Sugar, 4¼" . . . .$ 5.00- 8.00
2. Teapot, 7½" . . . .$ 35.00- 45.00
3. Creamer, 4¼" . . . .$ 5.00- 8.00

Row 2:
1. Shaker, 3½" . . . .$ 5.00- 7.00
2. Shaker, 3½" . . . .$ 5.00- 7.00
3. Cookie Jar, 9½" . . . . .$ 30.00- 40.00
4. Mug, 4¼" . . . .$ 6.00- 9.00

Row 3:
1. Bowl, 9" . . . .$ 15.00- 20.00
2. Bowl, 7" . . . .$ 10.00- 15.00
3. Bowl, 5" . . . .$ 5.00- 8.00

Row 4:
1. Divided Covered Casserole, 11½" . . . . .$ 25.00- 40.00
2. Bowl, 8½" . . . .$ 12.00- 18.00
3. Covered Casserole, 10" . . . .$ 30.00- 40.00

Page 112

Brochure Page, Ebb Tide

Row 1:
1. Cornucopia, 11¾" . . . .$ 35.00- 50.00
2. Pitcher, 14" . . . .$ 80.00-125.00

Row 2:
1. Candleholder, 2¾" . . .$ 8.00- 12.00
2. Console Bowl, 15¾"x9" . . . .$ 45.00- 80.00
3. Candleholder, 2¾" . . .$ 8.00- 12.00
4. Basket, 6¼" . . . .$ 35.00- 45.00
5. Basket, 16½" . . . .$ 65.00-100.00

Row 3:
1. Ashtray . . . .$ 35.00- 45.00
2. Vase, 7" . . . .$ 25.00- 35.00
3. Vase, 11" . . . .$ 35.00- 45.00
4. Vase, 9¼" . . . .$ 35.00- 50.00
5. Pitcher, 8¼" . . . .$ 35.00- 50.00

Row 4:
1. Teapot . . . .$ 60.00- 90.00
2. Sugar, 4" . . . .$ 20.00- 25.00
3. Creamer, 4" . . . .$ 20.00- 25.00
4. Bud Vase, 7" . . . .$ 22.00- 30.00
5. Cornucopia, 7½" . . . . .$ 35.00- 45.00

Page 113

Plate 63, Ebb Tide

Row 1:
1. Creamer, 4" . . . .$ 20.00- 25.00
2. Basket, 6¼" . . . .$ 35.00- 45.00
3. Sugar, 4" . . . .$ 20.00- 25.00

Row 2:
1. Candleholder, 2¾" . . .$ 8.00- 12.00
2. Console Bowl, 15¾" . .$ 45.00- 80.00
3. Candleholder, 2¾" . . .$ 8.00- 12.00

Row 3:
1. Basket, 16½" . . . .$ 65.00-100.00
2. Pitcher, 14" . . . .$ 80.00-125.00

Page 114

Brochure Page, Left, Blossom Flite

Row 1:
1. Pitcher, 6" . . . .$ 20.00- 30.00
2. Basket, 6" . . . .$ 22.00- 32.00
3. Pitcher, 8½" . . . .$ 35.00- 50.00
4. Basket, 8½" . . . .$ 45.00- 70.00
5. Vase, 10½" . . . .$ 40.00- 60.00

Row 2:
1. Creamer . . . .$ 15.00- 20.00
2. Teapot . . . .$ 40.00- 65.00
3. Sugar . . . .$ 15.00- 20.00
4. Planter, 10½" . . . .$ 30.00- 45.00

Row 3:
1. Basket, 10" . . . .$ 50.00- 75.00
2. Cornucopia, 10½" . . . .$ 30.00- 40.00
3. Basket, 8¼" . . . .$ 45.00- 70.00

Row 4:
1. Candleholder, 3" . . . . .$ 16.00- 20.00
2. Console Bowl, 16½" . .$ 45.00- 60.00
3. Candleholder, 3" . . . . .$ 16.00- 20.00
4. Ewer, 13½" . . . .$ 65.00- 95.00

Page 115

Plate 64, Classic

Row 1:
1. Vase, 6" . . . .$ 12.00- 16.00
2. Vase, 6" . . . .$ 12.00- 16.00
3. Ewer, 6" . . . .$ 12.00- 16.00
4. Vase, 6" . . . .$ 12.00- 16.00

Blossom Flite

Row 2:
1. Candleholder, 3" . . . . .$ 16.00- 20.00
2. Console Bowl, 16½" . .$ 45.00- 60.00
3. Candleholder, 3" . . . . .$ 16.00- 20.00

Row 3:
1. Basket, 6" . . . .$ 22.00- 32.00
2. Planter, 10½" . . . .$ 30.00- 45.00
3. Teapot, 8¼" . . . .$ 40.00- 65.00

Row 4:
1. Basket, 10" . . . .$ 50.00- 75.00
2. Ewer, 13½" . . . .$ 65.00- 95.00

Page 116

Plate 65, Butterfly
1. Serving Tray, 11½" . . .$ 35.00- 45.00

Brochure Page, Left, Butterfly

*Row 1:**
1. Bud Vase, 6¼" . . . .$ 20.00- 30.00
2. Cornucopia, 6¼" . . . . .$ 20.00- 25.00
3. Ashtray, 7" . . . .$ 20.00- 26.00
4. Bon Bon Dish, 6½" . . .$ 12.00- 16.00
5. Jardinier, 6" . . . .$ 20.00- 24.00

Row 2:
1. Flower Dish, 9¾" . . . .$ 20.00- 25.00
2. Window Box, 12¾" . . .$ 20.00- 30.00
3. Urn, 5½" . . . .$ 20.00- 25.00

Row 3:
1. Vase, 7" . . . .$ 20.00- 25.00
2. Basket, 8" . . . .$ 40.00- 60.00
3. Pitcher, 8¾" . . . .$ 40.00- 65.00

Row 4:
1. Lavabo, 16", (in original hanger . . . . $ 65.00- 95.00
2. Vase, 10½" . . . .$ 35.00- 50.00
3. Cornucopia, 10½" . . . .$ 30.00- 40.00
4. Pitcher, 13½" . . . .$ 70.00-100.00

Brochure Page, Right

Row 1:*
1. Creamer 1 16.00- 22.00
2. Teapot . . . .$ 50.00- 85.00
3. Sugar . . . .$ 16.00- 22.00

Row 2:
1. Serving Tray, 11½" . . .$ 45.00- 65.00
2. Vase, 9" . . . .$ 20.00- 30.00
3. Fruit Bowl, 10½" . . . . .$ 35.00- 50.00

Row 3:
1. Basket, 10½" . . . .$ 65.00-100.00
2. Candleholder . . . .$ 15.00- 20.00
3. Console Bowl . . . .$ 40.00- 60.00
4. Candleholder . . . .$ 15.00- 20.00

Page 117

Plate 66, Butterfly

Row 1:
1. Lavabo, 16", (In original hanger) . . . . $ 65.00- 95.00

Row 2:
1. Ashtray, 7" . . . .$ 20.00- 26.00
2. Pitcher, 8¾" . . . .$ 40.00- 65.00

Row 3:
1. Vase, 7" . . . .$ 20.00- 25.00
2. Pitcher, 13½" . . . .$ 70.00-100.00

Page 118

Plate 67, Serenade

Row 1:
1. Candleholders, 6½"(Pair) . . . .$ 36.00- 46.00
2. Fruit Bowl, 7" . . . .$ 40.00- 60.00

Brochure Page, Left, Serenade

Row 1:
1. Pitcher, 10½" . . . .$ 45.00- 70.00
2. Mug, 8 oz. . . . .$ 25.00- 35.00

Row 2:
1. Vase, 14" . . . .$ 40.00- 55.00
2. Ewer, 13¼" . . . .$ 125.00-180.00
3. Basket, 12"x11½" . . . .$ 110.00-170.00

Row 3:
1. Candleholder, 6½" . . .$ 18.00- 23.00
2. Fruit Bowl, 7" . . . .$ 40.00- 60.00
3. Candleholder, 6½" . . .$ 18.00- 23.00
4. Ashtray, 13"x10½" . . .$ 35.00- 45.00

Brochure Page, Right

Row 1:
1. Vase, 6½" . . . .$ 20.00- 26.00
2. Ewer, 6½" . . . .$ 25.00- 35.00
3. Urn, 5" . . . .$ 20.00- 30.00
4. Basket, 6¾" . . . .$ 30.00- 40.00
5. Vase, 5¼" . . . .$ 30.00- 40.00

Row 2:
1. Vase, 8½" . . . .$ 30.00- 40.00
2. Vase, 8½" . . . .$ 30.00- 40.00
3. Ewer, 8½" . . . .$ 30.00- 45.00
4. Candy Dish, 8¼" . . . . .$ 40.00- 60.00

Row 3:
1. Window Box,12½" . . . .$ 25.00- 35.00
2. Cornucopia, 11" . . . . . .$ 30.00- 40.00
3. Cornucopia, 11" . . . . . .$ 30.00- 40.00
4. Vase, 10½" . . . .$ 35.00- 50.00

Row 4:
1. Creamer, 3¼" . . . .$ 18.00- 25.00
2. Teapot, 5" . . . .$ 55.00- 85.00
3. Sugar, 3¼" . . . .$ 18.00- 25.00
4. Covered Casserole, 9" $ 35.00- 50.00

Page 119

Plate 68, Serenade

Row 1:
1. Vase, 6½" . . . .$ 20.00- 26.00
2. Ewer, 6½" . . . .$ 25.00- 35.00

Row 2:
1. Sugar, 3¼" . . . .$ 18.00- 25.00
2. Teapot, 5" . . . .$ 55.00- 85.00
3. Creamer, 3¼" . . . .$ 18.00- 25.00

Row 3:
1. Vase, 5¼" . . . .$ 30.00- 40.00
2. Ashtray, 13"x10½" . . .$ 35.00- 45.00
3. Candy Dish, 8¼" . . . . .$ 40.00- 60.00

Row 4:
1. Basket, 12"x11½" . . . .$ 110.00-170.00
2. Ewer, 13¼" . . . .$ 125.00-180.00
3. Pitcher, 10½" . . . .$ 45.00- 70.00

Page 120

Plate 69
1. Flower Frog, 10½" . . .$ 25.00- 35.00

Page 121

Plate 70, Novelty

Row 1:
1. Poodle Planter, 8" . . . .$ 20.00- 30.00
2. Planter, 10" . . . .$ 10.00- 12.00
3. Giraffe Planter, 8" . . . .$ 20.00- 30.00

Row 2:
1. Wall Pocket, 10½" . . .$ 20.00- 30.00
2. Vase, 8" . . . .$ 22.00- 35.00
3. Planter, 10½" . . . .$ 16.00- 20.00

Row 3:
1. Duck, 3½" . . . .$ 15.00- 20.00
2. Duck, 5"x7" . . . .$ 20.00- 28.00
3. Duck, 7" x 9" . . . .$ 25.00- 40.00
4. Wall Pocket, 6½" . . . .$ 25.00- 35.00

Row 4:
1. Leaf, 13" . . . .$ 16.00- 22.00
2. Planter, 9"x10½" . . . .$ 25.00- 35.00
3. Vase, 9¼" . . . .$ 18.00- 22.00

Page 123

Plate 71, Novelty

Row 1:
1. Baby Shoes, 3½" . . . .$ 25.00- 35.00
2. Clown Planter, 6¼" . . .$ 16.00- 22.00
3. Teddy Bear Planter, 7" $ 16.00- 22.00
4. Colt Figurine, 5½" . . . .$ 20.00- 28.00

Plate 72, Novelty

Row 1:
1. Siamese Cats, 5¾" . . .$ 35.00- 50.00

Row 2:
1. Love Birds Planter, 6" .$ 18.00- 24.00
2. Knight Planter, 8" . . . .$ 30.00- 40.00
3. Duck Candleholder, 3½" . . . .$ 18.00- 22.00

Row 3:
1. Basket, 8" . . . .$ 30.00- 45.00
2. Vase, 9" . . . .$ 30.00- 40.00
3. Basket, 6½" . . . .$ 25.00- 35.00

Page 124

Brochure Page: Novelty

Row 1:
1. Parrot Planter, 9½" . . .$ 20.00- 30.00
2. Pheasant Planter, 8" . .$ 20.00- 30.00
3. Pig Planter, 8" . . . .$ 14.00- 18.00
4. Little Girl Planter . . . . .$ 12.00- 15.00

Row 2:
1. Dog Planter, 8″ ...... $ 12.00- 15.00
2. Kitten Planter .... $ 12.00- 15.00
Row 3:
1. Little Girl Planter, 5½″ $ 12.00- 15.00
2. Little Boy Planter, 5½″ $ 12.00- 15.00
3. Elephant Planter ..... $ 10.00- 12.00
4. Elephant Planter ..... $ 10.00- 12.00
Row 4:
1. Wall Pocket......... $ 20.00- 30.00
2. Basket, 6½″ .... $ 20.00- 30.00
3. Baby Planter, 5½″ .... $ 14.00- 18.00
4. Baby Planter, 5½″ .... $ 14.00- 18.00
Row 5:
1. Vase, 10½″ .... $ 18.00- 25.00
2. Vase, 8¾″ .... $ 22.00- 32.00
3. Vase, 8¼″ .... $ 12.00- 15.00

Page 125

Plate 73, Novelty
Row 1:
1. Parrot Planter, 9½″ ... $ 20.00- 30.00
2. Geese Planter, 7¼″ .. $ 18.00- 26.00
3. Baby Planter, 5½″ .... $ 14.00- 18.00
4. Little Girl Planter, 5½″ $ 14.00- 18.00
Row 2:
1. Parrot Planter, 12½″ .. $ 25.00- 35.00
2. Dog Planter, 8″ ...... $ 12.00- 15.00
3. Pig Planter, 8″ .... $ 12.00- 15.00
Row 3:
1. Poodle Planter, 6¼″ .. $ 20.00- 30.00
2. Dachshund Figural, 6x14″ .... $ 45.00- 65.00
3. Kitten Planter, 6¼″ ... $ 20.00- 30.00
Row 4:
1. Vase, 8¼″ .... $ 12.00- 15.00
2. Planter, 12¼″ .... $ 25.00- 35.00
3. Vase, 10½″ .... $ 18.00- 25.00
4. Pheasant Planter, 8″ .. $ 20.00- 30.00

Page 126

Plate 74
Row 1:
1. Bud Vase, 9½″ ...... $ 20.00- 30.00
2. Vase, 4¼″ .... $ 10.00- 12.00
Row 2:
1. Console Bowl, 14½″ .. $ 25.00- 35.00
2. Wall Pocket, 8″ ...... $ 45.00- 65.00

Page 127

Plate 75, Royal
Row 1:
1. Wall Pocket, 7½″ .... $ 22.00- 28.00
2. Lavabo, 16″ (In original hanger) .... $ 40.00- 65.00
3. Vase, 7″ .... $ 16.00- 22.00
Row 2:
1. Cornucopia, 11″ ...... $ 20.00- 25.00
2. Window Box, 12½″ ... $ 12.00- 15.00
Row 3:
1. Basket, 8¾″ .... $ 25.00- 35.00
2. Vase, 10¾″ .... $ 25.00- 35.00
3. Ewer, 13½″ .... $ 50.00- 80.00
4. Jardinier, 7″ .... $ 20.00- 30.00

Page 129

Plate 76
Row 1:
1. Candy Dish, 6¾″ ..... $ 20.00- 25.00
2. Conch Shell, 7¼″ .... $ 15.00- 20.00
3. Jardinier, 6″ .... $ 16.00- 24.00
Row 2:
1. Window Box, 12½″ ... $ 15.00- 20.00
2. Window Box, 13″ ..... $ 12.00- 16.00
Row 3:
1. Planter, 13″ .... $ 18.00- 22.00
2. Double Bud Vase, 9″ .. $ 20.00- 30.00
3. Basket, 6¼″ .... $ 20.00- 25.00
Row 4:
1. Vase, 10½″ .... $ 50.00- 80.00
2. Fruit Bowl, 5¼″x10¼″ $ 20.00- 25.00
3. Vase, 12″ .... $ 16.00- 20.00

Page 130

Brochure Page, Left, Fiesta
Row 1:
1. Flower Pot, 4¼″ ..... $ 10.00- 12.00
2. Jardinier, 6″ .... $ 16.00- 24.00
3. Vase, 8½″ .... $ 25.00- 35.00
4. Vase, 5″x6½″ .... $ 25.00- 35.00
Row 2:
1. Jardinier, 6½″ .... $ 16.00- 24.00
2. Ewer, 8¾″ .... $ 25.00- 35.00
3. Cornucopia, 8½″ ..... $ 25.00- 35.00
Row 3:
1. Vase, 9½″ .... $ 30.00- 40.00
2. Garden Dish, 12½″ ... $ 20.00- 30.00

Brochure Page, Right
Row 1:
1. Madonna, 11½″ ...... $ 20.00- 32.00
2. St. Frances, 11½″ .... $ 20.00- 32.00
3. Urn, 5¾″ .... $ 8.00- 10.00
Row 2:
1. Jardinier, 6″ with Brass Stand .... $ 14.00- 18.00
2. Jardinier, 8″ with Brass Stand .... $ 15.00- 22.00
3. Jardinier, 7″ with Brass Stand .... $ 22.00- 35.00
4. Jardinier, 8″ with Brass Stand .... $ 20.00- 32.00
Row 3:
1. Jardinier, 10″ with Brass Stand .... $ 25.00- 35.00
2. Jardinier, 5½″ with Brass Stand .... $ 14.00- 18.00
3. Ashtray/Planter Combination, 26½″ .... $ 30.00- 45.00

Page 131

Plate 77
Row 1:
1. Urn, 4½″ .... $ 6.00- 10.00
2. Vase, 9″ .... $ 15.00- 18.00
3. Planter, 7¾″ .... $ 15.00- 18.00
Row 2:
1. Planter, 10¼″ .... $ 12.00- 16.00
2. Cornucopia, 8½″ ..... $ 25.00- 35.00
3. Vase, 6″ .... $ 15.00- 18.00
Row 3:
1. Basket, 12½″ .... $ 25.00- 35.00
2. Basket, 12½″ .... $ 20.00- 25.00
Row 4:
1. Bulb Bowls, 3¼″x7″ .. $ 15.00- 18.00
2. Vase, 9½″ .... $ 15.00- 20.00
3. Vase, 12″ .... $ 18.00- 24.00
4. Bulb Bowls, 3¼x10½″ $ 15.00- 18.00

Page 133

Plate 78
Row 1:
1. Flower Pot, 4¼″ ..... $ 10.00- 12.00
2. Basket, 7″ .... $ 20.00- 25.00
3. Planter 4½″ .... $ 6.00- 9.00
4. Bowl, 6″ .... $ 5.00- 8.00
Row 2:
1. Window Box, 12½″ ... $ 15.00- 25.00
2. Flower Pot, 3½″ ..... $ 3.00- 5.00
3. Planter, 12½″ .... $ 18.00- 22.00
Row 3:
1. Cornucopia, 10″ ...... $ 18.00- 22.00
2. Candy Dish, 9″ ...... $ 20.00- 30.00
3. Telephone Planter, 9″ . $ 30.00- 45.00
4. Planter 6¾″ .... $ 12.00- 18.00
Row 4:
1. Planter, 11¼″ .... $ 30.00- 40.00
2. Vase, 15″ .... $ 16.00- 22.00
3. Ashtray, 7″ .... $ 15.00- 20.00
4. Urn, 5″ .... $ 3.00- 5.00

Page 134

Brochure Page, Left, Tokay
*Row 1**:*
1. Cornucopia, 11″ ...... $ 25.00- 35.00
2. Basket, 10½″ .... $ 40.00- 65.00
3. Ewer, 12″ .... $ 90.00-140.00
Row 2:
1. Vase, 6″ .... $ 16.00- 24.00
2. Ewer, 8″ .... $ 30.00- 50.00
3. Cornucopia, 6½″ ..... $ 16.00- 24.00
Row 3:
1. Basket, 12″ .... $ 50.00- 80.00
2. Vase, 12″ .... $ 30.00- 45.00
3. Basket, 8″ .... $ 30.00- 40.00

Brochure Page, Right
Row 1:
1. Creamer .... $ 20.00- 30.00
2. Teapot.............. $ 50.00- 90.00
3. Sugar .... $ 20.00- 30.00
4. Candy Dish, 7″x8½″ .. $ 35.00- 55.00
Row 2:
1. Consolette, 15¾″ ..... $ 50.00- 90.00
2. Urn, 5½″ .... $ 22.00- 30.00
Row 3:
1. Vase, 8¼″ .... $ 25.00- 35.00
2. Vase, 10″ .... $ 30.00- 50.00
3. Fruit Bowl, 9½″ ..... $ 50.00- 90.00

Page 135

Plate 79, Tokay/Tuscany
Row 1:
1. Urn, 5½″ .... $ 22.00- 30.00
2. Creamer .... $ 20.00- 30.00
3. Sugar .... $ 20.00- 30.00
Row 2:
1. Cornucopia, 11″ ...... $ 25.00- 35.00
2. Ewer, 8″ .... $ 30.00- 50.00
3. Candy Dish, 7″x8½″ .. $ 35.00- 55.00
Row 3:
1. Vase, 10″ .... $ 30.00- 50.00
2. Leaf, 13″ .... $ 22.00- 32.00
3. Vase, 8¼″ .... $ 25.00- 35.00
Row 4:
1. Vase, 12″ .... $ 30.00- 45.00
2. Basket, 10½″ .... $ 40.00- 65.00
3. Ewer, 12″ .... $ 90.00-140.00

Page 136

Brochure Page, Tuscany
*Row 1***:*
1. Cornucopia, 6½″ ..... $ 16.00- 24.00
2. Vase, 6″ .... $ 16.00- 24.00
3. Ewer, 8″ .... $ 30.00- 50.00
4. Vase, 8¼″ .... $ 25.00- 35.00
5. Urn, 5½″ .... $ 22.00- 30.00
Row 2:
1. Basket, 8″ .... $ 30.00- 40.00
2. Fruit Bowl, 9½″ ..... $ 50.00- 90.00
3. Vase, 10″ .... $ 30.00- 50.00
4. Candy Dish, 7″x8½″ .. $ 35.00- 55.00
Row 3:
1. Cornucopia, 11″ ...... $ 25.00- 35.00
2. Basket, 10½″ .... $ 40.00- 65.00
3. Vase, 12″ .... $ 30.00- 45.00
4. Ewer, 12″ .... $ 90.00-140.00
Row 4:
1. Consolette, 15¾″ ..... $ 50.00- 90.00
2. Basket, 12″ .... $ 50.00- 80.00
3. Creamer .... $ 20.00- 30.00
4. Teapot.............. $ 50.00- 90.00
5. Sugar .... $ 20.00- 30.00

Page 137

Plate 80
1. Basket, 8″ .... $ 25.00- 45.00

Plate 81
1. Vase, 10″ .... $ 22.00- 32.00

Plate 82
Row 1:
1. Plate, 10½″ .... $ 8.00- 10.00
2. Pitcher, 8½″ .... $ 30.00- 55.00
Row 2:
1. Mug, 3¼″ .... $ 5.00- 6.00
2. Bowl, 5¼″ .... $ 4.00- 5.00
3. Saucer, 8¼″ .... $ 4.00- 5.00

Page 138

Brochure Page, Heritageware
Row 1:
1. Salad Bowl, 10″ ...... $ 12.00- 18.00

2. Bowl, 5¾″ .... $ 3.00- 5.00
Row 2:
1. Cookie Jar, 9¼″ ..... $ 35.00- 45.00
2. Nested Bowl, 6½″,7½″ and 8½″ .... $ 22.00- 32.00
3. Cruet Set, 6¼″ ...... $ 26.00- 36.00
4. Mug, 9 oz. .... $ 2.00- 3.00
5. Bowl, 7½″ .... $ 6.00- 8.00
6. Pitcher, 7″ .... $ 15.00- 20.00
7. Pitcher, 4½″ .... $ 12.00- 15.00
Row 3:
1. Cov. Casserole, 9½″ .. $ 20.00- 25.00
2. Grease Jar, 5¾″ ..... $ 20.00- 25.00
3. Shaker, 3½″ .... $ 4.00- 6.00
4. Shaker, 3½″ .... $ 4.00- 6.00

Page 139

Plate 83
Row 1:
1. Leaf, 8¾″ .... $ 6.00- 10.00
2. Bowl, 6½″ .... $ 4.00- 6.00
3. Leaf, 8¾″ .... $ 6.00- 10.00

Heritageware/Marcrest
Row 2:
1. Cruet, 6¼″ .... $ 13.00- 18.00
2. Cruet, 6¼″ .... $ 13.00- 18.00
3. Cookie Jar, 9¼″ ..... $ 35.00- 42.00
4. Grease Jar, 5¾″ ..... $ 20.00- 25.00
5. Shaker, 3½″ .... $ 4.00- 6.00
6. Shaker, 3½″ .... $ 4.00- 6.00
Row 3:
1. Mug, 3¼″ .... $ 2.00- 3.00
2. Mug, 3¼″ .... $ 2.00- 3.00
3. Pitcher, 7½″ .... $ 16.00- 22.00
4. Mug, 3¼″ .... $ 2.00- 3.00
5. Pitcher, 4½″ .... $ 12.00- 15.00
Row 4:
1. Pitcher, 7¾″ .... $ 25.00- 35.00
2. Cookie Jar, 9¼″ ..... $ 35.00- 45.00
3. Pitcher, 7″ .... $ 15.00- 20.00

Page 140

Plate 84, Continental/Tropicana
1. Basket, 12¾″ .... $ 45.00- 70.00
2. Planter, 15½″ .... $ 20.00- 25.00
3. Ewer, 12½″ .... $ 195.00-255.00

Brochure Page, Tropicana
Row 1:
1. Vase, 14½″ .... $ 110.00-195.00
2. Ewer, 12½″ .... $ 195.00-255.00
Row 2:
1. Basket, 12¾″ .... $ 160.00-225.00
2. Vase, 12½″ .... $ 120.00-215.00
Row 3:
1. Vase, 8½″ .... $ 90.00-155.00
2. Flower Bowl, 15½″ ... $ 90.00-155.00
Row 4:
1. Ashtray, 10″x7½″ .... $ 85.00-145.00

Page 141

Plate 85
Row 1:
1. Ashtray, 7″ .... $ 10.00- 12.00
2. Ashtray, 11¾″ .... $ 18.00- 22.00
3. Ashtray, 8″ .... $ 10.00- 15.00
Row 2:
1. Ashtray, 7″ .... $ 10.00- 15.00
2. Ashtray, 7″ .... $ 10.00- 12.00
3. Ashtray, 7″ .... $ 10.00- 12.00
4. Ashtray, 7″ .... $ 10.00- 12.00
Row 3:
1. Leaf, 10″ .... $ 10.00- 15.00
2. Leaf, 12¼″ .... $ 15.00- 20.00
3. Leaf, 7¼″ .... $ 4.00- 6.00
Row 4:
1. Leaf, 14″ .... $ 18.00- 25.00
2. Leaf, 14″ .... $ 18.00- 25.00

Page 142

Brochure Page, Top, Continental
Row 1:
1. Vase, 10″ .... $ 20.00- 25.00
2. Bud Vase, 9½″ ...... $ 20.00- 25.00
3. Consolette, 13¼″ ..... $ 30.00- 40.00
4. Vase, 9¾″ .... $ 18.00- 22.00
5. Vase, 12″ .... $ 28.00- 32.00
Row 2:
1. Flower Bowl, 9¼″ .... $ 20.00- 24.00
Row 3:
1. Ashtray, 12″ .... $ 25.00- 35.00
2. Ashtray, 13″ .... $ 25.00- 35.00

Brochure Page, Bottom Left
Row 1:
1. Vase, 15″ .... $ 25.00- 30.00
2. Vase, 15″ .... $ 25.00- 35.00
3. Leaf, 14″ .... $ 18.00- 25.00
Row 2:
1. Candy Dish, 8½″ ..... $ 25.00- 35.00
2. Flower Dish, 15½″ ... $ 20.00- 25.00
Row 3:
1. Candleholder/Vase, 10″ .... $ 20.00- 25.00
2. Ashtray, 7½″x10″ .... $ 25.00- 35.00
3. Ewer, 12½″ .... $ 50.00- 75.00

Brochure Page, Bottom Right
Row 1:
1. Basket, 12¾″ .... $ 40.00- 70.00
2. Vase, 13¾″ .... $ 25.00- 35.00
Row 2:
1. Candleholder/Vase, 10″ .... $ 20.00- 25.00
2. Vase, 12½″ .... $ 25.00- 32.00
3. Vase, 8½″ .... $ 18.00- 22.00
4. Planter, 5½″ .... $ 10.00- 15.00
Row 3:
1. Vase, 14½″ .... $ 25.00- 35.00
2. Ashtray, 10″ .... $ 25.00- 35.00
3. Ashtray, 8″ .... $ 25.00- 35.00

Page 143

Plate 86, Continental/Tropicana
Row 1:
1. Planter/Candleholder, 4″ .... $ 18.00- 22.00
2. Bud Vase, 9½″ ...... $ 20.00- 25.00
3. Planter/Candleholder, 4″ .... $ 18.00- 22.00
Row 2:
1. Basket, 12¾″ .... $ 160.00-225.00
2. Vase, 12½″ .... $ 120.00-215.00
3. Basket, 12¾″ .... $ 40.00- 70.00
Row 3:
1. Vase, 8½″ .... $ 18.00- 22.00
2. Vase, 14½″ .... $ 25.00- 35.00
3. Ewer, 12½″ .... $ 50.00- 75.00

Page 144

Plate 87
1. Ashtray, 8½″ .... $ 15.00- 20.00

Plate 88
1. Jardinier in Brass Stand, 21″ .... $ 25.00- 35.00
2. Ashtray/Planter Combination, 26″ .... $ 35.00- 55.00
3. Jardinier in Stand, 14″ $ 15.00- 22.00

Page 145

Plate 89
Row 1:
1. Ashtray, 6½″x10¼″ .. $ 25.00- 35.00
2. Ashtray, 6½″x10¼″ .. $ 25.00- 35.00
Row 2:
1. Ashtray, 6½″x10¼″ .. $ 25.00- 35.00
2. Ashtray, 6½″x10¼″ .. $ 25.00- 35.00
3. Ashtray, 6½″x10¼″ .. $ 25.00- 35.00
Row 3:
1. Ashtray, 12½″ .... $ 18.00- 25.00
2. Ashtray, 13″ .... $ 18.00- 25.00

Page 146

Brochure Page, Capri
Row 1:
1. Pitcher, 6¼″ .... $ 12.00- 15.00
2. Urn Vase, 5¾″ ...... $ 12.00- 15.00
3. Urn Vase, 9″ .... $ 18.00- 28.00
4. Vase, 12″ .... $ 15.00- 18.00
5. Ewer, 12″ .... $ 25.00- 40.00
6. Vase, 9¾″ .... $ 10.00- 12.00
7. Vase, 15″ .... $ 20.00- 25.00
8. Vase, 13¾″ .... $ 20.00- 25.00
9. Vase, 14½″ .... $ 20.00- 25.00
10. Vase, 10″ .... $ 18.00- 22.00
Row 2:
1. Llama Planter .... $ 22.00- 32.00
2. Covered Bowl .... $ 22.00- 32.00
3. Duck Planter .... $ 18.00- 28.00
4. Twin Swan Planter, 10½″ .... $ 20.00- 30.00
5. Bowl, 4½″ .... $ 5.00- 7.00
6. Candy Dish, 8½″ ..... $ 22.00- 32.00
7. Basket, 6¾″ .... $ 22.00- 32.00
8. Bowl, 5¼″x8″ .... $ 15.00- 18.00
Row 3:
1. Bowl, 4½″x8″ .... $ 10.00- 12.00
2. Vase, 4″x6″ .... $ 6.00- 9.00
3. Compote, 5½″ .... $ 7.00- 10.00
4. Ashtray, 7½″x10″ .... $ 15.00- 18.00
5. Basket, 12¼″ .... $ 22.00- 30.00
6. Leaf, 14″ .... $ 22.00- 30.00
Row 4:
1. Vase, 5¾″ .... $ 5.00- 7.00
2. Planter/Candleholder, 4″ .... $ 10.00- 12.00
3. Flower Dish, 8½″ .... $ 10.00- 12.00
4. Planter/Candleholder, 4″ .... $ 10.00- 12.00
5. Bowl, 4¼″ .... $ 5.00- 8.00
6. Swan, 3″ .... $ 4.00- 6.00
7. Swan, 8½″ .... $ 22.00- 28.00
8. Swan, 3″ .... $ 4.00- 6.00

Page 147

Plate 90
Row 1:
1. Experimental Glass, 3½″ .... $ 2.00- 5.00
2. Experimental Glass, 3½″ .... $ 2.00- 5.00
3. Experimental Glass, 3½″ .... $ 2.00- 5.00
4. Cruet, 4¾″ .... $ 10.00- 12.00
5. Experimental Glass, 3½″ .... $ 2.00- 5.00
6. Experimental Glass, 3½″ .... $ 2.00- 5.00
7. Experimental Glass, 3½″ .... $ 2.00- 5.00
Row 2:
1. Basket, 6½″ .... $ 20.00- 30.00
2. Basket, 12¼″ .... $ 22.00- 32.00
3. Planter, 5″ .... $ 25.00- 35.00
Row 3:
1. Swan, 8½″ .... $ 22.00- 28.00
2. Basket, 6¾″ .... $ 15.00- 20.00
3. Twin Swan Planter, 10½″ .... $ 20.00- 30.00
Row 4:
1. Ewer, 10½″ .... $ 16.00- 22.00
2. Vase, 13¾″ .... $ 20.00- 25.00
3. Vase, 11″ .... $ 35.00- 50.00
4. Urn Vase, 9″ .... $ 18.00- 28.00

Page 148

Brochure Page, Imperial
Row 1:
1. Jardinier, 7″ .... $ 8.00- 12.00
2. Jardinier, 9½″ .... $ 8.00- 12.00
3. Jardinier, 4½″ .... $ 4.00- 6.00
4. Urn, 5½″ .... $ 4.00- 6.00
5. Flower Pot, 3¾″ ..... $ 3.00- 5.00
6. Urn Jardinier, 5½″ ... $ 8.00- 12.00
Row 2:
1. Leaf, 14″ .... $ 18.00- 25.00
2. Vase, 10″ .... $ 8.00- 12.00
3. Flower Bowl, 3″x6″ ... $ 2.00- 3.00
4. Hanging Basket, 5¼″x8″ .... $ 12.00- 16.00
Row 3:
1. Swan, 8½″ .... $ 8.00- 12.00

2. Twin Swan Planter, 10½" ....$ 20.00- 30.00
3. Cherub Planter, 5¾" ..$ 10.00- 12.00
4. Cherub Planter, 5¾" ..$ 10.00- 12.00

Row 4:

1. Madonna, 9½" ....$ 15.00- 20.00

Page 149

Plate 91, Imperial

Row 1:

1. Swan, 6" ....$ 15.00- 20.00
2. Swan, 8½" ....$ 20.00- 32.00
3. Swan, 4" ....$ 5.00- 7.00
4. Swan, 4½" ....$ 2.00- 5.00

Row 2:

1. Madonna, 7" ....$ 15.00- 20.00
2. Madonna, 8¼" ....$ 20.00- 25.00
3. Planter, 5¼" ....$ 4.00- 6.00

Row 3:

1. Praying Hands Planter, 6" ....$ 10.00- 12.00
2. St. Frances Planter, 11" ....$ 20.00- 32.00
3. Madonna, 7" ....$ 16.00- 22.00

Row 4:

The following prices apply only to items listed, decorated by Shafer gold.

1. Vase, 5¾" ....$ 15.00- 20.00
2. Vase, 9" ....$ 15.00- 20.00
3. Vase, 5¾" ....$ 15.00- 20.00
4. Vase, 5" ....$ 15.00- 20.00

Page 150

Brochure, Imperial

Row 1:

1. Flower Bowl, 4¾" ....$ 2.00- 3.00
2. Planter, 4¾" ....$ 2.00- 3.00
3. Urn, 5" ....$ 2.00- 3.00
4. Vase, 8½" ....$ 5.00- 7.00

Row 2:

1. Vase, 10" ....$ 5.00- 8.00
2. Vase, 9" ....$ 10.00- 12.00
3. Vase, 10" ....$ 5.00- 8.00

Row 3:

1. Urn Vase, 5" ....$ 6.00- 8.00
2. Urn Vase, 6" ....$ 10.00- 12.00
3. Urn Vase, 7" ....$ 12.00- 14.00
4. Urn Vase, 8" ....$ 14.00- 18.00

Page 151

Plate 92

Row 1:

1. Planter, 3½" ....$ 3.00- 5.00
2. Planter, 6½" ....$ 5.00- 8.00
3. Planter, 5" ....$ 4.00- 6.00

Row 2:

1. Wall Pocket, 7" ......$ 18.00- 24.00
2. Window Box, 12½" ...$ 15.00- 20.00
3. Flower Pot, 4" ....$ 5.00- 7.00

Row 3:

1. Bowl, 9" ....$ 4.00- 6.00
2. Planter, 6¼" ....$ 15.00- 20.00
3. Urn Vase, 5" ....$ 6.00- 8.00

Row 4:

1. Planter, 3¼" ....$ 4.00- 6.00
2. Window Box, 8" ......$ 8.00- 10.00
3. Planter, 3¼" ....$ 4.00- 6.00

Row 5:

1. Vase, 7¾" ....$ 18.00- 28.00
2. Wall Pocket, 8½" ....$ 25.00- 35.00
3. Vase, 9" ....$ 10.00- 12.00
4. Cornucopia, 8½" .....$ 18.00- 24.00

Page 152

Brochure Page, House 'n Garden

Row 1:

1. Steak Plate, 11¾" ....$ 2.00- 3.00
2. Divided Vegetable Bowl, 10¾" ....$ 3.00- 4.00
3. Baker, 10" ....$ 3.00- 4.00

Row 2:

1. Covered Casserole, 10" ....$ 5.00- 7.00
2. Bowl, 10¼" ....$ 4.00- 6.00

Row 3:

1. Covered Casserole, 10" ....$ 6.00- 10.00
2. Teapot, 5 cup........$ 5.00- 7.00
3. Covered Jar, 12 oz....$ 2.00- 2.50

Page 153

Plate 93

Row 1:

1. Plate, 10½" ....$ 2.00- 3.00
2. Mug, 3¼" ....$ 1.50- 2.00
3. Plate, 10" ....$ 3.00- 5.00

Row 2:

1. Bowl, 6½" ....$ 1.00- 2.00
2. Bowl, 5¼" ....$ 1.00- 2.00
3. Plate, 10½" ....$ 2.00- 3.00
4. Saucer, 6½" ....$ 1.00- 2.00
5. Mug, 3¼" ....$ 1.00- 2.00

Plate 94

Row 1:

1. Skillet Tray, 9¼"x15½" ....$ 35.00- 50.00
2. Skillet Tray, 9¼"x15½" ....$ 35.00- 50.00

Row 2:

1. Skillet Tray, 9¼"x15½" ....$ 35.00- 50.00
2. Skillet Tray, 9¼"x15½" ....$ 35.00- 50.00

Page 154

Plate 95

1. Carafe, 6½" ....$ 14.00- 18.00

Brochure Page, House 'n Garden

Row 1:

1. Carafe, 6½" ....$ 14.00- 18.00
2. Baker, 32 oz.........$ 3.00- 5.00
3. Covered Casserole, 32 oz...................$ 4.00- 6.00
4. Carafe Set..........$ 15.00- 20.00

Row 2:

1. Bowl, 6" ....$ 1.00- 1.50
2. Steak Plate, 14" ......$ 4.00- 6.00
3. Shakers, 3¼" (set) ...$ 2.00- 3.00

Row 3:

1. Cup, 7 oz............$ 1.00- 1.50
2. Saucer, 5⅞" ....$ .75- 1.00
3. Plate, 9⅜" ....$ 1.00- 2.00

Plate 155

Plate 96, House 'n Garden

Row 1:

1. Butter, 7¾" ....$ 5.00- 8.00
2. Teapot, 5 cup........$ 5.00- 7.00
3. Soup 'n Sandwich Set.$ 4.00- 6.00

Row 2:

1. Tray, 11" ....$ 3.00- 5.00
2. Shaker, 3¼" ....$ 1.00- 1.50
3. Spoon Rest, 6¾" .....$ 3.00- 5.00
4. Shaker, 3¼" ....$ 1.00- 1.50
5. Luncheon Plate, 8½" .$ 1.50- 2.00

Row 3:

1. Pitcher, 7½" ....$ 8.00- 12.00
2. Coffee Pot, 11" ......$ 18.00- 25.00
3. Bud Vase, 9" ....$ 5.00- 7.00
4. Tid Bit, 10" ....$ 12.00- 15.00

Row 4:

1. Canister Set, 6",7",8" and 9" ....$ 40.00- 65.00

Page 156

Plate 97

1. Stand, 6½"x8" ....$ 15.00- 20.00

Page 157

Plate 98, Experimentals

Row 1:

1. Candy Dish, 6¾" .....$ 30.00- 40.00

Row 2:

1. Planter, 4¾" ....$ 30.00- 40.00
2. Planter, 4¾" ....$ 30.00- 40.00

Row 3:

1. Planter, 4½" ....$ 16.00- 22.00
2. Leaf, 12" ....$ 25.00- 35.00
3. Vase, 8" ....$ 30.00- 40.00

Row 4:

1. Plate, 10½" ....$ 10.00- 12.00
2. Plate, 10½" ....$ 10.00- 12.00

Plate 159

Plate 100, Experimentals

1. Vase, 8½" ....$ 30.00- 40.00
2. Vase, 8½" ....$ 30.00- 40.00

Plate 101

1. Plate, 10½" ....$ 20.00- 25.00
2. Plate, 10½" ....$ 20.00- 25.00

Plate 102

Experimental Lids Used for Test Glazes

Page 161

Brochure Page, Top, Blue Band

Row 1:

1. Bowl, 4" ....$ 10.00- 16.00
2. Bowl, 5½" ....$ 14.00- 20.00
3. Bowl, 6¼" ....$ 16.00- 24.00
4. Bowl, 7¼" ....$ 20.00- 28.00
5. Bowl, 8¼" ....$ 22.00- 32.00

Row 2:

1. Bowl, 9¼" ....$ 25.00- 35.00
2. Bowl, 10¼" ....$ 30.00- 40.00

Row 3:

1. Bowl, 11¼" ....$ 35.00- 45.00
2. Bowl, 12⅝" ....$ 40.00- 50.00
3. Bowl, 13½" ....$ 40.00- 60.00

Brochure Page, Bottom Panelled

Row 1:

1. Bowl, 5⅜" ....$ 14.00- 20.00
2. Bowl, 6¼" ....$ 16.00- 24.00
3. Bowl, 7½" ....$ 20.00- 28.00

Row 2:

1. Bowl, 8½" ....$ 25.00- 35.00
2. Bowl, 9⅝" ....$ 30.00- 40.00
3. Bowl, 10⅝" ....$ 35.00- 45.00

Page 163

Brochure Page, Top, Blue Band

Row 1:

1. Bowl, 4" ....$ 10.00- 16.00
2. Bowl, 5⅛" ....$ 14.00- 20.00
3. Bowl, 6¼" ....$ 20.00- 28.00

Row 2:

1. Bowl, 7¼" ....$ 20.00- 28.00
2. Bowl, 8¼" ....$ 22.00- 32.00

Brochure Page, Bottom

Row 1:

1. Nappy, 4¼" ....$ 10.00- 16.00
2. Nappy, 5¼" ....$ 14.00- 20.00
3. Nappy, 6¼" ....$ 16.00- 24.00
4. Nappy, 7¼" ....$ 20.00- 28.00

Row 2:

1. Nappy, 8½" ....$ 22.00- 32.00
2. Nappy, 9⅜" ....$ 25.00- 35.00

Page 165

Brochure Page, Top, Blue Band

Row 1:

1. Nappy, 4¼" ....$ 10.00- 16.00
2. Nappy, 5¼" ....$ 14.00- 20.00
3. Nappy, 6¼" ....$ 16.00- 24.00
4. Nappy, 7¼" ....$ 20.00- 28.00

Row 2:

1. Nappy, 8½" ....$ 22.00- 32.00
2. Nappy, 9⅜" ....$ 25.00- 35.00

Brochure Page, Bottom

Row 1:

1. Jug, 48's,¾ pt.......$ 30.00- 35.00
2. Jug, 42's, 1 pt.......$ 35.00- 45.00
3. Jug, 36's, 1½ pt.....$ 40.00- 45.00

Row 2:

1. Jug, 30's, 2½ pt.....$ 45.00- 60.00
2. Jug, 24's, 4 pt.......$ 50.00- 75.00
3. Jug, 18's, 5 pt.......$ 60.00- 80.00

Page 167

Brochure Page, Top, Blue Band

Row 1:

1. Covered Butter, 6⅝" ..$ 65.00- 80.00
2. Covered Butter, 7¼" ..$ 85.00-105.00
3. Covered Butter, 7⅞" ..$ 90.00-110.00

Row 2:
1. Custard, No. 1 . . . . $ 10.00- 12.00
2. Custard, No. 2 . . . . $ 10.00- 15.00

Brochure Page, Bottom, Yellow Ware

Row 1:
1. Bowl, 4⅛" . . . . $ 10.00- 16.00
2. Bowl, 5⅛" . . . . $ 14.00- 20.00
3. Bowl, 6¼" . . . . $ 16.00- 24.00
4. Bowl, 7¼" . . . . $ 20.00- 28.00
5. Bowl, 8¼" . . . . $ 22.00- 32.00

Row 2:
1. Bowl, 9¼" . . . . $ 25.00- 35.00
2. Bowl, 10" . . . . $ 30.00- 40.00

Row 3:
1. Bowl, 11⅛" . . . . $ 35.00- 45.00
2. Bowl, 12¼" . . . . $ 40.00- 50.00
3. Bowl, 13⅜" . . . . $ 40.00- 60.00

Page 169

Brochure Page, Top, Grecian Border/Cereal Ware

Row 1:
1. Canister . . . . $ 35.00- 50.00
2. Spice Jar . . . . $ 25.00- 35.00
3. Cruet . . . . $ 40.00- 60.00
4. Salt Box . . . . $ 65.00- 90.00
5. Cruet . . . . $ 40.00- 60.00
6. Spice Jar . . . . $ 25.00- 35.00
7. Canister . . . . $ 35.00- 50.00

Row 2:
1. Spice Jar . . . . $ 25.00- 35.00
2. Spice Jar . . . . $ 25.00- 35.00

Row 3:
1. Canister . . . . $ 35.00- 50.00
2. Spice Jar . . . . $ 25.00- 35.00
3. Canister . . . . $ 35.00- 50.00
4. Canister . . . . $ 35.00- 50.00
5. Spice Jar . . . . $ 25.00- 35.00
6. Canister . . . . $ 35.00- 50.00

Brochure Page, Bottom

Row 1:
1. Canister . . . . $ 35.00- 50.00
2. Spice Jar . . . . $ 25.00- 35.00
3. Cruet . . . . $ 40.00- 60.00
4. Salt Box . . . . $ 65.00- 90.00
5. Cruet . . . . $ 40.00- 60.00
6. Spice Jar . . . . $ 25.00- 35.00
7. Canister . . . . $ 35.00- 50.00

Row 2:
1. Spice Jar . . . . $ 25.00- 35.00
2. Spice Jar . . . . $ 25.00- 35.00

Row 3:
1. Canister . . . . $ 35.00- 50.00
2. Spice Jar . . . . $ 25.00- 35.00
3. Canister . . . . $ 35.00- 50.00
4. Canister . . . . $ 35.00- 50.00
5. Spice Jar . . . . $ 25.00- 35.00
6. Canister . . . . $ 35.00- 50.00

Page 170

Brochure Page

Row 1:
1. Custard, 3" . . . . $ 5.00- 7.00
2. Jug, 1 pint . . . . $ 22.00- 28.00
3. Jug, 1 quart . . . . $ 32.00- 38.00
4. Jug, ¾ pint . . . . $ 18.00- 24.00
5. Ramekin, 4" . . . . $ 5.00- 8.00

Row 2:
1. Pie Plate, 9" . . . . $ 16.00- 22.00
2. Pie Plate, 10" . . . . $ 18.00- 26.00
3. French Casserole, 5" . $ 16.00- 20.00
4. Bean Pot, 6" . . . . $ 24.00- 34.00
5. French Casserole, 4" . $ 10.00- 15.00
6. Baked Apple, 5" . . . . . $ 5.00- 8.00

Row 3:
1. Nested Bowl, 5",6",7",8", and 9" . . . $ 50.00- 80.00
2. Covered Casserole, 8" $ 24.00- 34.00
3. Covered Casserole, 7" $ 22.00- 32.00
4. Plate, 7" . . . . $ 8.00- 12.00
5. Covered Casserole, 6" $ 20.00- 25.00

Row 4:
1. Bake Set Bowls, 6",7",8", and 9" . . . . . $ 45.00- 65.00
2. Bean Pot, 5" . . . . $ 22.00- 26.00
3. Bean Pot, 7" . . . . $ 26.00- 36.00
4. Bean Pot, 4" . . . . $ 18.00- 22.00
5. Nested Deep Bowls, 4",5",6",and 7" . . . . . . $ 45.00- 65.00

Page 171

Brochure Page, Top, Double Border Cereal Ware

Row 1:
1. Canister . . . . $ 35.00- 50.00
2. Spice Jar . . . . $ 25.00- 35.00
3. Cruet . . . . $ 40.00- 60.00
4. Salt Box . . . . $ 65.00- 90.00
5. Cruet . . . . $ 40.00- 60.00
6. Spice Jar . . . . $ 25.00- 35.00
7. Canister . . . . $ 25.00- 35.00

Row 2:
1. Spice Jar . . . . $ 25.00- 35.00
2. Spice Jar . . . . $ 25.00- 35.00

Row 3:
1. Canister . . . . $ 35.00- 50.00
2. Spice Jar . . . . $ 25.00- 35.00
3. Canister . . . . $ 35.00- 50.00
4. Canister . . . . $ 35.00- 50.00
5. Spice Jar . . . . $ 25.00- 35.00
6. Canister . . . . $ 35.00- 50.00

Brochure Page, Bottom

Row 1:
1. Canister . . . . $ 35.00- 50.00
2. Spice Jar . . . . $ 25.00- 35.00
3. Cruet . . . . $ 40.00- 60.00
4. Salt Box . . . . $ 65.00- 90.00
5. Cruet . . . . $ 40.00- 60.00
6. Spice Jar . . . . $ 25.00- 35.00
7. Canister . . . . $ 35.00- 50.00

Row 2:
1. Spice Jar . . . . $ 25.00- 35.00
2. Spice Jar . . . . $ 25.00- 35.00

Row 3:
1. Canister . . . . $ 35.00- 50.00
2. Spice Jar . . . . $ 25.00- 35.00
3. Canister . . . . $ 35.00- 50.00
4. Canister . . . . $ 35.00- 50.00
5. Spice Jar . . . . $ 25.00- 35.00
6. Canister . . . . $ 35.00- 50.00

Page 173

Brochure Page, Top, Double Border Cereal Ware

Row 1:
1. Canister . . . . $ 35.00- 50.00
2. Spice Jar . . . . $ 25.00- 35.00
3. Cruet . . . . $ 40.00- 60.00
4. Salt Box . . . . $ 65.00- 90.00
5. Cruet . . . . $ 40.00- 60.00
6. Spice Jar . . . . $ 25.00- 35.00
7. Canister . . . . $ 35.00- 50.00

Row 2:
1. Spice Jar . . . . $ 25.00- 35.00
2. Spice Jar . . . . $ 25.00- 35.00

Row 3:
1. Canister . . . . $ 35.00- 50.00
2. Spice Jar . . . . $ 25.00- 35.00
3. Canister . . . . $ 35.00- 50.00
4. Canister . . . . $ 35.00- 50.00
5. Spice Jar . . . . $ 25.00- 35.00
6. Canister . . . . $ 35.00- 50.00

Brochure Page, Bottom, Blue Bird Cereal Ware

Row 1:
1. Canister . . . . $ 40.00- 60.00
2. Spice Jar . . . . $ 30.00- 45.00
3. Cruet . . . . $ 50.00- 75.00
4. Salt Box . . . . $ 85.00-125.00
5. Cruet . . . . $ 50.00- 75.00
6. Spice Jar . . . . $ 30.00- 45.00
7. Canister . . . . $ 40.00- 60.00

Row 2:
1. Spice Jar . . . . $ 30.00- 45.00
2. Spice Jar . . . . $ 30.00- 45.00

Row 3:
1. Canister . . . . $ 40.00- 60.00
2. Spice Jar . . . . $ 30.00- 45.00
3. Canister . . . . $ 40.00- 60.00
4. Canister . . . . $ 40.00- 60.00
5. Spice Jar . . . . $ 30.00- 45.00
6. Canister . . . . $ 40.00- 60.00

Page 175

Brochure Page, Top, Delft Cereal Ware

Row 1:
1. Canister . . . . $ 40.00- 60.00
2. Spice Jar . . . . $ 30.00- 45.00
3. Cruet . . . . $ 50.00- 75.00
4. Salt Box . . . . $ 85.00-125.00
5. Cruet . . . . $ 50.00- 75.00
6. Spice Jar . . . . $ 30.00- 45.00
7. Canister . . . . $ 40.00- 60.00

Row 2:
1. Spice Jar . . . . $ 30.00- 45.00
2. Spice Jar . . . . $ 30.00- 45.00

Row 3:
1. Canister . . . . $ 40.00- 60.00
2. Spice Jar . . . . $ 30.00- 45.00
3. Canister . . . . $ 40.00- 60.00
4. Canister . . . . $ 40.00- 60.00
5. Spice Jar . . . . $ 30.00- 45.00
6. Canister . . . . $ 40.00- 60.00

Brochure Page, Bottom, Salt Boxes

Row 1:
1. Round Salt Box . . . . . . $ 65.00- 95.00
2. Round Salt Box . . . . . . $ 65.00- 95.00
3. Round Salt Box . . . . . . $ 90.00-140.00
4. Round Salt Box . . . . . . $ 90.00-140.00

Row 2:
1. Panelled Salt Box . . . . $ 75.00-100.00
2. Panelled Salt Box . . . . $ 75.00-100.00
3. Panelled Salt Box . . . . $ 90.00-140.00
4. Panelled Salt Box . . . . $ 90.00-140.00

Page 176

Brochure Page, Hotel/Toiletware
1. Combinet . . . . $ 50.00- 90.00
2. Mug . . . . $ 10.00- 12.00
3. Jug . . . . $ 25.00- 35.00
4. Covered Chamber . . . . $ 50.00- 90.00

Page 177

Brochure Page, Top, Cuspidors

Row 1:
1. Cuspidor . . . . $ 50.00- 80.00
2. Cuspidor . . . . $ 50.00- 80.00
3. Cuspidor . . . . $ 50.00- 80.00
4. Cuspidor . . . . $ 50.00- 80.00

Row 2:
1. Cuspidor . . . . $ 70.00-110.00
2. Cuspidor . . . . $ 70.00-110.00

Row 3:
1. Cuspidor . . . . $ 50.00- 80.00
2. Cuspidor . . . . $ 50.00- 80.00
3. Cuspidor . . . . $ 50.00- 80.00
4. Cuspidor . . . . $ 50.00- 80.00

Brochure Page, Bottom, Zane Grey

Row 1:
1. Covered Jar, ½ Gallon . . . . $ 45.00- 65.00
2. Covered Jar, 1 Gallon . $ 60.00- 90.00
3. Covered Jar, 1½ Gallon . . . . $ 80.00-120.00
4. Covered Jar, 2 Gallon . $ 110.00-150.00
5. Covered Jar, 3 Gallon . $ 125.00-200.00

Page 178

Brochure Page, Zane Grey
1. Covered Jar, 4 Gallon . $ 200.00-260.00
2. Covered Jar, 5 Gallon . $ 240.00-300.00
3. Covered Jar, 6 Gallon . $ 280.00-350.00

Page 179

Brochure Page, Top, Zane Grey

Row 1:
1. Bowl, 4⅛" . . . . $ 10.00- 16.00

2. Bowl, 5⅛″ .... $ 14.00- 20.00
3. Bowl, 6¼″ .... $ 16.00- 24.00
4. Bowl, 7¼″ .... $ 22.00- 28.00
5. Bowl, 8¼″ .... $ 22.00- 32.00

Row 2:

1. Bowl, 9⅛″ .... $ 25.00- 35.00
2. Bowl, 10″ .... $ 30.00- 40.00

Row 3:

1. Bowl, 11½″ .... $ 35.00- 45.00
2. Bowl, 12¼″ .... $ 40.00- 50.00
3. Bowl, 13⅝″ .... $ 40.00- 60.00

Brochure Page, Bottom

Row 1:

1. Jug, ¾ pt .... $ 30.00- 35.00
2. Jug, 1 pt .... $ 35.00- 45.00
3. Jug, 1½ pt .... $ 40.00- 45.00

Row 2:

1. Jug, 2½ pt .... $ 45.00- 60.00
2. Jug, 4 pt .... $ 50.00- 75.00
3. Jug, 5 pt .... $ 60.00- 80.00

Page 180

Brochure Page, Top, Zane Gray

Row 1:

1. Butter, 6⅝″ .... $ 65.00- 85.00
2. Butter, 7¼″ .... $ 85.00-105.00
3. Butter, 7⅞″ .... $ 90.00-110.00

Row 2:

1. Custard, No. 1 .... $ 10.00- 12.00
2. Custard, No. 2 .... $ 12.00- 15.00

Brochure Page, Bottom

1. Salt Box .... $ 75.00-110.00
2. Cuspidor .... $ 50.00- 80.00

Page 181

Brochure Page, Top Left, Rainbow

1. Plate 10½″ .... $ 2.00- 3.00
2. Mug, 9 oz. .... $ 1.00- 1.50
3. Bowl, 6½″ .... $ 1.00- 1.50

Brochure Page, Top Right

Row 1:

1. Plate, 8½″ .... $ 2.00- 3.00
2. Cup, 6 oz .... $ 1.00- 1.50
3. Saucer, 5½″ .... $ .75- 1.00

Row 2:

1. Leaf, 7¼″ .... $ 4.00- 6.00
2. Leaf Chip 'n Dip, 12¼″ $ 15.00- 20.00
3. Tip Bit Tray, 10″ ..... $ 12.00- 15.00

Row 3:

1. Bowl, 8″ .... $ 4.00- 6.00
2. Bowl, 7″ .... $ 3.00- 4.00
3. Bowl, 6″ .... $ 2.00- 4.00

Row 4:

1. Leaf Tray, 12″ .... $ 15.00- 20.00

Brochure Page, Bottom, Left to Right, Crestone

Row 1:

1. Plate, 10¼″ .... $ 2.00- 4.00
2. Plate, 7½″ .... $ 1.50- 2.50
3. Mug, 9 oz .... $ 1.50- 2.00
4. Bowl, 6″ .... $ 1.00- 1.50
5. Plate, 6½″ .... $ .75- 1.00
6. Carafe, 2 cup, 6½″ ... $ 15.00- 22.00
7. Pitcher, 38 oz. .... $ 15.00- 20.00
8. Stein, 14 oz .... $ 4.00- 6.00
9. Covered French Casserole, 9 oz. ...... $ 4.00- 5.00
10. Cup, 7 oz .... $ 1.50- 2.00
11. Saucer, 5⅞″ .... $ .75- 1.00
12. Plate 9⅜″ .... $ 2.00- 3.00

Row 2:

1. Open Baker, 32 oz. ... $ 3.00- 4.00
2. Cov. Casserole, 32 oz. $ 5.00- 7.00
3. Individual Covered Casserole; 9 oz ...... $ 3.00- 4.00
4. Gravy Boat/Syrup, 10 oz .... $ 3.00- 4.00
5. Saucer, 6½″ .... $ .75- 1.25
6. French Casserole, 9 oz $ 3.00- 4.00
7. Bowl, 9¾″ .... $ 5.00- 8.00
8. Teapot, 5 cup .... $ 22.00- 30.00
9. Covered Jar .... $ 3.00- 4.00
10. Butter Dish, ¼ lb .... $ 8.00- 12.00
11. Bowl, 9 oz .... $ 1.50- 2.00
12. Carafe Set .... $ 20.00- 25.00

Row 3:

1. Custard, 6 oz .... $ 1.00- 2.00
2. Shaker Set, 3¾″ ..... $ 4.00- 8.00
3. Creamer, 8 oz .... $ 2.00- 4.00
4. Sugar, 8 oz .... $ 2.00- 4.00
5. Leaf Chip 'n Dip, 14¼″ $ 18.00- 22.00
6. Coffee Server, 8 cup .. $ 18.00- 25.00

Page 182

Brochure Page, Top Left, House 'n Garden

Row 1:

1. Bowl, 6½″ .... $ 1.00- 1.50
2. Plate, 10¼″ .... $ 2.00- 3.00
3. Mug, 9 oz .... $ 1.00- 1.50
4. Bowl, 5¼″ .... $ 1.00- 1.50
5. Plate, 6½″ .... $ .75- 1.00
6. Cookie Jar, 94 oz ..... $ 10.00- 15.00

Row 2:

1. Jug, 5 pt .... $ 8.00- 10.00
2. Jug, 2 pt .... $ 5.00- 7.00
3. Creamer, 8 oz .... $ 1.00- 2.00
4. Sugar, 12 oz......... $ 1.00- 2.00
5. Bean Pot, 2 qt .... $ 4.00- 6.00
6. Individual Covered Bean Pot, 12 oz .... $ 2.00- 2.50
7. Coffee Pot, 8 cup ..... $ 18.00- 25.00

Row 3:

1. Covered French Casserole, 5¼″ ...... $ 1.50- 2.50
2. Open French Casserole, 5¼″ .... $ 1.00- 1.50
3. Jug, 2 qt. .... $ 8.00- 12.00
4. Shaker Set, 3¾″ ..... $ 2.00- 3.00
5. Leaf Chip 'n Dip, 15″ . $ 15.00- 20.00
6. Stein, 16 oz .... $ 1.00- 2.00

Brochure Page, Top Right

Row 1:

1. Bud Vase, 9″ .... $ 5.00- 7.00
2. Steak Plate, 11¾″ .... $ 2.00- 3.00
3. Divided Vegetable, 10¾″ .... $ 3.00- 4.00
4. Covered Casserole, 10″, 2 pt .... $ 5.00- 7.00

Row 2:

1. Bowl, 10¼″ .... $ 4.00- 6.00
2. Covered Casserole, 10″, 2 qt. .... $ 6.00- 10.00
3. Teapot .... $ 5.00- 7.00

Row 3:

1. Covered Jar, 12 oz ... $ 2.00- 2.50
2. Butter, ¼ lb .... $ 5.00- 8.00
3. Ashtray, 8″ .... $ 10.00- 15.00
4. Pie Plate, 9¼″ .... $ 2.00- 2.50

Row 4:

1. Snack Set .... $ 3.00- 4.00
2. Covered French Casserole, 3 pt .... $ 5.00- 8.00
3. Covered French Casserole with Warmer $ 18.00- 25.00
4. Open French Casserole, 3 pt .... $ 8.00- 10.00
5. Dutch Oven, 3 pt ..... $ 2.00- 3.50
6. Open Baker, 3 pt ..... $ 1.50- 2.00

Brochure Page, Bottom Left

1. Soup 'n Sancwich .... $ 4.00- 6.00
2. Snack Set .... $ 4.00- 6.00
3. Toast 'n Cereal ...... $ 4.00- 6.00

Page 183

Brochure Page, Top Left, House 'n Garden

Row 1:

1. Salad Bowl, 6½″ ..... $ 1.00- 2.00
2. Continental Mug, 10 oz .... $ 2.00- 3.00
3. Custard .... $ .75- 1.00
4. Corn Dish, 9¼″ ...... $ 1.00- 2.50
5. Chip 'n Dip, 11½″ .... $ 4.00- 5.00

Row 2:

1. Double Server, 14½″ . $ 5.00- 7.00
2. Sauce Bowl, 5½″ .... $ 1.00- 1.50
3. Tray, 11″x12″ .... $ 8.00- 10.00
4. Chip 'n Dip, 11″x12″ .. $ 10.00- 12.00

Row 3:

1. Gravy Boat Saucer, 10¼″ .... $ 1.00- 2.00
2. Gravy Boat, 16 oz .... $ 1.50- 2.50
3. Gravy Boat Set .... $ 3.00- 4.00
4. Open Roaster, 7 pt ... $ 2.00- 3.00
5. Covered Roaster, 7 pt . $ 6.00- 10.00

Row 4:

1. Server, 13⅜″ .... $ 3.00- 4.00
2. Server with Chicken Cover, 13⅜″ .... $ 20.00- 30.00
3. Open Baker, 13⅜″ .... $ 3.00- 4.00
4. Server with Chicken Cover, 13⅜″ .... $ 20.00- 30.00

Brochure Page, Top Right

Row 1:

1. Bowl, 6½″ .... $ 1.00- 1.50
2. Plate, 10¼″ .... $ 2.00- 3.00
3. Mug, 9 oz .... $ 1.00- 1.50
4. Bowl, 5¼″ .... $ .75- 1.00
5. Plate, 6½″ .... $ .75- 1.00
6. Cookie Jar, 94 oz ..... $ 10.00- 15.00

Row 2:

1. Plate, 8½″ .... $ 1.50- 2.00
2. Cup, 6 oz .... $ 1.00- 1.50
3. Saucer, 5½″ .... $ .75- 1.00
4. Bowl, 6″ .... $ 1.00- 1.50
5. Plate, 9⅜″ .... $ 1.50- 2.50
6. Cup, 7 oz .... $ 1.00- 1.50
7. Saucer, 5⅞″ .... $ .75- 1.00
8. Bean Pot, 2 qt .... $ 4.00- 6.00

Row 3:

1. Shaker, Set.......... $ 2.00- 3.00
2. Shaker, Set.......... $ 2.00- 3.00
3. Sugar, 12 oz......... $ 1.00- 2.00
4. Creamer, 8 oz .... $ 1.00- 2.00
5. Butter Dish, ¼ lb ..... $ 5.00- 8.00
6. Individual Bean Pot, 12 oz .... $ 2.00- 2.50
7. Covered Jar, 12 oz ... $ 2.00- 2.50

Row 4:

1. Custard, 6 oz .... $ .75- 1.00
2. Pie Plate, 9¼″ .... $ 2.00- 2.50
3. Soup 'n Sandwich .... $ 4.00- 6.00
4. Bake and Serve, 6½″ . $ 1.00- 1.50
5. Server, 10″ .... $ 2.00- 2.50

Brochure Page, Bottom Left

Row 1:

1. Stein, 16 oz .... $ 1.00- 2.00
2. Continental Mug, 10 oz $ 2.00- 3.00
3. Covered Hen Casserole .... $ 15.00- 20.00
4. Covered Duck Casserole, 2 pt....... $ 15.00- 20.00
5. Covered Duck Casserole, 2 qt....... $ 20.00- 25.00
6. Covered Chicken Casserole, 2 qt....... $ 20.00- 25.00

Row 2:

1. Divided Vegetable, 10¾″ .... $ 3.00- 4.00
2. Gravy Boat Set .... $ 3.00- 4.00
3. Piggy Bank .... $ 12.00- 15.00
4. Corky Piggy Bank .... $ 12.00- 15.00
5. Jumbo Corky Piggy Bank .... $ 15.00- 20.00

Row 3:

1. Bowl, 10¼″ .... $ 4.00- 6.00
2. Steak Plate, 14″ ..... $ 4.00- 6.00
3. Steak Plate, 11¾″ .... $ 2.00- 3.00

Row 4:

1. Dutch Oven, 3 pt ..... $ 2.50- 3.50
2. Baker, 3 pt .... $ 1.50- 2.00
3. Covered Casserole, 2 pt .... $ 3.00- 4.00
4. Covered Casserole, 2 qt. .... $ 6.00- 10.00

Brochure Page, Bottom Right
Row 1:
1. Jug, 2 qt . . . .$ 8.00- 12.00
2. Jug, 2 pt . . . .$ 5.00- 7.00
3. Jug, 5 pt . . . .$ 8.00- 10.00
4. Coffee Pot, 8 cup . . . . .$ 18.00- 25.00
Row 2:
1. Covered Casserole, 32 oz. . . . .$ 2.40- 3.50
2. Open Casserole, 32 oz $ 2.00- 2.50
3. Bowl, 6″ . . . .$ 1.00- 2.50
4. Bowl, 7″ . . . .$ 2.00- 4.00
5. Bowl, 8″ . . . .$ 3.00- 4.00
Row 3:
1. Covered French Casserole, 3 pt. with Warmer . . . .$ 18.00- 25.00
2. Covered French Casserole, 3 pt . . . .$ 8.00- 10.00
3. Covered French Casserole, 5¼″ . . . . . .$ 1.50- 2.00
4. Open French Casserole, 5¼″ . . . .$ 1.00- 1.50
Row 4:
1. Leaf Chip 'n Dip, 15″ .$ 15.00- 20.00
2. Ashtray, 8″ . . . .$ 10.00- 15.00
3. Teapot, 5 cup . . . .$ 5.00- 7.00

Page 184

Brochure Page, Top Left, Imperial
Row 1:
1. Leaf . . . .$ 15.00- 20.00
2. Open Front Vase . . . . .$ 4.00- 5.00
3. Planter . . . .$ 3.00- 4.00
4. Bowl Planter . . . .$ 3.00- 4.00
Row 2:
1. Vase . . . .$ 8.00- 10.00
2. Jardinier . . . .$ 25.00- 30.00
3. Jardinier and Pedestal .$ 25.00- 35.00
4. Jardinier and Pedestal .$ 40.00- 60.00
Row 3:
1. Swan . . . .$ 8.00- 12.00
2. Figural Planter . . . .$ 20.00- 32.00
Row 4:
1. Llama Planter . . . .$ 22.00- 32.00
2. Twin Swan Planter . . . .$ 20.00- 30.00
3. St. Frances Planter . . .$ 20.00- 32.00

Brochure Page, Top Right
Row 1:
1. Urn, 5½″ . . . .$ 8.00- 12.00
2. Bowl, 6″ . . . .$ 1.00- 2.00
3. Planter, 4¾″ . . . .$ 1.00- 2.00
4. Planter, 6¾″ . . . .$ 1.00- 2.00
Row 2:
1. Compote, 4¼″ . . . .$ 1.00- 2.00
2. Urn, 7″ . . . .$ 1.50- 2.50
3. Vase, 4¾″ . . . .$ 1.00- 2.00
4. Urn, 4¾″ . . . .$ 1.00- 2.00
Row 3:
1. Planter, 5″ . . . .$ 1.00- 2.00
2. Basket, 7″ . . . .$ 8.00- 12.00
3. Planter, 7″ . . . .$ 1.50- 2.50
4. Urn, 4¾″ . . . .$ 1.00- 2.00
Row 4:
1. Bowl, 4½″ . . . .$ 1.00- 2.00
2. Bowl, 3⅞″ . . . .$ 1.00- 2.00
3. Urn, 5½″ . . . .$ 1.50- 2.50

Brochure Page, Bottom Left
Row 1:
1. Flower Dish, 11¾″ . . .$ 2.00- 3.00
2. Flower Dish, 14″ . . . . .$ 3.00- 4.00
3. Flower Dish, 6½″ . . . .$ 1.00- 2.00
Row 2:
1. Flower Dish, 7″ . . . . . .$ 1.00- 2.00
2. Flower Dish, 8¼″ . . . .$ 1.00- 2.00
3. Flower Dish, 7″ . . . . . .$ 1.00- 2.00
4. Flower Dish, 7″ . . . . . .$ 1.00- 2.00
Row 3:
1. Flower Dish, 8¼″ . . . .$ 1.50- 2.50
2. Flower Dish, 12″ . . . . .$ 2.00- 3.00
3. Flower Bowl, 8¼″ . . . .$ 1.00- 2.00
4. Candleholder, 4½″ . . .$ 1.00- 2.00
Row 4:
1. Flower Dish, 8¾″ . . . .$ 1.00- 2.00
2. Flower Dish, 5″ . . . . . .$ 1.00- 2.00
3. Flower Dish, 6¼″ . . . .$ 1.00- 2.00
4. Flower Dish, 6½″ . . . .$ 1.00- 2.00
5. Flower Dish, 6½″ . . . .$ 1.00- 2.00
Row 5:
1. Flower Dish, 8¼″ . . . .$ 1.00- 2.00
2. Flower Dish, 10″ . . . . .$ 1.00- 2.00
3. Planter, 7½″ . . . .$ 1.50- 2.50

Brochure Page, Bottom Right
Row 1:
1. Swan, 3″ . . . .$ 1.00- 2.00
2. Swan, 3″ . . . .$ 1.00- 2.00
3. Swan, 8½″ . . . .$ 8.00- 12.00
4. Leaf . . . .$ 10.00- 12.00
Row 2:
1. Twin Swan Planter, 10½″ . . . .$ 20.00- 30.00
2. Vase, 10″ . . . .$ 2.00- 3.00
3. Madonna, 9½″ . . . .$ 15.00- 20.00
Row 3:
1. Vase, 8¾″ . . . .$ 1.00- 2.00
2. Ivy Bowl, 10″ . . . .$ 1.00- 2.00
3. Dutch Shoe Planter, 8″ $ 2.50- 3.50
4. Jardinier in Stand, 22½″ . . . .$ 25.00- 35.00
5. Jardinier, 10½″ . . . . . .$ 20.00- 32.00
Row 4:
1. Vase, 10¾″ . . . .$ 2.00- 3.00
2. Vase, 9″ . . . .$ 2.00- 3.00
3. Pitcher, 11¾″ . . . .$ 6.00- 8.00
4. Vase, 10⅞″ . . . .$ 4.00- 5.00

Page 185

Brochure Page, Top Left, Imperial
Row 1:
1. Urn, 5″ . . . .$ 1.00- 2.00
2. Basket, 7″ . . . .$ 4.00- 5.00
3. Planter, 4¾″ . . . .$ 1.00- 2.00
Row 2:
1. Leaf Bowl, 9¾″ . . . . . .$ 2.00- 3.00
2. Low Bowl, 9¾″ . . . . . .$ 1.00- 2.00
3. Planter, 6″ . . . .$ 1.00- 2.00
Row 3:
1. Flower Bowl, 7½″ . . . .$ 1.00- 2.00
2. Jardinier, 4¼″ . . . .$ 1.00- 2.00
3. Dish Garden, 6″ . . . . . .$ 1.00- 2.00
4. Dish Garden, 6½″ . . . .$ 1.00- 2.00
5. Compote, 7½″ . . . .$ 1.40- 2.50
Row 4:
1. Swan, 4″ . . . .$ 1.50- 2.00
2. Swan, 7½″ . . . .$ 8.00- 12.00
3. Swan, 7½″ . . . .$ 15.00- 20.00
4. Madonna, 7½″ . . . .$ 15.00- 20.00

Brochure Page, Top Right
Row 1:
1. Planter, 5″ . . . .$ 1.00- 2.00
2. Urn, 4¾″ . . . .$ 1.00- 2.00
3. Planter, 4¾″ . . . .$ 1.00- 2.00
4. Urn . . . .$ 2.00- 3.00
Row 2:
1. Urn, 7″ . . . .$ 1.50- 2.50
2. Urn, 5½″ . . . .$ 1.50- 2.50
3. Compote, 4¼″ . . . .$ 1.00- 2.00
Row 3:
1. Vase, 9″ . . . .$ 2.00- 3.00
2. Vase, 10″ . . . .$ 2.00- 3.00
3. Vase, 10⅞″ . . . .$ 4.00- 5.00
4. Vase, 11¾″ . . . .$ 4.00- 5.00
Row 4:
1. Madonna, 6¼″ . . . .$ 4.00- 5.00
2. Madonna, 7¼″ . . . .$ 15.00- 20.00
3. Madonna, 9½″ . . . .$ 15.00- 20.00

Brochure Page, Bottom Left
Row 1:
1. Flower Dish, 12″ . . . . .$ 2.00- 3.00
2. Flower Dish, 11¾″ . . .$ 2.00- 3.00
3. Flower Dish, 14″ . . . . .$ 3.00- 4.00
Row 2:
1. Flower Dish, 10″ . . . . .$ 1.50- 2.40
2. Flower Dish, 8″ . . . . . .$ 1.00- 2.00
3. Flower Dish, 8¼″ . . . .$ 1.00- 2.00
4. Flower Dish, 8¼″ . . . .$ 1.00- 2.00
5. Flower Dish, 8″ . . . . . .$ 1.00- 2.00
Row 3:
1. Flower Dish, 8¼″ . . . .$ 1.00- 2.00
2. Flower Dish, 8¼″ . . . .$ 1.00- 2.00
3. Flower Dish, 7″ . . . . . .$ 1.00- 2.00
4. Flower Dish, 6½″ . . . .$ 1.00- 2.00
5. Flower Dish, 7″ . . . . . .$ 1.00- 2.00
Row 4:
1. Flower Dish, 7″ . . . . . .$ 1.00- 2.00
2. Flower Dish, 6½″ . . . .$ 1.00- 2.00
3. Flower Bowl, 6¾″ . . . .$ 1.00- 2.00
4. Flower Dish, 6½″ . . . .$ 1.00- 2.00
5. Flower Dish, 6¼″ . . . .$ 1.00- 2.00
Row 5:
1. Flower Bowl, 6½″ . . . .$ 1.00- 2.00
2. Flower Bowl, 6″ . . . . . .$ 1.00- 2.00
3. Flower Bowl, 5″ . . . . . .$ 1.00- 2.00
4. Planter, 6¾″ . . . .$ 1.00- 2.00
5. Flower Dish, 6½″ . . . .$ 1.00- 2.00

Brochure Page, Bottom Right
Row 1:
1. Vase, 3¾″ . . . .$ 1.00- 2.00
2. Planter, 3½″ . . . .$ 1.00- 2.00
3. Planter 3½″ . . . .$ 1.00- 2.00
4. Planter, 3½″ . . . .$ 1.00- 2.00
5. Planter, 4¾″ . . . .$ 1.00- 2.00
6. Compote, 6″ . . . .$ 1.00- 2.00
Row 2:
1. Low Flower Arranger, 12¼″ . . . .$ 1.40- 2.50
2. Low Flower Arranger, 9″ . . . .$ 1.00- 2.00
3. Low Bowl, 7¾″ . . . . . .$ 1.00- 2.00
4. Low Bowl, 8¼″ . . . . . .$ 1.00- 2.00
Row 3:
1. Flower Dish, 6″ . . . . . .$ 1.00- 2.00
2. Flower Dish, 10½″ . . .$ 1.50- 2.50
3. Planter, 8″ . . . .$ 1.50- 2.50
4. Planter, 6¼″ . . . .$ 1.00- 2.00
Row 4:
1. Swan, 3″ . . . .$ 1.00- 2.00
2. Swan, 3″ . . . .$ 1.00- 2.00
3. Swan, 8″ . . . .$ 8.00- 12.00
4. Twin Swan Planter, 10½″ . . . .$ 20.00- 30.00

Page 186

Brochure Page, Top Left, Imperial
Row 1:
1. Flower Dish, 6¼″ . . . .$ 1.00- 2.00
2. Flower Dish, 6¾″ . . . .$ 1.00- 2.00
3. Flower Dish, 6¾″ . . . .$ 1.00- 2.00
4. Flower Dish, 8¼″ . . . .$ 1.00- 2.00
Row 2:
1. Flower Dish, 8½″ . . . .$ 1.00- 2.00
2. Vase, 6″ . . . .$ 1.00- 2.00
3. Garden Dish . . . .$ 1.00- 2.00
4. Garden Dish, 8½″ . . . .$ 1.00- 2.00
Row 3:
1. Garden Dish, 7″ . . . . . .$ 1.00- 2.00
2. Garden Dish, 7″ . . . . . .$ 1.00- 2.00
3. Garden Dish, 7¾″ . . . .$ 1.00- 2.00
4. Garden Dish, 7″ . . . . . .$ 1.00- 2.00
Row 4:
1. Garden Dish, 6¼″ . . . .$ 1.00- 2.00
2. Planter, 6½″ . . . .$ 1.00- 2.00
3. Planter, 6¾″ . . . .$ 1.00- 2.00
4. Garden Dish, 7″ . . . . . .$ 1.00- 2.00
Row 5:
1. Garden Dish, 7½″ . . . .$ 1.00- 2.00
2. Garden Dish . . . .$ 1.00- 2.00
3. Flower Bowl, 7¼″ . . . .$ 1.00- 2.00
4. Flower Bowl, 6½″ . . . .$ 1.00- 2.00

Brochure Page, Top Right
Row 1:
1. Planter, 6¼" ....$ 1.00- 2.00
2. Planter, 7¼" ....$ 1.50- 2.50
3. Planter, 7⅝" ....$ 1.50- 2.50
4. Planter, 8⅛" ....$ 1.50- 2.50

Row 2:
1. Planter, 6¾" ....$ 1.00- 2.00
2. Planter, 5¼" ....$ 1.50- 2.50
3. Planter, 3½" ....$ 1.00- 2.00
4. Compote, 3½" ....$ 1.00- 2.00

Row 3:
1. Owl Planter, 6⅛" .....$ 2.00- 3.00
2. Planter ....$ 2.00- 3.00
3. Planter ....$ 1.00- 2.00
4. Jardinier, 6¾" ....$ 3.00- 4.00

Row 4:
1. Flower Dish, 8" ......$ 1.00- 2.00
2. Garden Dish, 10" .....$ 1.50- 2.50
3. Garden Dish, 8½" ....$ 1.00- 2.00

Row 5:
1. Garden Dish, 11¾" ...$ 2.00- 3.00
2. Flower Dish, 12" .....$ 2.00- 3.00
3. Garden Dish, 14" .....$ 3.00- 4.00

Brochure Page, Bottom Left
Row 1:
1. Garden Dish ....$ 1.00- 2.00
2. Garden Dish ....$ 1.00- 2.00
3. Garden Dish ....$ 1.00- 2.00
4. Garden Dish ....$ 1.00- 2.00

Row 2:
1. Garden Dish ....$ 2.00- 3.00
2. Flower Bowl ....$ 1.50- 2.50
3. Garden Dish ....$ 1.00- 2.00
4. Flower Pot ....$ 1.00- 2.00

Row 3:
1. Garden Dish ....$ 1.00- 2.00
2. Candleholder/Planter, 4" ....$ 1.50- 2.50
3. Planter, 8½" ....$ 1.50- 2.50
4. Candleholder/Planter, 4" ....$ 1.50- 2.50

Row 4:
1. Garden Dish, 11¾" ...$ 2.00- 3.00
2. Garden Dish, 14" .....$ 3.00- 4.00

Row 5:
1. Garden Dish ....$ 1.00- 2.00
2. Garden Dish ....$ 1.00- 2.00
3. Garden Dish ....$ 1.00- 2.00

Brochure Page, Bottom Right
Row 1:
1. Madonna, 8½" ....$ 15.00- 20.00
2. Pitcher Set, 5½" .....$ 5.00- 8.00
3. Swan, 4" ....$ 1.50- 2.00
4. Swan, 4" ....$ 1.50- 2.00
5. Swan, 7½" ....$ 8.00- 12.00

Row 2:
1. Vase, 5½" ....$ 1.00- 2.00
2. Planter, 4¾" ....$ 1.00- 2.00
3. Planter, 3½" ....$ 1.00- 2.00
4. Flower Bowl, 7½" ....$ 1.00- 2.00
5. Flower Bowl, 8¾" ....$ 1.00- 2.00

Row 3:
1. Planter, 4⅜" ....$ 1.00- 2.00
2. Planter, 4⅜" ....$ 1.00- 2.00
3. Compote, 4¼" ....$ 1.00- 2.00
4. Planter, 5⅝" ....$ 1.00- 2.00

Row 4:
1. Vase, 12" ....$ 3.00- 5.00
2. Swan, 4" ....$ 1.00- 2.00
3. Swan, 4" ....$ 1.00- 2.00
4. Swan, 8½" ....$ 8.00- 12.00
5. Vase, 9¼" ....$ 2.50- 3.50

Page 187

Brochure Page, Top Left, Imperial
Row 1:
1. Flower Bowl, 5" ......$ 1.00- 2.00
2. Flower Dish, 6¼" ....$ 1.00- 2.00
3. Planter, 6¾" ....$ 1.00- 2.00
4. Flower Arranger, 6½" .$ 1.00- 2.00

Row 2:
1. Flower Dish, 7" ......$ 1.00- 2.00
2. Dish Garden, 8½" ....$ 1.00- 2.00
3. Flower Dish, 8" ......$ 1.00- 2.00
4. Flower Dish, 7" ......$ 1.00- 2.00

Row 3:
1. Flower Dish, 6½" ....$ 1.00- 2.00
2. Flower Dish, 6½" ....$ 1.00- 2.00
3. Flower Dish, 7" ......$ 1.00- 2.00
4. Flower Dish, 8¼" ....$ 1.00- 2.00

Row 4:
1. Flower Dish, 8" ......$ 1.00- 2.00
2. Dish Garden, 11¾" ...$ 2.00- 3.00
3. Dish Garden, 10" .....$ 1.40- 2.50

Row 5:
1. Dish Garden, 12" .....$ 2.00- 3.00
2. Dish Garden, 12¼" ...$ 3.00- 4.00
3. Flower dish, 14" ......$ 3.00- 4.00

Brochure Page, Top Right
Row 1:
1. Flower Bowl, 6¾" ....$ 1.00- 2.00
2. Planter, 3" ....$ 1.00- 2.00
3. Planter, 3½" ....$ 1.00- 2.00
4. Planter, 3½" ....$ 1.00- 2.00
5. Planter, 3½" ....$ 1.00- 2.00
6. Flower Arranger, 5" ...$ 1.00- 2.00

Row 2:
1. Flower Arranger, 5"x7" $ 1.00- 2.00
2. Flower Arranger, 5" ...$ 1.00- 2.00
3. Planter, 4¾" ....$ 1.00- 2.00
4. Vase, 5¼" ....$ 1.00- 2.00
5. Vase, 5" ....$ 1.00- 2.00

Row 3:
1. Compote, 3⅜" ....$ 1.00- 2.00
2. Dish Garden, 7" ......$ 1.00- 2.00
3. Flower Bowl, 7½" ....$ 1.00- 2.00
4. Low Bowl, 7¾" ......$ 1.00- 2.00

Row 4:
1. Bulb Bowl, 7½" ......$ 1.00- 2.00
2. Low Bowl, 8¾" ......$ 1.00- 2.00
3. Flower Bowl, 6" ......$ 1.00- 2.00
4. Flower Bowl, 6½" ....$ 1.00- 2.00

Row 5:
1. Swan, 4" ....$ 1.00- 2.00
2. Swan, 4" ....$ 1.00- 2.00
3. Swan, 8½" ....$ 8.00- 12.00
4. Planter, 6¼" ....$ 1.00- 2.00

Brochure Page, Bottom Left
Row 1:
1. Flower Bowl, 5¾" ....$ 1.00- 2.00
2. Flower Dish, 7" ......$ 1.00- 2.00
3. Dish Garden, 7" ......$ 1.00- 2.00
4. Dish Garden, 7¾" ....$ 1.00- 2.00

Row 2:
1. Flower Dish, 6¼" ....$ 1.00- 2.00
2. Flower Dish, 6½" ....$ 1.00- 2.00
3. Dish Garden, 7" ......$ 1.00- 2.00
4. Flower Dish, 7" ......$ 1.00- 2.00

Row 3:
1. Flower Bowl, 6½" ....$ 1.00- 2.00
2. Flower Dish, 8" ......$ 1.00- 2.00
3. Flower Dish, 7" ......$ 1.00- 2.00
4. Flower Dish, 8¼" ....$ 1.00- 2.00

Row 4:
1. Dish Garden, 8½" ....$ 1.00- 2.00
2. Dish Garden, 10" .....$ 1.50- 2.50
3. Dish Garden, 11¾" ...$ 2.00- 3.00

Row 5:
1. Dish Garden, 12¼" ...$ 3.00- 4.00
2. Flower Dish, 12" .....$ 2.00- 3.00
3. Flower Dish, 14" .....$ 3.00- 4.00

Brochure Page, Bottom Right
Row 1:
1. Planter, 4¾" ....$ 1.00- 2.00
2. Swan Candleholder, 8¾" ....$ 2.00- 3.00
3. Flower Bowl, 7¾" ....$ 1.50- 2.50
4. Swan Candleholder, 8¾" ....$ 2.00- 3.00
5. Jardinier, 4⅝" ....$ 1.00- 2.00

Row 2:
1. Scoop Planter, 4¾" ...$ 2.00- 3.00
2. Chickadee Planter, 6" .$ 4.00- 5.00
3. Penguin Planter, 6" ...$ 4.00- 5.00
4. Chickadee Planter, 5¼" ....$ 4.00- 5.00
5. Praying Hands Planter, 6" ....$ 10.00- 12.00

Row 3:
1. Compote, 3¾" ....$ 1.00- 2.00
2. Planter, 3½" ....$ 1.00- 2.00
3. Planter, 3½" ....$ 1.00- 2.00
4. Compote, 3⅜" ....$ 1.00- 2.00

Row 4:
1. Planter, 6¾" ....$ 1.00- 2.00
2. Bulb Bowl, 7½" ......$ 1.00- 2.00
3. Flower Bowl, 7½" ....$ 1.00- 2.00
4. Low Bowl, 7¾" ......$ 1.00- 2.00

Row 5:
1. Cornucopia, 9½" .....$ 4.00- 6.00
2. Bowl, 5¾" ....$ 1.00- 2.00
3. Arranger/Ashtray, 6⅝" ....$ 2.00- 2.50
4. Flower Bowl, 9¼" ....$ 2.00- 2.40

Page 188

Brochure Page, Top Left, Imperial
Row 1:
1. Garden dish, 6½" ....$ 1.00- 2.00
2. Garden Dish, 7" ......$ 1.00- 2.00
3. Garden Dish, 6¼" ....$ 1.00- 2.00
4. Garden Dish, 6¼" ....$ 1.00- 2.00

Row 2:
1. Garden Dish, 7¼" ....$ 1.00- 2.00
2. Garden Dish, 7" ......$ 1.00- 2.00
3. Garden Dish, 7⅛" ....$ 1.00- 2.00
4. Garden Dish, 7¼" ....$ 1.00- 2.00

Row 3:
1. Garden Dish, 6⅞" ....$ 1.00- 2.00
2. Garden Dish, 7" ......$ 1.00- 2.00
3. Garden Dish, 7" ......$ 1.00- 2.00
4. Garden Dish, 7" ......$ 1.00- 2.00

Row 4:
1. Garden Dish, 7¼" ....$ 1.00- 2.00
2. Garden Dish, 7½" ....$ 1.00- 2.00
3. Garden Dish, 7" ......$ 1.00- 2.00
4. Planter, 6¾" ....$ 1.00- 2.00
5. Garden Dish, 7¾" ....$ 1.00- 2.00

Brochure Page, Top Right
Row 1:
1. Madonna, 8½" ....$ 15.00- 20.00
2. Pitcher Set, 5½" .....$ 5.00- 8.00
3. Swan, 4" ....$ 1.50- 2.00
4. Swan, 4" ....$ 1.50- 2.00
5. Swan, 7½" ....$ 8.00- 12.00

Row 2:
1. Basket, 7" ....$ 3.00- 4.00
2. Bowl, 8¾" ....$ 1.50- 2.50
3. Planter, 6½" ....$ 1.00- 2.50
4. Planter, 7¼" ....$ 1.50- 2.00
5. Vase, 9½" ....$ 2.00- 3.00

Row 3:
1. Planter, 4½" ....$ 1.00- 2.00
2. Planter, 4⅜" ....$ 1.00- 2.00
3. Planter, 5⅝" ....$ 1.00- 2.00
4. Planter, 7½" ....$ 1.00- 2.00
5. Planter, 7½" ....$ 1.00- 2.00
6. Planter, 7¾" ....$ 1.50- 2.50

Row 4:
1. Vase, 10" ....$ 3.00- 4.00
2. Planter, 8⅛" ....$ 1.50- 2.50
3. Vase, 9" ....$ 1.50- 2.50
4. Vase, 8½" ....$ 1.50- 2.50
5. Pitcher, 10" ....$ 8.00- 12.00

Brochure Page, Bottom Left
Row 1:
1. Planter, 7¾" ....$ 1.50- 2.50
2. Planter, 7½" ....$ 1.00- 2.00

3. Compote, 7½″ . . . . . . $ 1.00- 2.00
4. Planter, 5¼″ . . . . $ 1.00- 2.00
5. Planter, 4½″ . . . . $ 1.00- 2.00
6. Planter, 5″ . . . . $ 1.00- 2.00

Row 2:
1. Basket, 7″ . . . . $ 3.00- 4.00
2. Flower Bowl, 9¼″ . . . . $ 1.00- 2.00
3. Planter, 5½″ . . . . $ 1.00- 2.00
4. Cornucopia, 8¼″ . . . . . $ 2.00- 3.00
5. Planter, 7″ . . . . $ 1.00- 2.00
6. Bud Vase, 6½″ . . . . . . $ 1.00- 2.00
7. Vase, 9¼″ . . . . $ 1.50- 2.50

Row 3:
1. Madonna, 8½″ . . . . $ 15.00- 20.00
2. Pitcher Set, 5½″ . . . . . $ 5.00- 8.00
3. Pitcher Set, 7″ . . . . $ 8.00- 12.00
4. Basket, 9″ . . . . $ 3.00- 5.00
5. Swan, 4″ . . . . $ 1.50- 2.00
6. Swan, 7½″ . . . . $ 8.00- 12.00

Row 4:
1. Vase, 10½″ . . . . $ 3.00- 4.00
2. Planter, 8⅛″ . . . . $ 1.50- 2.50
3. Vase, 9⅛″ . . . . $ 1.50- 2.50
4. Vase, 8½″ . . . . $ 1.50- 2.50
5. Pitcher, 10″ . . . . $ 8.00- 12.00

Brochure Page, Bottom Right

Row 1:
1. Garden Dish, 7″ . . . . . . $ 1.00- 2.00
2. Garden Dish, 6¼″ . . . . $ 1.00- 2.00
3. Garden Dish, 7″ . . . . . . $ 1.00- 2.00
4. Garden Dish, 6½″ . . . . $ 1.00- 2.00
5. Planter, 3½″ . . . . $ 1.00- 2.00

Row 2:
1. Planter, 6¾″ . . . . $ 1.00- 2.00
2. Garden Dish, 7″ . . . . . . $ 1.00- 2.00
3. Garden Dish, 7″ . . . . . . $ 1.00- 2.00
4. Garden Dish, 7″ . . . . . . $ 1.00- 2.00
5. Garden Dish, 7¼″ . . . . $ 1.00- 2.00

Row 3:
1. Garden Dish, 7½″ . . . . $ 1.00- 2.00
2. Garden Dish, 7″ . . . . . . $ 1.00- 2.00
3. Garden Dish, 7¾″ . . . . $ 1.00- 2.00
4. Garden Dish, 8″ . . . . . . $ 1.00- 2.00
5. Garden Dish, 9¾″ . . . . $ 1.00- 2.00

Row 4:
1. Garden Dish, 7¾″ . . . . $ 1.00- 2.00
2. Garden Dish, 10½″ . . . $ 1.00- 2.00
3. Flower Bowl, 7½″ . . . . $ 1.00- 2.00
4. Flower Bowl, 8⅛″ . . . . . $ 1.00- 2.00
5. Flower Bowl, 6½″ . . . . $ 1.00- 2.00

Page 189

Brochure Page, Top Left, Imperial

Row 1:
1. Garden Dish, 8¾″ . . . . $ 1.00- 2.00
2. Candleholder/Planter, 4″ . . . . $ 1.50- 2.50
3. Flower Dish, 8½″ . . . . $ 1.50- 2.50
4. Candleholder/Planter 4″ . . . . $ 1.50- 2.50

Row 2:
1. Flower Dish, 11¾″ . . . $ 2.00- 3.00
2. Flower Dish, 14″ . . . . . $ 3.00- 4.00
3. Flower Dish, 6½″ . . . . $ 1.00- 2.00

Row 3:
1. Flower Dish, 7″ . . . . . . $ 1.00- 2.00
2. Flower Dish, 8¼″ . . . . $ 1.00- 2.00
3. Flower Dish, 7″ . . . . . . $ 1.00- 2.00

Row 4:
1. Flower Dish, 7″ . . . . . . $ 1.00- 2.00
2. Flower Dish, 7″ . . . . . . $ 1.00- 2.00
3. Flower Dish, 8¼″ . . . . $ 1.00- 2.00
4. Flower Dish, 12″ . . . . . $ 2.00- 3.00

Brochure Page, Top Right

Row 1:
1. Vase, 10″ . . . . $ 3.00- 4.00
2. Swan, 4″ . . . . $ 1.00- 2.00
3. Swan, 8½″ . . . . $ 8.00- 12.00
4. Swan, 4″ . . . . $ 1.00- 2.00
5. Vase, 9½″ . . . . $ 1.50- 2.50

Row 2:
1. Vase, 5½″ . . . . $ 1.00- 2.00
2. Planter, 6″ . . . . $ 1.00- 2.00
3. Flower Bowl, 7¾″ . . . . $ 1.50- 2.50
4. Planter, 6½″ . . . . $ 1.00- 2.00
5. Compote, 7½″ . . . . $ 1.00- 2.00
6. Planter, 5⅝″ . . . . $ 1.00- 2.00

Row 3:
1. Vase, 5½″ . . . . $ 1.00- 2.00
2. Planter, 6″ . . . . $ 1.00- 2.00
3. Flower Bowl, 7¾″ . . . . $ 1.50- 2.50
4. Planter, 6½″ . . . . $ 1.00- 2.00
5. Compote, 7½″ . . . . $ 1.00- 2.00
6. Planter, 5⅝″ . . . . $ 1.00- 2.00

Row 4:
1. Swan, 4″ . . . . $ 1.50- 2.00
2. Swan, 7½″ . . . . $ 8.00- 12.00
3. Swan, 4″ . . . . $ 1.50- 2.00
4. Madonna, 9½″ . . . . $ 10.00- 12.00

Brochure Page, Bottom Left

Row 1:
1. Dish Garden, 8½″ . . . . $ 1.00- 2.00
2. Vase, 6″ . . . . $ 1.00- 2.00
3. Dish Garden, 6½″ . . . . $ 1.00- 2.00
4. Dish Garden, 8½″ . . . . $ 1.00- 2.00

Row 2:
1. Dish Garden, 7″ . . . . . . $ 1.00- 2.00
2. Flower Bowl, 5¾″ . . . . $ 1.00- 2.00
3. Flower Dish, 7″ . . . . . . $ 1.00- 2.00
4. Dish Garden, 7¾″ . . . . $ 1.00- 2.00

Row 3:
1. Flower Dish, 6½″ . . . . $ 1.00- 2.00
2. Flower Dish, 6¼″ . . . . $ 1.00- 2.00
3. Planter, 6¾″ . . . . $ 1.00- 2.00
4. Flower Dish, 7″ . . . . . . $ 1.00- 2.00

Row 4:
1. Flower Dish, 8″ . . . . . . $ 1.00- 2.00
2. Dish Garden, 7″ . . . . . . $ 1.00- 2.00
3. Flower Bowl, 6½″ . . . . $ 1.00- 2.00
4. Flower Dish, 8¼″ . . . . $ 1.00- 2.00

Row 5:
1. Dish Garden, 10″ . . . . . $ 1.50- 2.50
2. Flower Dish, 7″ . . . . . . $ 1.00- 2.00
3. Dish Garden, 8½″ . . . . $ 1.00- 2.00
4. Dish Garden, 11¾″ . . . $ 2.00- 3.00

Row 6:
1. Dish Garden, 12¼″ . . . $ 3.00- 4.00
2. Flower Dish, 12″ . . . . . $ 2.00- 3.00
3. Flower Dish, 14″ . . . . . $ 3.00- 4.00

Brochure Page, Bottom Right

Row 1:
1. Chickadee Planter, 6″ . $ 4.00- 5.00
2. Planter, 4⅜″ . . . . $ 1.00- 2.00
3. Planter, 4¾″ . . . . $ 1.00- 2.00
4. Chicadee Planter, 5¼″ $ 4.00- 5.00

Row 2:
1. Planter, 3½″ . . . . $ 1.00- 2.00
2. Flower Bowl, 3″ . . . . . . $ 1.00- 2.00
3. Flower Bowl, 3⅞″ . . . . . $ 1.00- 2.00
4. Planter, 3¼″ . . . . $ 1.00- 2.00

Row 3:
1. Bowl, 6⅜″ . . . . $ 1.00- 2.00
2. Planter, 3½″ . . . . $ 1.00- 2.00
3. Flower Bowl, 7½″ . . . . $ 1.00- 2.00
4. Jardinier, 3⅞″ . . . . $ 1.00- 2.00

Row 4:
1. Pitcher Set, 5½″ . . . . . $ 5.00- 8.00
2. Jardinier, 4½″ . . . . $ 1.00- 2.00
3. Scoop Planter, 7″ . . . . $ 2.00- 3.00
4. Boy Planter, 8″ . . . . . . $ 3.00- 4.00

Row 5:
1. Cornucopia, 9½″ . . . . . $ 4.00- 6.00
2. Planter, 4½″ . . . . $ 1.00- 2.00
3. Planter, 4⅜″ . . . . $ 1.00- 2.00
4. Vase, 6½″ . . . . $ 2.00- 3.00

Page 190

Brochure Page, Top Left, Imperial

Row 1:
1. Planter, 3½″ . . . . $ 1.00- 2.00
2. Planter, 4½″ . . . . $ 1.00- 2.00
3. Planter, 3½″ . . . . $ 1.00- 2.00
4. Planter, 4¾″ . . . . $ 1.00- 2.00
5. Planter, 6¼″ . . . . $ 1.00- 2.00
6. Planter, 4⅛″ . . . . $ 1.00- 2.00

Row 2:
1. Garden Dish, 8¾″ . . . . $ 1.00- 2.00
2. Garden Dish, 9¼″ . . . . $ 1.00- 2.00
3. Flower Dish, 9″ . . . . . . $ 1.00- 2.00
4. Garden Dish, 8½″ . . . . $ 1.00- 2.00
5. Flower Dish, 8¼″ . . . . $ 1.00- 2.00

Row 3:
1. Garden Dish, 10″ . . . . . $ 1.50- 2.50
2. Garden Dish, 14″ . . . . . $ 3.00- 4.00

Row 4:
1. Garden Dish, 15″ . . . . . $ 3.00- 4.00
2. Garden Dish, 11¾″ . . . $ 2.00- 3.00

Row 4:
1. Flower Dish, 12″ . . . . . $ 2.00- 3.00
2. Garden Dish, 10½″ . . . $ 1.50- 2.50
3. Garden Dish, 11½″ . . . $ 2.00- 3.00
4. Planter, 5″ . . . . $ 1.00- 2.00
5. Planter, 6¼″ . . . . $ 1.00- 2.00

Brochure Page, Top Right

Row 1:
1. Garden Dish, 8¾″ . . . . $ 1.00- 2.00
2. Garden Dish, 8½″ . . . . $ 1.00- 2.00
3. Garden Dish, 8½″ . . . . $ 1.00- 2.00
4. Garden Dish, 8½″ . . . . $ 1.00- 2.00
5. Flower Dish, 8¼″ . . . . $ 1.00- 2.00

Row 2:
1. Garden Dish, 10″ . . . . . $ 1.50- 2.50
2. Garden Dish, 11¾″ . . . $ 2.00- 3.00
3. Flower Dish, 10½″ . . . $ 1.50- 2.50
4. Garden Dish, 14″ . . . . . $ 3.00- 4.00

Row 3:
1. Flower Dish . . . . $ 2.00- 3.00
2. Garden Dish, 10½″ . . . $ 1.50- 2.50
3. Garden Dish . . . . $ 2.00- 3.00
4. Planter, 5″ . . . . $ 1.00- 2.00
5. Planter, 4¾″ . . . . $ 1.00- 2.00

Row 4:
1. Planter, 3½″ . . . . $ 1.00- 2.00
2. Planter, 3½″ . . . . $ 1.00- 2.00
3. Planter, 4¾″ . . . . $ 1.00- 2.00
4. Planter, 4½″ . . . . $ 1.00- 2.00
5. Vase, 5½″ . . . . $ 1.00- 2.00
6. Planter, 4¾″ . . . . $ 1.00- 2.00

Brochure Page, Bottom Left

Row 1:
1. Planter, 7¾″ . . . . $ 1.50- 2.50
2. Planter, 7½″ . . . . $ 1.00- 2.00
3. Planter, 5¼″ . . . . $ 1.00- 2.00
4. Planter, 5¾″ . . . . $ 1.00- 2.00
5. Planter, 5″ . . . . $ 1.00- 2.00

Row 2:
1. Vase, 9¼″ . . . . $ 1.50- 2.50
2. Planter, 7″ . . . . $ 1.00- 2.00
3. Planter, 6¼″ . . . . $ 1.00- 2.00
4. Basket, 7″ . . . . $ 3.00- 4.00
5. Basket, 7½″ . . . . $ 3.00- 4.00
6. Basket, 9″ . . . . $ 3.00- 5.00

Row 3:
1. Planter, 8½″ . . . . $ 1.50- 2.50
2. Planter, 5¾″ . . . . $ 1.00- 2.00
3. Planter, 5″ . . . . $ 1.00- 2.00
4. Planter, 4½″ . . . . $ 1.00- 2.00
5. Planter, 5¾″ . . . . $ 1.00- 2.00
6. Planter, 5¼″ . . . . $ 1.00- 2.00

Row 4:
1. Planter, 4″ . . . . $ 1.00- 2.00
2. Planter, 3½″ . . . . $ 1.00- 2.00
3. Planter, 4¾″ . . . . $ 1.00- 2.00
4. Planter, 3½″ . . . . $ 1.00- 2.00
5. Pitcher Set, 5½″ . . . . . $ 5.00- 8.00
6. Pitcher Set, 7″ . . . . $ 8.00- 12.00

Row 5:
1. Garden Dish, 7″ . . . . . . $ 1.00- 2.00
2. Garden Dish, 6¼″ . . . . $ 1.00- 2.00
3. Garden Dish, 6½″ . . . . $ 1.00- 2.00
4. Garden Dish, 6½″ . . . . $ 1.00- 2.00

5. Garden Dish, 7" . . . . . . $ 1.00- 2.00

Brochure Page, Bottom Right

Row 1:

1. Garden Dish, 7¼" . . . . $ 1.00- 2.00
2. Garden Dish, 7" . . . . . . $ 1.00- 2.00
3. Garden Dish, 7½" . . . . $ 1.00- 2.00
4. Garden Dish, 7" . . . . . . $ 1.00- 2.00
5. Garden Dish, 7" . . . . . . $ 1.00- 2.00

Row 2:

1. Garden Dish, 7¾" . . . . $ 1.00- 2.00
2. Garden Dish, 8" . . . . . . $ 1.00- 2.00
3. Garden Dish, 7¾" . . . . $ 1.00- 2.00
4. Garden Dish, 8½" . . . . $ 1.00- 2.00
5. Flower Dish, 8¼" . . . . $ 1.00- 2.00

Row 3:

1. Garden Dish, 8¾" . . . . $ 1.00- 2.00
2. Flower Dish, 9" . . . . . . $ 1.00- 2.00
3. Garden Dish, 11½" . . . $ 2.00- 3.00
4. Garden Dish, 10½" . . . $ 1.50- 2.50

Row 4:

1. Flower Bowl, 6½" . . . . $ 1.00- 2.00
2. Flower Bowl, 8⅛" . . . . . $ 1.00- 2.00
3. Planter, 3½" . . . . $ 1.00- 2.00
4. Planter, 4⅛" . . . . $ 1.00- 2.00
5. Planter, 5½" . . . . $ 1.00- 2.00

Row 5:

1. Flower Bowl, 9¼" . . . . $ 1.00- 2.00
2. Bowl, 7⅝" . . . . $ 1.00- 2.00
3. Planter, 6¾" . . . . $ 1.00- 2.00
4. Flower Dish, 9" . . . . $ 1.00- 2.00
5. Flower Bowl, 7½" . . . . $ 1.00- 2.00

Row 6:

1. Flower Dish, 12" . . . . . $ 2.00- 3.00
2. Garden Dish, 14" . . . . . $ 3.00- 4.00
3. Garden Dish, 11¾" . . . $ 2.00- 3.00

Page 191

Brochure Page, Top Left, Imperial

Row 1:

1. Garden Dish, 6½" . . . . $ 1.00- 2.00
2. Garden Dish, 7" . . . . . . $ 1.00- 2.00
3. Garden Dish, 6¼" . . . . $ 1.00- 2.00
4. Garden Dish, 6¼" . . . . $ 1.00- 2.00
5. Garden Dish, 7¼" . . . . $ 1.00- 2.00

Row 2:

1. Garden Dish, 7" . . . . . . $ 1.00- 2.00
2. Garden Dish, 7¼" . . . . $ 1.00- 2.00
3. Garden Dish, 7" . . . . . . $ 1.00- 2.00
4. Garden Dish, 7" . . . . . . $ 1.00- 2.00
5. Garden Dish, 7" . . . . . . $ 1.00- 2.00

Row 3:

1. Garden Dish, 7½" . . . . $ 1.00- 2.00
2. Garden Dish, 7" . . . . . . $ 1.00- 2.00
3. Garden Dish, 7¾" . . . . $ 1.00- 2.00
4. Planter, 6¾" . . . . $ 1.00- 2.00
5. Garden Dish, 8" . . . . . . $ 1.00- 2.00

Row 4:

1. Flower Bowl, 6½" . . . . $ 1.00- 2.00
2. Flower Bowl, 8⅛" . . . . . $ 1.00- 2.00
3. Garden Dish, 7¾" . . . . $ 1.00- 2.00
4. Garden Dish, 10½" . . . $ 1.00- 2.00
5. Flower Bowl, 7½" . . . . $ 1.00- 2.00

Brochure Page, Top Right

Row 1:

1. Madonna, 8½" . . . . $ 15.00- 20.00
2. Pitcher Set, 5½" . . . . . $ 5.00- 8.00
3. Basket, 9" . . . . $ 3.00- 5.00
4. Jardinier, 4½" . . . . $ 1.00- 2.00
5. Swan, 4" . . . . $ 1.50- 2.00
6. Swan, 7½" . . . . $ 8.00- 12.00

Row 2:

1. Basket, 7" . . . . $ 3.00- 4.00
2. Flower Bowl, 8¾" . . . . $ 1.00- 2.00
3. Planter, 4" . . . . $ 1.00- 2.00
4. Compote, 4" . . . . $ 1.00- 2.00
5. Bud Vase, 6½" . . . . . . $ 1.00- 2.00
6. Vase, 8" . . . . $ 1.50- 2.50
7. Vase, 9" . . . . $ 1.50- 2.50

Row 3:

1. Planter, 4⅜" . . . . $ 1.00- 2.00
2. Urn, 5¾" . . . . $ 1.00- 2.00
3. Planter, 5⅝" . . . . $ 1.00- 2.00
4. Planter, 4⅜" . . . . $ 1.00- 2.00
5. Compote, 4¼" . . . . $ 1.00- 2.00
6. Planter, 7¾" . . . . $ 1.50- 2.50

Row 4:

1. Vase, 10" . . . . $ 3.00- 4.00
2. Planter, 8⅛" . . . . $ 1.50- 2.50
3. Vase, 9⅛" . . . . $ 1.50- 2.50
4. Vase, 8½" . . . . $ 1.50- 2.50
5. Pitcher, 10" . . . . $ 8.00- 12.00

Brochure Page, Bottom Left, Victorian

Row 1:

1. Pitcher Set, 9" . . . . $ 8.00- 12.00
2. Vase, 5" . . . . $ 1.00- 2.00
3. Planter, 6½" . . . . $ 1.00- 2.00

Row 2:

1. Basket, 9" . . . . $ 3.00- 5.00
2. Dish Garden, 7" . . . . . . $ 1.00- 2.00
3. Bowl, 7¾" . . . . $ 1.00- 2.00

Row 3:

1. Vase, 9" . . . . $ 1.50- 2.50
2. Garden Dish, 9½" . . . . $ 2.00- 3.00
3. Vase, 9" . . . . $ 1.50- 2.50

Row 4:

1. Basket, 9" . . . . $ 3.00- 5.00
2. Planter, 7½" . . . . $ 1.00- 2.00
3. Planter, 5⅜" . . . . $ 1.00- 2.00
4. Planter, 5¾" . . . . $ 1.00- 2.00
5. Planter, 4⅜" . . . . $ 1.00- 2.00
6. Planter, 5" . . . . $ 1.00- 2.00

Row 5:

1. Pitcher Set, 7" . . . . $ 8.00- 12.00
2. Pitcher Set, 5½" . . . . . $ 5.00- 8.00
3. Planter, 3½" . . . . $ 1.00- 2.00
4. Planter, 5" . . . . $ 1.00- 2.00
5. Planter, 4¾" . . . . $ 1.00- 2.00
6. Planter, 3½" . . . . $ 1.00- 2.00

Brochure Page, Bottom Right

Row 1:

1. Garden Dish, 7" . . . . . . $ 1.00- 2.00
2. Garden Dish, 6¼" . . . . $ 1.00- 2.00
3. Garden Dish, 6½" . . . . $ 1.00- 2.00
4. Garden Dish, 6½" . . . . $ 1.00- 2.00
5. Garden Dish, 7" . . . . . . $ 1.00- 2.00

Row 2:

1. Garden Dish, 7" . . . . . . $ 1.00- 2.00
2. Garden Dish, 7" . . . . . . $ 1.00- 2.00
3. Garden Dish, 7" . . . . . . $ 1.00- 2.00
4. Planter, 3½" . . . . $ 1.00- 2.00
5. Planter, 4⅛" . . . . $ 1.00- 2.00

Row 3:

1. Garden Dish, 7¾" . . . . $ 1.00- 2.00
2. Garden Dish, 8" . . . . . . $ 1.00- 2.00
3. Garden Dish, 7¾" . . . . $ 1.00- 2.00
4. Garden Dish, 8½" . . . . $ 1.00- 2.00
5. Flower Dish, 8¼" . . . . $ 1.00- 2.00

Row 4:

1. Garden Dish, 8¾" . . . . $ 1.00- 2.00
2. Flower Dish, 9" . . . . . . $ 1.00- 2.00
3. Garden Dish, 11½" . . . $ 2.00- 3.00
4. Garden Dish, 10½" . . . $ 1.50- 2.50

Row 5:

1. Flower Bowl, 9¼" . . . . $ 1.00- 2.00
2. Bowl, 7⅝" . . . . $ 1.00- 2.00
3. Flower Bowl, 6½" . . . . $ 1.00- 2.00
4. Flower Bowl, 7½" . . . . $ 1.00- 2.00

Row 6:

1. Flower Dish, 12" . . . . . $ 2.00- 3.00
2. Garden Dish, 14" . . . . . $ 3.00- 4.00
3. Garden Dish, 11¼" . . . $ 2.00- 3.00

* - High range applies to matte with turquoise interior.

** - High range applies to pink-green combinations.

*** - High range applies to pink-gray-green combinations.

Schroeder's Antiques Price Guide

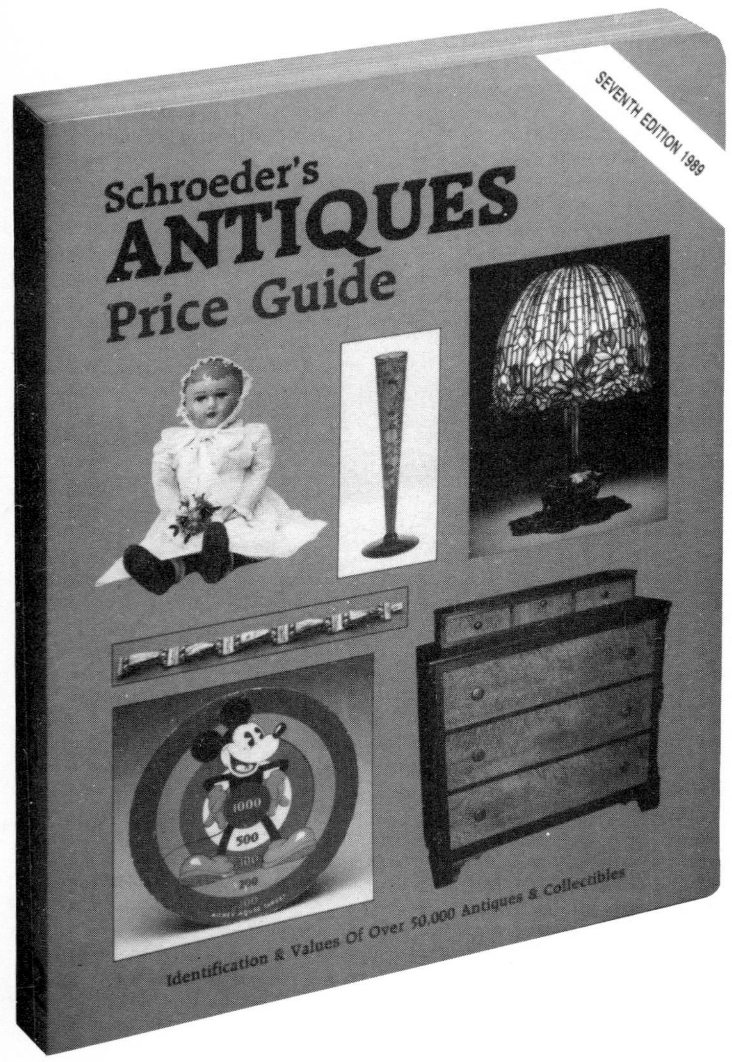

Schroeder's Antiques Price Guide has climbed its way to the top in a field already supplied with several well-established publications! The word is out, *Schroeder's Price Guide* is the best buy at any price. Over 500 categories are covered, with more than 50,000 listings. But it's not volume alone that makes Schroeder's the unique guide it is recognized to be. From ABC Plates to Zsolnay, if it merits the interest of today's collector, you'll find it in Schroeder's. Each subject is represented with histories and background information. In addition, hundreds of sharp original photos are used each year to illustrate not only the rare and the unusual, but the everyday "fun-type" collectibles as well -- not postage stamp pictures, but large close-up shots that show important details clearly.

Each edition is completely re-typeset from all new sources. We have not and will not simply change prices in each new edition. All new copy and all new illustrations make Schroeder's THE price guide on antiques and collectibles.

The writing and researching team behind this giant is proportionately large. It is backed by a staff of more than seventy of Collector Books' finest authors, as well as a board of advisors made up of well-known antique authorities and the country's top dealers, all specialists in their fields. Accuracy is their primary aim. Prices are gathered over the entire year previous to publication, from ads and personal contacts. Then each category is thoroughly checked to spot inconsistencies, listings that may not be entirely reflective of actual market dealings, and lines too vague to be of merit. Only the best of the lot remains for publication. You'll find *Schroeder's Antiques Price Guide* the one to buy for factual information and quality.

No dealer, collector or investor can afford not to own this book. It is available from your favorite bookseller or antiques dealer at the low price of $12.95. If you are unable to find this price guide in your area, it's available from Collector Books, P. O. Box 3009, Paducah, KY 42001 at $12.95 plus $2.00 for postage and handling.

8½ x 11, 608 Pages $12.95

COLLECTOR BOOKS

A Division of Schroeder Publishing Co., Inc.